Rousseau as Author

LETTRES

ÉCRITES DE LA

MONTAGNE.

PAR J. J. ROUSSEAU.

EN DEUX PARTIES.

VITAM
IMPENDERE
VERO.

A AMSTERDAM,
Chez MARC MICHEL REY.
MDCCLXIV.

ROUSSEAU AS AUTHOR

Consecrating One's Life to the Truth

Christopher Kelly

The University of Chicago Press
Chicago and London

CHRISTOPHER KELLY is professor of political science at Boston College. He is the author of *Rousseau's Exemplary Life* (1987) and the general coeditor of *The Collected Writings of Rousseau*.

The University of Chicago Press, Chicago 60637
The University of Chicago Press, Ltd., London
© 2003 by The University of Chicago
All rights reserved. Published 2003
Printed in the United States of America

12 11 10 09 08 07 06 05 04 03   1 2 3 4 5

ISBN: 0-226-43023-5 (cloth)
ISBN: 0-226-43024-3 (paper)

Library of Congress Cataloging-in-Publication Data

Kelly, Christopher, 1950–
   Rousseau as author : consecrating one's life to the truth / Christopher Kelly.
     p. cm.
Includes bibliographical references and index.
   ISBN 0-226-43023-5 (cloth : alk. paper)—ISBN 0-226-43024-3 (pbk. : alk. paper)
   1. Rousseau, Jean-Jacques, 1712–1778—Ethics.   2. Rousseau, Jean-Jacques, 1712–1778—Views on authorship.   3. Authorship.   1. Title.
   PQ2056.E85 K45 2003
   848'.509—dc21   2002007098

∞ The paper used in this publication meets the minimum requirements of the American National Standard for Information Sciences—Permanence of Paper for Printed Library Materials, ANSI Z39.48-1992.

Frontispiece: Title page from Jean-Jacques Rousseau's *Letters Written from the Mountain*. Amsterdam: Marc-Michel Rey, 1764.

CONTENTS

List of Abbreviations *vii*

Acknowledgments *ix*

Introduction *1*

CHAPTER ONE
Responsible and Irresponsible Authors *8*

CHAPTER TWO
The Case for (and against) Censorship *29*

CHAPTER THREE
The Case against (and for) the Arts *51*

CHAPTER FOUR
Heroic and Antiheroic Citizens *82*

CHAPTER FIVE
"A Hermit Makes a Very Peculiar Citizen":
Rousseau and Literary Citizenship *116*

CHAPTER SIX
Philosophic Good and Bad Faith *140*

Postscript: Philosophers and the Friend of the Truth *172*

Notes *183*

Bibliography *199*

Index *207*

ABBREVIATIONS

CW	*Collected Writings of Rousseau.* 9 volumes to date. Edited by Roger D. Masters and Christopher Kelly. Hanover, N.H.: University Press of New England, 1991–.
d'Alembert	*Politics and the Arts: Letter to d'Alembert on the Theatre.* Edited by Allan Bloom. Ithaca: Cornell University Press, 1960.
Emile	*Emile, or On Education.* Edited by Allan Bloom. New York: Basic Books, 1979.
Leigh	*Correspondance complète de Jean-Jacques Rousseau.* Edited by R. A. Leigh. 51 vols. Geneva: Institut et Musée Voltaire, 1965–95.
Pl.	*Oeuvres complètes.* Vols. 1–5. Paris: NRF-Editions de la Pléiade, 1959–95. Translations from this edition are my own unless otherwise indicated.

ACKNOWLEDGMENTS

Unlike Rousseau, I have been the willing and grateful recipient of material support for my research. I am happy to have this opportunity to thank the National Endowment for the Humanities, the Earhart Foundation, and the George A. and Eliza Gardner Howard Foundation for fellowships that allowed me to devote time to this project. I also thank the Camargo Foundation for its warm hospitality during my residence as a fellow.

Henry Higuera and Ruth Grant read the manuscript and made more helpful suggestions than I have been able to incorporate. The readers for University of Chicago Press (one of whom, as a good Rousseauist, insisted on not being anonymous) challenged my argument in ways that forced me to clarify my position.

Earlier versions of parts of some of the chapters were originally published elsewhere. I would like to thank the original publishers for permission to reprint. Part of chapter 2 appeared in the *Journal of Politics* 59, no. 4 (November 1997): 1232–51. Parts of chapter 3 appeared in the *American Journal of Political Science* 31, no. 2 (May 1987): 321–35; and *The Legacy of Rousseau*, edited by Clifford Orwin and Nathan Tarcov, 20–44 (Chicago: University of Chicago Press, 1997). Parts of chapter 4 appeared in *Eighteenth-Century Studies* 33, no. 1 (fall 1999): 85–101; and *Polity* 30, no. 2 (winter 1997): 347–66. Parts of chapter 6 appeared in *Interpretation* 23, no. 3 (spring 1996): 417–44; and *Pensée Libre*, no. 8 (2001): 101–13.

INTRODUCTION

"To consecrate one's life to the truth": this is the way Rousseau translated "*vitam impendere vero,*" taken from Juvenal's *Satires* (*d'Alembert* 132; Pl. 5:120). Rousseau announced to the world that this was his motto in his *Letter to d'Alembert* and reaffirmed it in *Emile* and *Letters Written from the Mountain*. He had it put on a seal that he used on his correspondence and in his last work, the *Reveries of the Solitary Walker*, devoted a long discussion to whether he had lived up to it. This motto is at the center of Rousseau's ideas of authorship and responsibility. To understand its significance is the ultimate goal of this work.

This motto elicits at least three overlapping issues. The first of these is Rousseau's notorious sincerity, his openness about the details of his intimate life and feelings. The second is his devotion to a life of philosophic inquiry. The third is his remarkable boldness in stating things that risked persecution. While it is impossible to ignore the first two of these issues, the third will be the focus here. It is also the one that predominates in Juvenal, who uses it in connection with his character Crispus in the fourth *Satire*. Crispus is presented as having the capacity to offer useful advice to rulers, but also as failing to do so because of the danger of speaking the truth to a tyrant. He lived a long life as a courtier precisely because he was not one who consecrated his life to the truth. By adopting as a motto the attribute denied to Crispus, Rousseau indicated his own willingness to take risks as an author. Understanding Rousseau's authorship entails understanding how he thought one must go about doing this.

The argument of this book is that for Rousseau, "consecrating one's life to the truth" meant both publicly taking responsibility for what one publishes and, also, publishing only those things that will be of public benefit.

Thus, it involves both openness and discretion. To put this another way, Rousseau insisted that publication of a book was a public act and that it therefore carried with it weighty responsibilities. He thought through the implications of this view and acted upon them with a remarkable thoroughness. As a result, he arrived at a new understanding of citizenship and a radical critique of contemporary authors who regarded the relations among the truth, their own interest, and good citizenship as less problematic than he did.

Rousseau's authorship is distinctive in numerous other ways. Although he wrote both before and after what could be called his career as a publishing author, he began this career only when nearing the age of forty and he renounced it less than fifteen years later. During this period he wrote academic discourses, polemical pamphlets, plays, an opera, a fairy tale, open letters, novels, a dictionary, and treatises. He was successful in most of these genres and experimented with several others. Virtually every one of his publications created a public sensation and had large or, in some cases, enormous sales. The range of his works is a good indication of his ambition as a writer, which gives the appearance of having been to rewrite the major works of European literature. His *Emile* is a redoing of Plato's *Republic* that turns the original on its head;[1] his *Julie, or the New Heloise*, gives a new turn to one of history's most famous love stories; and his *Confessions* usurps the title of Saint Augustine's work while profoundly altering the understanding of human life contained in the original. To this can be added his attacks on the classical theater and music of France that propose new alternatives to the established forms. In spite of the diversity of the genres he adopted, Rousseau cultivated and acquired a distinct and unified persona as an author. His readers were drawn to his books because of their view of the author.

Rousseau's contemporaries recognized very quickly that there was something new in his way of being an author, although they varied in their assessment of it. Even his friends greeted his sudden acquisition of fame upon the publication of the *Discourse on the Sciences and the Arts* in 1751 with a mixture of delight and puzzlement. Shortly after the publication of the *Discourse*, Denis Diderot, who had encouraged him to write it and had handled the details of its publication,[2] wrote the ailing Rousseau a note saying, "It is succeeding beyond the skies; there is no precedent for such a success" (*Confessions*, CW 5:304; Pl. 1:363). After two years of polemics during which the *Discourse* was attacked by writers ranging from minor provincial academics to the father-in-law of the king of France, Rousseau found himself—at the age of forty—as one of Europe's leading intellectual figures.[3]

The puzzlement of Rousseau's friends at this success can be explained, to begin with, by how unexpected it was. He had arrived in Paris almost ten years earlier filled with ambition and armed with his invention of a new system of musical notation. Unfortunately, the Academy of Sciences met the *Plan Regarding New Signs for Music* with indifference. Rousseau's subsequent attempts to advance in high society by memorizing poetry and playing chess were even less successful. After spending a year in Venice as the secretary to the French ambassador, he was either dismissed or resigned and returned to Paris, where he wrote an opera that got no further than a rehearsal at which it was derided by the famous composer Rameau. After these failures Rousseau seemed to have found his level as a secretary for the wealthy and intellectually ambitious Dupin family, at whose dinners he was able to observe famous writers such as Fontenelle, Buffon, and perhaps Voltaire. He conducted historical research for Mme. Dupin, helped M. Dupin on a refutation of Montesquieu, and attended chemistry courses with Dupin's son from an earlier marriage. Mme. Dupin later admitted that, in spite of almost daily contact with Rousseau over several years, she had never suspected him of having any noteworthy talent (*Confessions*, CW 5:98; Pl. 1:116). There is little reason to believe that anyone—other than perhaps Diderot, who commissioned him to write some articles on music for his planned *Encyclopédie*—would have disagreed with her assessment. The most that could be said about this decade of striving is that it put Rousseau in a position of being able to make a very modest living. Any hopes he had beyond this rested in the opportunity for a more lucrative position with the Dupins rather than in any possible literary endeavors.

The tardiness of Rousseau's blossoming is sufficient by itself to account for his acquaintances' puzzlement, but it was not the only cause for wonder and even uneasiness. All of Rousseau's critics noted the apparent paradox contained in the *Discourse* of great literary skill being used to attack literature. Diderot may, at first, have been untroubled by the position Rousseau took, but d'Alembert (his coeditor of the *Encyclopédie*) felt obliged to explain it away. In the "Preliminary Discourse" of the *Encyclopédie*, he refers to "an eloquent and philosophical writer who accused the sciences and the arts of corrupting human mores" and hastens to add that Rousseau's contributions to the *Encyclopédie* constitute an endorsement of this work.[4] Both Rousseau's critics and his friends contrasted his actions to his argument in order to dismiss the latter.

In the short run this focus on Rousseau's behavior rather than his arguments allowed his acquaintances to embrace him as a fellow literary man in spite of his continued attack on literature, but in the longer run his behavior proved to be even more troubling than his arguments. This was so because Rousseau insisted on behaving in ways that differed markedly from other successful authors. Later he explained the increasing tension between himself and his friends by saying, "It was less my literary celebrity than my personal reform, whose period I mark here, that attracted their jealousy to me: perhaps they would have pardoned me for shining in the art of writing; but they could not pardon me for using my behavior to give an example which seemed to be troublesome to them" (*Confessions*, CW 5:304; Pl. 1:362). This example consisted in making his behavior harmonize with his principles and in setting out "alone in a new route" as an author. In his last work, the *Reveries*, Rousseau contrasts his own authorship with that of his contemporaries by saying, "When [their book] was done and published, its content no longer interested them in any way, unless it were to make others adopt it and to defend it in case it were attacked; but for the rest, they drew nothing from it for their own use and were not even concerned whether this content were false or true—provided it was not refuted. As for me, when I desired to learn, it was in order to know and not in order to teach" (*Reveries*, CW 8:18; Pl. 1:1013). In sum, he saw himself as a new sort of author and challenged his contemporaries to evaluate themselves in light of his standard.

Rousseau's "new route" forms the main subject of this book. One of the marks of Rousseau's authorship is the great seriousness with which he took every aspect of it. Several years before beginning his literary career, he began his preparations for that career by writing an "Idea of the Method in the Composition of a Book." He wrote poetry as an "exercise for getting used to elegant inversions and for learning to write better prose" (*Confessions*, CW 5:132; Pl. 1:157). Feeling "the need to learn how to write," he translated Tacitus and other masters of style (Pl. 5:1227). He wrote several works devoted to the discussion of the nature and limits of expressiveness in language. When it came to the publication of his works, he gave detailed instructions to the artists who prepared illustrations; he paid careful attention to typesetting and quality of paper; and he quarreled with both publishers and censors over issues ranging from the relative importance of clarity, rhythm, and good grammar to the responsibility a novelist has for opinions espoused by his characters. It would be hard to find an author who had more evidence of having thought about every aspect of his activity.

Some of the complexity of Rousseau's idea of authorship is shown in two different aspects of his career. The first is his celebrated boldness and independence. Although he was careful in his dealings with legal authorities, he renounced many of the strategies of self-protection practiced by his contemporaries such as anonymous or pseudonymous publication or the cultivation of prestigious institutional ties. I will begin the discussion of Rousseau's authorship in chapter 1 with a description of the distinctiveness of

Rousseau's practice and the understanding that lies behind it. The second aspect is Rousseau's claim that he has promised to tell the truth "in every useful thing, as long as it is in me" (*Beaumont*, CW 9:52; Pl. 4:967). In addition to supporting Rousseau's boldness, this promise also led him to a thorough consideration of the circumstances in which the truth is morally useful and those in which it is not. This consideration led him to a sort of self-restraint that accompanies his boldness. To put this another way, as will be argued below, Rousseau was convinced that authorship was an essentially public and political activity and that the pursuit of truth was essentially a private and personal activity. Thus, after describing Rousseau's activity as an author, in subsequent chapters I will attempt to show the political significance he attributed to his books. A part of this discussion will involve a new interpretation of Rousseau's concept of citizenship, for which, I will argue, his own writing serves as a model. Finally, in the concluding chapter I will turn to Rousseau's view of the relation between his literary activity and his philosophic activity.

Some readers might find it useful for me to distinguish my approach from that taken by other scholars of Rousseau. Rousseau's understanding of the reasons for his activity as an author has not been an issue for the best known, most influential, and—in some respects—most impressive interpretations of Rousseau to appear in the past fifty years. For example, while Jean Starobinski's pathbreaking *Jean-Jacques Rousseau: La Transparence et l'obstacle*[5] does deal with Rousseau's literary activity in a comprehensive way, it is concerned less with Rousseau's account of the reasons for his activity than with the playing out of a personal existential dilemma of feeling that issued in writing. In many ways Jacques Derrida's *De la grammatologie*[6] is a reversal of Starobinski's psychological-literary approach, but it is a reversal that moves much further away from any notion of a reflective author by focusing on the unruliness of language that escapes authorial control. As a result of these two important works, there is now no shortage of psychological or deconstructionist studies of Rousseau. Other scholars—usually those interested in Rousseau's political thought—have made valuable contributions to understanding parts of his rhetoric in particular works, but few of them have felt compelled to address his manner of presenting this thought in a systematic way. My goal here is to let the buried question of authorial intention emerge more clearly.[7] That my approach need not close itself off to the legitimate insights offered by alternatives will, I hope, be made clear by the amount I have learned from the readings made possible by these different approaches.

One area of scholarship that does give close attention to the more or less reflective practices of authors in their relation with the public has been historical work on the formation of the "public sphere" in the eighteenth century or earlier. Recently, increasing attention has been paid to the early history of the publishing business and interrelations among authors, publishers, and government censors.[8] Historians of prerevolutionary France, inspired in part by Jürgen Habermas's *Structural Transformation of the Public Sphere: An Inquiry into a Category of Bourgeois Society*,[9] have taken a great interest in the discovery, invention, or formation of public opinion by writers and their readers. I have benefited from these historians, but my approach differs from theirs because it pays particular attention to what distinguishes Rousseau from his contemporaries and his explanations of these differences. Rousseau himself insisted upon his uniqueness, and even his enemies did not disagree with him on this point. Neither the Enlightenment itself nor the historical study of the Enlightenment has succeeded in making Rousseau conform to its model of behavior. In fact, one of the most interesting recent attempts to describe the workings of the eighteenth-century "republic of letters" takes as its point of departure a defense of those features of the "republic" most condemned by Rousseau.[10] Beyond the fact that I will be treating the untypical case represented by Rousseau, my approach differs from that of historians interested in the formation of the public sphere by being concerned with the seriousness of the case that Rousseau makes for himself rather than with his influence or representative character.

In my effort to describe Rousseau's arguments and actions as an author, I will have occasion to contrast his positions with those of contemporaries such as Diderot, d'Alembert, and Voltaire. In doing so, I concede that these writers confronted the same set of problems as Rousseau, but insist that they disagreed sharply about the solution to the problems and the reasons justifying these solutions. My treatment of these other writers is meant only to show their positions, or Rousseau's understanding of their positions, as they contrast with Rousseau's own. Only a full-scale treatment of the views of each of them could do justice to their seriousness and consistency.

Finally, my approach here can be contrasted with the one I myself took in an earlier book dedicated to Rousseau's *Confessions*.[11] In that book I attempted to show the philosophic importance of the *Confessions* by treating it less as an autobiography to be measured against either the established facts of Rousseau's life or independent understanding of his personality than as a sort of philosophic novel meant to give a concrete illustration of his understanding of human nature in general. In interpreting the *Confessions* this way, I deliberately refrained from considering other sources of information about his life such as his correspondence; instead, I interpreted the *Confessions* in light of the theoretical issues raised by works like *Emile*. I have come to appreciate the fact that Rousseau's actions should not be so radically separated from his account of his actions in the *Confessions*. Once he began his career as an author, he took advantage of his celebrity to present a particular image of authorial responsibility. In particular, he wrote his letters knowing that they would be circulated and probably published, and he took steps to make sure that they would be preserved, intending to use many of his letters as an appendix to the *Confessions*. Thus, what seem to be private communications are written with publication in mind. As a consequence, I have made extensive use of his correspondence to illustrate both his deeds and his explanations of their meaning. I have not, however, used the correspondence to arrive at conclusions that are not at least implicit in the published works. The argument of this book will be that consideration of apparently trivial matters connected with writing leads close to the heart of the most important issues of Rousseau's thought. In an effort to demonstrate this, my discussions alternate between accounts of Rousseau's decisions about putting his name on his books and the relation between these decisions and technical issues of his political theory. They also alternate between discussions of practical matters of publication and the philosophic basis of Rousseau's view of the interrelations among politics, the arts, and writing. Rather than focusing on one book and its meaning, I will treat Rousseau's literary career as a whole. This different method, however, is guided by the same concern as my earlier book, although it has caused me to reevaluate some of my conclusions.

CHAPTER ONE

RESPONSIBLE AND IRRESPONSIBLE AUTHORS

Rousseau's life was full of quarrels with former friends and associates, including the vanguard of the Enlightenment in the eighteenth century, people such as Grimm, Diderot, Hume, d'Holbach, d'Alembert, and Voltaire. Anyone with reverence for intellectual life who examines these episodes closely must be dismayed by the petty vindictiveness, refusal to tolerate disagreement, and unscrupulous actions that frequently characterized them. In this regard, the intellectual quarrels of the eighteenth century hardly differ from those with which we are familiar today. Because of Rousseau's pattern of difficult and sometimes even undeniably paranoid behavior, it is tempting to explain away his side in these quarrels as simply a function of his peculiar personality. Nonetheless, profound differences on matters of principle frequently played a large role in them in ways that are not always readily apparent. A prime illustration of the mixture of deeply personal matters and important principles can be found in a series of entanglements between Rousseau and Voltaire centering on the issues of anonymity, false attributions, and naming names.

These events allow Rousseau's understanding of authorship to stand out in sharp relief in comparison to the very different understanding held by Voltaire, the most famous writer among his contemporaries.[1] Both men behaved with remarkable consistency, but in entirely opposite ways. The consistency of their behavior reveals profoundly different understandings of authorship and responsibility. We can grasp the nature and significance of these alternative understandings if we call into question our own anachronistic assumption that it is natural for an author's name to appear on a book.

I. Naming Names

Not long after Rousseau fled from France following the condemnation of *Emile* in June 1762, a woman who had been very moved by the "Profession of Faith of the Savoyard Vicar" composed a letter to him expressing her admiration and seeking spiritual guidance. Not knowing where Rousseau had settled and apparently believing in the solidarity of men of letters, she mailed the letter to Rousseau in care of Voltaire. Upon receiving this testimony of regard for a man he no longer respected, Voltaire responded by mailing the pious woman a copy of the *Oath of the Fifty*, a scandalous antireligious work he had published anonymously the year before and that he had publicly denied he had written. Because Voltaire had not indicated that the pamphlet was from him, the astonished woman assumed that it had been sent by Rousseau and may have thought that he was its author. Straightening out this misunderstanding caused Rousseau a certain amount of trouble at a time when his life had been disrupted.

This was not the first time Voltaire had encouraged the attribution of one of his own anonymous works to Rousseau. Earlier the same year he had published another attack on Christianity, *Catechism of the Honest Man*, putting on the title page initials that pointed to Rousseau as the author of this antireligious book. Readers more than two centuries later are likely to be amazed by Voltaire's behavior in these cases, but in the eighteenth century this was only a striking example of widespread practice and could be justified as sensible prudence accompanied by a degree of personal malice. Neither of these actions was at all out of character for Voltaire. He regularly published works anonymously and then denied his authorship, and he frequently attributed works he wished to disown to other people with or without their consent.

Less than a year after Voltaire's prank concerning the *Oath of the Fifty*, Rousseau retaliated in a fashion when he published *Letters Written from the Mountain*, which defends the *Social Contract* and *Emile* against their censorship by Geneva. In the fifth letter Rousseau suggests that the Genevan authorities had been foolish in their rush to condemn *Emile*. He says that, rather than acting so rashly, they should have consulted Voltaire (who at that time lived just outside of Geneva and was in regular contact with leading members of the government), who would have responded by calming them. Rousseau then puts into Voltaire's mouth a speech in which the latter asserts that works of reasoning such as Rousseau's do no harm because so few people understand them and points out that the Genevans had tolerated much more daring works written by Voltaire himself. In the midst of this speech, Rousseau's Voltaire exclaims:

> Of all the follies of men, to reason is the one that harms the human race the least, and one sees even wise people infatuated with that folly sometimes. I do not reason, myself, that is true, but others do reason; what harm comes from it? See such, such, and such work; are there anything but pleasantries in these Books? Myself in the end, if I do not reason, I do better; I make my readers reason. See my chapter on the Jews [in the *Essay on Morals*]; see the same chapter more developed in the *Oath of the Fifty*. (*Mountain*, CW 9:225; Pl. 3:799)

By inventing this speech, Rousseau appears to make Voltaire himself admit that he was the author of a work he had frequently denied writing.

It would be hard to exaggerate Voltaire's rage when he read this. While his opinion of Rousseau had never been extremely high and their relations had been steadily deteriorating for several years, he now decided that Rousseau was not only insane, but also a traitor of the worst sort. To the terms of ridicule he had previously heaped on Rousseau in correspondence with mutual acquaintances, he now added the additional one of "police informer" (*délateur*). He used this term in numerous letters in which he complained about Rousseau's attribution of the *Oath* to him. Within days of reading the offending passage in *Letters Written from the Mountain*, he published (anonymously, of course) the pamphlet *Sentiment of the Citizens*, in which he revealed personal secrets about Rousseau, told some half-truths, and simply fabricated some scandalous stories about him. In addition, not being satisfied with accusing Rousseau of being a police informer, he decided to become one himself. This time he wrote to Genevan authorities in his own name urging that they take action against the departures from religious orthodoxy in *Letters Written from the Mountain*, implying that Rousseau should be sentenced to death in absentia. Although there is little reason to believe that Voltaire seriously wished to have Rousseau executed, he certainly did want to stir up trouble for him, and in this he was quite successful. The ferocity of his retaliation indicates Voltaire's outrage at the possible danger caused by this breach of his anonymity, in spite of the fact that his authorship of the *Oath* was known to Rousseau only because it was a quite open secret already. Having spent six months in the Bastille and a period of time in exile years before, Voltaire was acutely sensitive to the risks involved in writing controversial works. In fact, his decision to reside near Geneva was influenced by his desire to be close to foreign territory if a rapid flight from France became necessary.

Rousseau was deeply wounded by the anonymous *Sentiment of the Citizens*, although he never learned the identity of its author. Dismissing as preposterous the rumor that such a clumsy work had been written by

Voltaire, he attributed the pamphlet to the Genevan minister Jacob Vernes, who had been publicly saying some of the things contained in it. Rousseau decided to retaliate against Vernes by having the pamphlet reprinted in Paris (where he assumed his public reputation would cause people to dismiss the slanders against him) and named Vernes as the author (*Confessions*, CW 5:530; Pl. 1:632). Although he gave up this plan after receiving assurances from Vernes and others that he was mistaken, Rousseau persisted in his belief and softened his attribution only to a statement of the reasons that led him to suspect Vernes.

A final episode in the sequence of events involving Rousseau and Voltaire occurred a couple of years later. After Rousseau took refuge in England in 1766, Voltaire struck once again. He published the *Lettre de M. de Voltaire au docteur Jean-Jacques Pansophe* (published immediately in England as *A Letter from Mr. Voltaire to Mr. Jean-Jacques Rousseau*).[2] A few months later, in a letter to David Hume, Rousseau made the plausible accusation that Voltaire had published this work in an effort to turn the English against him. Rousseau's complaint was made public not by Rousseau himself, but by Hume's publication of his letter as part of his own quarrel with Rousseau. Voltaire responded by publishing the *Letter from M. de Voltaire to Mr. Hume* in which he denied that he was the author of the *Letter to Pansophe* and cited Rousseau's attribution of the work to him as proof that Rousseau was an unscrupulous liar. Moreover, Voltaire continued his effort to discredit Rousseau by writing to friends denying his authorship of the *Letter to Pansophe* and giving suggestions about who might have written it. He even wrote to these supposed authors accusing them of stirring up trouble for him by using his name.

Rousseau's behavior throughout this sequence of events is very consistent. In a book he published under his own name, he named Voltaire as the author of a work the latter had in fact written. He responded to an anonymous attack by publicly naming its presumed author and to a nonanonymous attack by complaining about it privately. While Rousseau was inflexible with regard to naming himself on his own works, he was not always so intransigent with respect to others. He exposed Voltaire and Vernes because their (in the case of Vernes) presumed attacks were so personal in nature. In other cases he was reasonably careful to leave anonymous authors with their anonymity intact. For example, he almost always carefully referred to "the author of the *Pensées philosophiques*" or "the author of *De l'esprit*," even though it was well known that Diderot and Helvétius were the authors of these works. In a reference to *The Spirit of the Laws* in the *Second Discourse*, he shows his respect for the fact that Montesquieu had published this work anonymously by referring only to an "illustrious philosopher" (CW 3:21; Pl. 3:136). At the end of his life, Rousseau returned to the issue of authors' concealment of their identities in the *Reveries*. While he persisted in condemning such practices and used the example of Montesquieu's anonymous *Temple de Gnide* to illustrate them, he did so without naming Montesquieu as the author. Thus, as Victor Gourevitch has observed, Rousseau's personal commitment to honesty did not require that he expose everyone else's secrets; although, as we have seen, it did permit exposure under certain circumstances.³

Voltaire's behavior was equally consistent in the opposite direction. He denied writing works he had written and attributed them to others. He clearly regarded Rousseau's openness as not only imprudent but as wickedly irresponsible because it encouraged persecutors. While it might be tempting to dismiss this lamentable sequence of events by referring to Rousseau's supposed paranoia and Voltaire's characteristic vindictiveness, the consistency of their behavior is evidence of profoundly different understandings of authorship. They, along with some of their contemporaries, shared the perception that public opinion could become a force in the world and the desire to use their own status as authors to shape this new force. We can gain insight into their views by examining features of their authorship and the explanations they gave for these features.

II. Anonymity and Responsibility

If we open a first edition of one of Rousseau's books—for example, the *Social Contract*—on the title page we see the name of the book, Rousseau's name along with the designation "Citizen of Geneva," and the indication that the book was published in Amsterdam by the publisher Rey in 1762. None of this is likely to be taken as very noteworthy by a reader today, but we should not allow expectations based on our normal experience to conceal the importance of this title page. Rousseau's decision to open his works with accurate and complete information was a distinct departure from the practice of many of his contemporaries who wrote controversial books. This is not to deny that there were some instances in which Rousseau departed from or allowed publishers to depart from his rule of complete openness, but generally he consented to such practices only reluctantly and when yielding to advice against his better judgment. What is striking about Rousseau's case is the relatively few exceptions to his policy of openness.

Today the anonymous publication of a book like *Primary Colors* is likely to cause a sensation, but in the century or so leading up to the beginning of Rousseau's literary career in 1750, seminal books of the Enlightenment such as Descartes's *Discourse on Method,* Spinoza's *Tractatus,* Locke's *Two Treatises on Government,* Hume's *Treatise of Human Nature,* and Montesquieu's *Spirit of the Laws* and *Persian Letters* all were originally published anonymously. By the time Rousseau's first important works were published, his best friend Diderot had published numerous books such as the *Pensées philosophiques, Les Bijoux indiscrets,* and the *Lettre sur les aveugles,* all of them anonymously and some clandestinely or with a false indication of place of publication.[4] It may always be true that one cannot judge a book by its cover, but in Rousseau's day one could also not judge it by its title page, which could lie about the author, publisher, place and date of publication. Indeed, at times prohibited books made new appearances under a misleading title so that one could not even be confident that the title on the title page was genuine.[5]

These deceptive practices were, in large part, responses to a complex system of censorship.[6] Legal publication in France and elsewhere usually required prior consent from government-appointed censors who could deny publication for a variety of reasons. By law, books could be suppressed on the grounds that they undermined the government, morals, or religion, or because they attacked individuals. In practice, however, there are examples of censors preventing the publication of books on the grounds that they were poorly written or because someone with influence did not want them to be published. Voltaire's observation that legal permission to publish depended on whether the censor happened to be the friend of one's friend or the friend of one's enemy was an accurate one. This arbitrary and capricious system made publication into a sort of lottery. It must be added that success in running the obstacle course of prior censorship did not confer immunity from prosecution. Helvétius, for example, found cold comfort in the tacit permission he received for the publication of *De l'esprit* in 1758 when the book was condemned immediately after publication, and he avoided prosecution only by making a public disavowal of its contents.

Chrétien-Guillaume de Lamoignon de Malesherbes—whose tenure in the position of director of publishing corresponded with the major part of Rousseau's literary career—attempted to make liberal use of this illiberal system that he inherited from his predecessors.[7] Malesherbes was guided both by his sympathy for unorthodox books and by his concern for French commercial interests. Part of the function of the office of the book trade was to help French publishing against foreign competition, and if a book was denied permission for publication in France, it was quite possible that it would be published abroad and, therefore, that sales would benefit publishers in other countries. Malesherbes was acutely aware of this tension between censorship and support of a national publishing industry. His concern went hand in hand with his desire to increase the circulation of enlightenment in France.

As a consequence of these two concerns, Malesherbes governed the book trade with what Rousseau called "as much enlightenment as gentleness, and to the great satisfaction of literary people" (*Confessions*, CW 5:428; Pl. 1:511). For example, he made frequent use of censors who were sympathetic to controversial causes. In one notable instance, he appointed d'Alembert as the censor of Rousseau's *Letter to d'Alembert on the Theatre*, and d'Alembert announced that he approved the work for publication even without reading it. In this instance and others, Rousseau was the beneficiary of Malesherbes's administration, although when *Emile* was attacked by the Parlement of Paris, Malesherbes showed that his loyalty was more to the system than to Rousseau. In any event, from the beginning Rousseau's satisfaction did not extend to the system Malesherbes administered.

Malesherbes was particularly troubled by one peculiar consequence of prior censorship: when his office let a book pass censorship, it not only allowed publication, but also (in effect) endorsed its contents. In other words, official permission appeared to be a recommendation, a sort of Good Housekeeping seal of approval. Because of this, censors might be tempted to avoid taking sides on every conceivable intellectual dispute by simply turning down any questionable book. To address this problem, Malesherbes greatly extended the use of tacit, or as he called it "illegal," permission to publish. When the office controlling the book trade was willing to tolerate a book but wanted to avoid giving the appearance of endorsing its contents, it notified the publisher that permission for publication was denied but also unofficially informed him (or in some cases, her) that it would not prosecute a discreet publication. Books published with tacit permission often gave a foreign city as the place of publication and usually were published anonymously to avoid punishment for the author if the book happened to be suppressed by some other public authority later on. Michel Foucault has argued that during this period "anonymity was of interest only as a puzzle to be solved," but it might be more accurate to say that anonymity was embraced as the solution to the problem posed by censorship.[8] In sum, books published with tacit permission were books whose very existence depended on no one taking public responsibility for them, not the censors, not the publisher, and most definitely not the author.

One reason that the authorities did not object to anonymous publication of controversial works is that these books would often appear and disappear unnoticed, whereas books known to be written by a famous author would be read more seriously and by more people. Consequently, when the censors knew that a famous author's name was going to appear on a book, they looked at it especially closely because they knew it would be popular. As might be expected, Rousseau's policy of naming himself as an author led him into regular clashes with both the censors and his publishers. Friends, publishers, and even sympathetic government officials constantly urged him to behave as everyone else did, but he insisted on confronting the entire system of censorship head-on. He was quite resentful of friends who reproached him for putting his name on *Emile* (*Confessions*, CW 5:482; Pl. 1:526). When, at the prompting of Malesherbes himself, his publisher advised him to drop his name from the title page of the *Social Contract*, he refused. He was irritated at the decision of another publisher (also in response to urging from Malesherbes) to publish an edition of *Emile* in France with the pretense that it was printed in Holland.[9]

Most successful writers, unlike Rousseau, were content to adapt to the repressive conditions in which they found themselves by embracing this evasion of responsibility. Rousseau's acquaintance the baron d'Holbach, for example, attributed his own works of antireligious materialism (which were published clandestinely and abroad) to other writers, sometimes to authors of sound reputation and impeccable orthodoxy who had recently died and could not deny the attribution. Voltaire, in particular, incessantly counseled his followers that "one must never present anything under one's name."[10] He chided anyone foolish enough to ignore this advice. In a marginal note to his copy of the *Letter to Beaumont*, he blamed Rousseau for bringing persecution on himself by naming himself as author of his books, unlike Spinoza, who "did not name himself."[11] As we have seen, he himself regularly used pseudonyms, false attributions, and anonymity. Not only did he frequently issue public statements denying his authorship of books he had in fact written, but he also made such denials to friends so that, without knowing that they were doing so, they would spread the lie. While Voltaire is, perhaps, the most expert practitioner of this strategy, he was far from being the only one. In fact, he was quite willing to give lessons to other writers in these tactics.

Within the context of censorship and the danger of imprisonment, the basic reasons behind Voltaire's policy of anonymity and false attribution are easy enough to grasp. He spelled them out clearly in a series of letters he wrote to Helvétius in 1763.[12] In these letters Voltaire stresses that not only is there no disharmony between devotion to truth and concern for one's own safety, but, in fact, service to enlightenment depends on attending to one's own interest. Because the strength of its opponents depends crucially on their good reputation among the powerful, enlightenment will be served well only if it destroys this support. Therefore, it is necessary to make these opponents look ridiculous through the use of satire and even possibly libelous attacks. There are two dangers in pursuing this policy. First, there is the obvious one of running afoul of the censors or prosecutors. Second, there is the less obvious, but equally important, fact that one's own reputation can suffer if one is known as the author of works indulging in purely personal attacks. Anonymity solves both problems. Voltaire's analysis leads directly to his avowed maxim, "Strike and conceal your hand."[13]

III. "MY NAME . . . WILL EVEN CONSTITUTE ITS TITLE"

Although Voltaire's letters to Helvétius were written thirteen years after Rousseau's *First Discourse* and the situation for writers had begun to worsen in the intervening years, these letters still capture the atmosphere in which Rousseau began his literary career. In fact, the early stages of this career followed a well-traveled path similar to the one advised by Voltaire. When Rousseau was twenty-seven—long before he became famous—he published an autobiographical poem, "Le Verger de Madame la Barrone de Warens." Not only did he publish this work anonymously, but its title page indicates that it was published in London by a nonexistent publisher when it was, in fact, published in either Lyons or Chambéry. Later he did publish his *Dissertation on Modern Music* and some poems with his name attached, but none of these works were of the sort that could cause trouble for an author.

Shortly before Rousseau had the "illumination" that led to the writing of the *First Discourse*, he and Diderot planned a joint publication of a journal called *Le Persiffleur* (the Banterer) modeled on the *Spectator*. In Rousseau's draft of what was intended to be the first issue, he refers to "the two principal dispositions" of the presumably single author. He says, "By the first I find myself wisely foolish, by the other foolishly wise" (Pl. 1:1110). Although this and other similar statements are often read as an early account of the oscillation of Rousseau's own personality, it seems simpler and more plausible to read them as an account of two different writers publishing under a single pseudonym.

A large part of the draft consists of a statement of principles in which Rousseau insists on the importance of impartial criticism of books and the need to banish from the journal "every personal criticism or observation" concerning authors (Pl. 1:1107). He concludes that the effort to preserve impartiality requires that the identity of the author of *Le Persiffleur* remain unknown. At this point Rousseau saw anonymity as a crucial contribution to "consulting only reason and speaking only the truth" (Pl. 1:1112). Prior to the "illumination," then, Rousseau fully embraced what could be called the conventional practices of authors of even mildly unconventional works.

Rousseau's clear reflection on issues involved in anonymous publishing is strong evidence that when he changed his practice, he did so because of his deepening reflection on the significance of the practice he was rejecting, rather than because of an unreflective attachment to self-exposure. In any event, it is clear that Rousseau took some time to convert himself to his new position. In the *Confessions* he says that once the *First Discourse* had made him a celebrity, he undertook a complete moral reform, but that he only gradually put his behavior into harmony with his principles (*Confessions*, CW 5:303–8; Pl. 1:362–68). As part of this reform, he decided to use his fame to set a new example of behavior for literary people.

It seems clear that a part of this reform was the decision to attach his name to his publications, a decision that he implemented more and more consistently from 1751–53 (see table, next page). Because Rousseau was relatively inexperienced as a published author and, moreover, was quite ill, Diderot attended to the details of the publication of the *First Discourse*. Given that Diderot himself had only recently been released from a prison term brought about by his *Letter on the Blind*, it is hardly surprising that Rousseau's *Discourse* was published (in January 1751) with no indication of who the author was beyond the statement "By a Citizen of Geneva." By the end of the year, however, the work had been reissued several times, the last one with Rousseau's name attached.

Over the next couple of years, Rousseau anonymously published the first of his replies to critics of the *Discourse* and several pamphlet contributions to the quarrel between the adherents of French and Italian music. By the end of both series of publications, Rousseau attached his name to his contributions. During the same period he allowed his opera *The Village Soothsayer* and his play *Narcissus* to be performed without attribution, but he openly acknowledged both upon their publication in 1753. He even took great pride in proclaiming his authorship of the play when it flopped. With only one exception, after the anonymous publication of the *Letter from a Symphonist* in September 1753,[14] he always put his name on his publications, even owning works such as "The Queen Fantastic" when they were published without his permission. In short, over this period of frantic literary activity during which he published a new work every couple of months, he completed the reversal of a policy that he had earlier accepted without reservation.

In several of the key publications of this period, Rousseau instituted what became a favorite practice of putting his name into the very title of his work. He later gave a strong endorsement of this practice in a response to

This table is meant to be a representative, rather than exhaustive, list of Rousseau's publications from 1751–53.

Month of Publication	Work	Authorial Identification
1751		
January	Discourse which Won the Prize of the Academy of Dijon in the year 1750 on the Question proposed by that Academy: Has the restoration of the Sciences and Arts tended to purify Morals?*	By a Citizen of Geneva
June	Letter to M. the Abbé Raynal Author of the Mercury of France	Anonymous
July	Articles on music for volume 1 of the Encyclopédie	Identified as author in d'Alembert's "Preliminary Discourse"
October	Observations by Jean-Jacques Rousseau of Geneva on the Reply Made to His Discourse	Named in title
November	Letter from J. J. Rousseau of Geneva to M. Grimm on the refutation of his Discourse by M. Gautier Professor of Mathematics and History and member of the Royal Academy of Literature of Nancy	Named in title
1752		
April	Letter to M. Grimm on the Subject of the Remarks Added to His Letter on "Omphale"	Anonymous
April	Final Reply	J. J. Rousseau of Geneva
May	Letter by Jean-Jacques Rousseau of Geneva About a New Refutation of His Discourse by a Member of the Academy of Dijon	Named in title
1753		
January or February	Narcissus or The Lover of Himself	By J. J. Rousseau
September	Letter from a Symphonist of the Royal Academy of Music to His Comrades in the Orchestra	Anonymous
November	Letter on French Music	By J. J. Rousseau
?	The Village Soothsayer Interlude Presented at Fontainbleau before their Majesties the 18th and 24th October 1752 and at Paris	By J. J. Rousseau

*The *Discourse* was reissued several times that year by a variety of publishers. The last of these editions included Rousseau's name as author.

an inquiry from his publisher Rey, who had asked if Rousseau wished to publish his *Letter to d'Alembert* anonymously. Rousseau answered, "Not only will you be able to name me; but my name will be in and will even constitute its title" (Leigh 5:70). The actual title of the *Letter* is, then, *J. J. Rousseau Citizen of Geneva, To M. d'Alembert of the French Academy, the Royal Academy of Sciences of Paris, the Prussian Academy, the Royal Society of London, the Royal Academy of Literature of Sweden, and the Institute of Bologna: On his Article GENEVA in the Seventh Volume of the Encyclopedia and Particularly on the project of establishing a Dramatic Theater in that City*. Similarly the actual title of the *Letter to Beaumont* is *Jean-Jacques Rousseau, Citizen of Geneva, to Christophe de Beaumont, Archbishop of Paris, Duke of St. Cloud, Peer of France, Commander of the Order of the Holy Spirit, Provider of the Sorbonne, Etc.* In the titles of these works, he makes explicit the juxtaposition between his own status as a simple Genevan to the exalted conventional status of his opponent. In each of these works, the juxtaposition sets the stage for a radical reversal of status.

If Foucault is right when he declares, "Speeches and books were assigned real authors, other than mythical or important religious figures, only when the author became subject to punishment,"[15] Rousseau is a prime example of someone who embraced the risks of authorship and, thereby, brought its role in society to the fore. He made authorship into a public identity and made a willingness to risk punishment for what one published into a crucial part of this identity.

IV. Anonymous Kings and Named Authors

Rousseau's effort to make authorship into a particular sort of public identity necessarily entailed an effort to raise the status of this identity. In this, as in other things, his approach can be understood in relation to that of Voltaire. The latter's change of name from Arouet to the more noble-sounding Arouet de Voltaire brought him some respect, but it also earned some ridicule even from supporters like Diderot. Very early in his career, Voltaire was brutally taught the lesson that the acknowledgment of his talent counted for little among French aristocrats when talent came into conflict with the privileges connected with a title.[16] His writings frequently lament the precedence of hereditary privilege over talent, but he remained extremely sensitive about his status. Thus, he left himself open to the charge made by Stendhal that "one is only too much aware that Voltaire would have traded all his genius for noble birth."[17]

When he was eighteen, Rousseau briefly attempted to pass himself off as a Parisian musician with the more noble-sounding name of Vaussore de Villeneuve with comically disastrous results (*Confessions*, CW 5:124–25; Pl. 1:147–50); but when he reached maturity, he made no effort to imitate Arouet de Voltaire. While Rousseau received no beatings at the hands of the servants of aristocrats (although one employer, the count de Montaigu, threatened to have him thrown out of a window), he also learned early that the prerogatives of rank and nobility took precedence over both talent and justice in France (*Confessions*, CW 5:273–76; Pl. 1:323–28). Nevertheless, he was willing to let his own genius and his own name stand against kings and refused to listen to the objection that "since I am only a man of the people, I have nothing to say that deserves the attention of readers" (*Confessions*, CW 5:586; Pl. 1:1150).

Rousseau first undertook his elevation of the status of author in the very work that could be said to have introduced his policy of rejecting anonymity: the first pamphlet in which he went so far as to make his own name part of his title, *Observations by Jean-Jacques Rousseau of Geneva on the Reply Made to His Discourse*. This was a response to a criticism of the *Discourse on the Sciences and the Arts* written by a well-known anonymous author of a very special sort, the former King Stanislaus of Poland, who was also the father of the queen of France. Although Stanislaus had published his "Reply" anonymously, Rousseau was quickly informed of the identity of his opponent and knew that the public would also be aware of it. Rousseau later said, "I seized the occasion I was offered to teach the public how a private man could defend the cause of truth even against a sovereign" (*Confessions*, CW 5:307; Pl. 1:366). Given that his *Observations* takes issue with a figure of such stature, it is not surprising that Rousseau's friends urged him not merely to remain anonymous but to refrain from publication altogether.

Precisely because he is writing in opposition to an author who is both anonymous and known to be a king, Rousseau opens the *Observations* by arguing that social status should have no significance in intellectual disputes. Taking this opportunity to make his earliest published statement on natural equality, he insists that his deference to his opponent will not affect his response because "whenever reason is at issue, men return to the right of Nature and resume their original equality" (*Observations*, CW 2:37; Pl. 3:35). Social status is irrelevant because all authors are equal in principle. He adds to this rejection of authority by dismissing Stanislaus's appeal to the names of famous writers to support his position (CW 2:50; Pl. 3:52). Neither the title of one's opponent nor the famous names of his authorities carry any weight in rational debate.

One might think that this insistence on equality could lead to an endorsement of anonymity comparable to the one given in *Le Persiffleur*. Anonymity would be the solution to the problems caused by inequality of social status or reputation—anonymous authors being in principle indistinguishable and therefore equal. In fact, Rousseau does assert, "Truth is so independent of those who attack it and those who defend it, that the Authors who dispute over it ought mutually to forget each other" (CW 2:40; Pl. 3:40).[18] He immediately says that this rule is impossible to follow in the present situation. Even though Stanislaus had published anonymously, his identity was known. As a result, truth cannot be the simply decisive factor in their public debate. Rousseau must find something other than natural equality to level the playing field, or to tip it in his favor.

Accordingly, after his preliminary effort to dismiss authority based on either political status or literary reputation by appealing to natural equality, Rousseau takes the second step of constructing a rival form of authority based on personal conviction and exemplary behavior rather than conventional status. He does this not by praising himself directly, but by describing the success of Christianity in spreading a doctrine that, like his own, does not favor the learned or the powerful. He says, "Twelve poor fishermen and artisans undertook to instruct and convert the world. Their method was simple. They preached without Art but with an earnest heart; and of all the miracles with which God honored their faith, the most striking was the saintliness of their life" (CW 2:45; Pl. 3:45). Thus earnestness and living one's life as a model for emulation can be sources of personal authority that can convert large numbers. Rousseau himself devotes much of his art to developing a reputation for artlessness and earnestness. In sum, he sees a connection between the success of his doctrine and his status as a new kind of author whose authority is linked with his personal character rather than his credentials.

While Rousseau was correct in his judgment that Stanislaus would not attempt retribution, his effrontery in usurping the superior status of the king did not escape the attention of a young writer living under Stanislaus's patronage. In 1755 the young playwright Charles Palissot de Montenoy satirized Rousseau's behavior and even his lack of an aristocratic name in his play *Le Cercle ou Les Originaux*. A character easily identifiable as Rousseau, but called simply "The Philosopher," says, "I have given several works to the public; and while one sees so many authors who blush at their name, because they do not find it noble enough, I had the courage to affix mine, and to teach anyone who wanted to know that I am called Blaise-Gilles-Antoine, the cosmopolitan." His noble interlocutor replies to this plebian name, "One needs philosophy indeed to put up with a name like that one."[19] In spite of such mockery, or assisted by the additional publicity it gave him, Jean-Jacques, as he came to be generally known, was immensely successful at using his common name to win over readers.

Rousseau's distinctive practice of putting his own name on his books is coupled with an equally distinctive practice of refusing to dedicate those books to influential patrons or potential patrons. Rousseau's only works containing dedications are *The Village Soothsayer*, dedicated to his friend Charles Duclos, who had been instrumental in arranging a performance of this opera, and the *Second Discourse*, dedicated to the republican city of Geneva. This decision to shun protectors was consciously made (*Confessions*, CW 5:321; Pl. 1:382), and Rousseau steadfastly refused to listen to hints that dedications and works written in praise of the powerful could be useful to him (*Confessions*, CW 5:463; Pl. 1:554). He insisted on standing alone without the sort of supports aspired to by other writers.

The insistence on attaching his name to his books and on renouncing dedications to the powerful were only two elements in Rousseau's bold policy of defying or reversing authority. When censors demanded alterations in order to allow publication, he frequently resisted. For example, he refused to accept most of the suggested changes to *Julie* on the grounds that the censor was attempting to rewrite his novel.[20] When the government censor of his abridgment of the abbé de Saint-Pierre's *Project for Perpetual Peace* demanded that he change a sentence, Rousseau refused and suggested that his wording be left as it stood and that the censor's version be inserted on a separate sheet as an erratum (*Saint-Pierre*, Pl. 3:580 n. 1 to p. 580).[21] It is hardly surprising that Rousseau's suggestion was rejected since it would increase the provocative character of his original formulation by making his disagreement with the censor as conspicuous as possible.

This is not to say that Rousseau failed to exercise any caution. As Heinrich Meier has shown in his definitive edition of the *Second Discourse*, Rousseau removed excessively bold passages from his works even at late stages of the publication process.[22] Also, he was occasionally willing to use others as a partial cloak for opinions he wished to support. This was his intention when he undertook to edit the abbé de Saint-Pierre's works, although in this instance he quickly concluded that this strategy was a mistake (*Confessions*, CW 5:342, 356; Pl. 1:407, 423–24). He did use characters such as the Savoyard Vicar and Julie as the mouthpieces for unorthodox religious teachings. Rousseau complained bitterly when the opinions expressed by his characters were attributed to him, and both characters do express some opinions that Rousseau did not share (*Dialogues*, CW 1:70; Pl. 1:749–50; and *Beaumont*, CW 9:100; Pl. 4:1029).[23] Nevertheless, even in these cases, he insisted on taking responsibility for the publication of those ideas in his role as presumed editor. Thus, even when coming closest to Voltaire's policy, Rousseau diverged from it in the crucial sense by taking responsibility for the publication, if not the origination, of the ideas in question.

His most significant precaution against persecution was to live in one country (France), be a citizen of a second (Geneva), and publish his books in a third (Holland). In the *Second Discourse* he even took the further step of dating his dedication from a fourth country (Savoy). Rousseau thought that this policy maximized his freedom to write what he wished because the Genevan government would have no grounds for objecting to what he published in another country and the French government should see no reason to prosecute a foreigner (*Confessions*, CW 5:341; Pl. 1:406). He believed that the independence he gained from his situation allowed him to avoid the need to resort to anonymity. In the end, such precautions failed to disarm the reaction to Rousseau's boldness. They did, however, allow him to make himself into a symbol of all victims of unjust oppression in a way that someone who published anonymously while living safely in high society could not. Shortly after the publication of the *Social Contract* and *Emile* in 1762, in a step that was extreme even by the standards of the day, censors across Europe decided that these books must be burned.[24] Rousseau reacted to the suppression of his books by writing defenses of them that were, in their turn, suppressed. His *Letters Written from the Mountain*, which attacked the censors, had the remarkable distinction of being declared unworthy of being burned by the public hangman in Geneva (*Confessions*, CW 5:522; Pl. 1:623). Numerous other cities—less solicitous of the hangman's sensibilities—did have the *Letters* burned. With each successive defense, Rousseau persisted in his claims that the suppression of his works was both unjust and a violation of accepted legal procedure.

Rousseau was well aware of the distinctiveness of his own behavior and in the *Letter to Beaumont* claimed that he was "the only Author of my century and many others who wrote in good faith" (*Beaumont*, CW 9:51; Pl. 4:965). Although this is more modest than the first draft of this passage in which he refers not merely to many centuries, but to "perhaps almost all" centuries full of authors who wrote in bad faith (Pl. 4:1741), it seems hyperbolic when one considers the extent of the difficulties felt by all controversial writers in the Old Regime. Nevertheless, other writers who were not particularly friendly to Rousseau tended to accept his self-characterization. D'Alembert, for example, who admitted that the threat of prosecution prevented him from saying more than one-quarter of the truth, declared that Rousseau was perhaps the only writer who dared to speak his mind.[25] This is so because "fear of outraging established opinions, of shocking through paradoxes, of passing as a cynic, of making enemies and trouble for himself, none of all that stops him."[26] Diderot—who once described his own writing by saying, "I saved myself by means of the most glib ironic tone I could achieve, generalities, laconism, and obscurity"—also regarded Rousseau as an exemplar of openness in his writings.[27] Whether they attributed its source to recklessness, a desire for celebrity, or singular devotion to the truth, virtually everyone agreed that an unrivaled boldness was the hallmark of Rousseau's writing.

More recently, some who wish to offer a sympathetic explanation of Rousseau's policy are tempted to attribute it to a simple desire for openness and distaste for covert maneuvering, an interpretation that Rousseau did much to encourage.[28] Such an explanation, while it contains a good deal of truth, has the danger of leading to a picture of a rather naive Rousseau in contrast to a sophisticated Voltaire. Both sides of this picture would fail to do justice to its subjects: the positions of both men resulted from careful reflection on the concrete circumstances in which they found themselves as writers in the eighteenth century and from well-thought-out views of the social responsibility of authors. In fact, it should be pointed out that other writers such as d'Alembert and Diderot also were compelled to reflect deeply about their own position in the world, and each arrived at a different strategy for combining safety and effectiveness. D'Alembert, for example, wrote "Essay on the Society of Literary People and the Great," exposing many of the same problems identified by Rousseau and Voltaire.[29] Whatever the truth might be about Rousseau's vanity, desire for martyrdom, or love of transparency, he also gave careful arguments to justify his idiosyncratic insistence on taking responsibility for what he wrote. These arguments show why he attempted to undermine the understanding of authorial irresponsibility that greased the wheels of publishing in the ancien régime.

Given the novelty of Rousseau's openness and the risks to which it exposed him, it is not surprising that on numerous occasions he presented the reasons that led him to this policy. These discussions show clearly enough that it would be a mistake to attribute his conduct simply to vanity or some sort of desire for a Socrates-like martyrdom, although it must be conceded that his contemporaries were quick to seize on one or the other of these explanations, with his enemies favoring the first and his supporters the second of these alternatives.[30]

The most straightforward explanation of this practice of publishing under his own name occurs in the so-called "Second Preface" to *Julie*. This "preface," which was published independently of the novel, consists of a dialogue between Rousseau and a man of letters who has been plausibly identified as Diderot and, in any event, like Diderot is a supporter of the use of anonymity.³¹ The first question raised in the dialogue concerns whether *Julie* is fact or fiction. In a manner that helped to stimulate interest in both the novel and its putative editor, whom readers found it easy to identify with the hero of the novel, Rousseau fails to give a direct answer to the interlocutor's question about the truth of this collection of letters (see *Confessions*, CW 5:458; Pl. 1:548). Presenting a novel as a factual account was a common practice, and, contrary to what one might assume today, Rousseau's distinctiveness consisted more in his refusal simply to lie by saying that his book was a true account rather than in his willingness to let his readers think it was.

Having dodged the issue of the truth of the letters, Rousseau turns the discussion to the merits of the book and what it can hope to accomplish. After pointing out how far the lessons of this novel are from current standards of behavior, the interlocutor urges him to conceal his identity even as the editor of the book and offers to keep the secret. Rousseau responds, "I am naming myself at the head of this book, not to claim it as mine; but to answer for it. If it contains evil, let it be imputed to me; if good, I do not plan to boast of it." In the shorter preface that accompanied the novel, he says in addition, "Every honorable man must acknowledge the books he publishes" (*Julie*, CW 6:19, 3; Pl. 2:26–27, 5).³² The implication that other writers (such as Voltaire and Diderot, for example, but also Spinoza, Descartes, Hume, and Montesquieu) were dishonorable was a challenge to and rebuke of publishers, the censors, and especially all other writers who had no qualms about adapting to the system. It is not surprising that Voltaire understood Rousseau's insistence on naming names as a sort of declaration of war.

In *Letters Written from the Mountain* and the *Letter to Beaumont*, works written in response to the suppression of the *Social Contract* and *Emile*, Rousseau spells out his reasons for refusing to come to terms with a system of censorship that thrives on anonymity in terms that show his opposition to the position adopted by Voltaire. The censors in Geneva had argued that their prohibition and public burning of the *Social Contract* did not require that they question Rousseau in advance about his authorship and the contents of his book. Their argument rested on a distinction between the author and the book. Because a penalty inflicted on a book (such as being burned) has no effect on its author, public authorities have no need to concern themselves excessively with real authorship or actual contents of books. Rousseau points out that such a condemnation can hardly fail to damage the reputation of anyone known to be the author. It is only in the case of anonymity that the fate of the book can have no consequences for the authors, who "are even in the practice of avowing these Books in order to do themselves honor with them, and of disavowing them in order to put themselves under cover" (*Mountain*, CW 9:219; Pl. 3:792). Rousseau's point would be supported by the case of Montesquieu, who published the *Persian Letters* anonymously but used it as his major credential for election to the French Academy, even though acknowledging it would have cost him votes.[33] If this is true of an author respected by Rousseau, how could it not apply to lesser authors who, even when they are apparently bitter critics of the government, tend to be merely clamoring for a larger share of the benefits that come with celebrity as a writer. Such social critics and the public authorities who order the burning of their books can share a good laugh at dinner over the prosecution that took place in the morning. Authorial vanity is not damaged by this arrangement because there are ways of making one's authorship a very open secret without running any risk. Because there are no consequences for anyone, authors can write without worrying about being held accountable for what they say and authorities can prosecute and burn without worrying about the justice of what they do. The apparent adversaries are in fact joined in a system of irresponsibility that serves both sides well. Only "clumsy" and "imprudent" authors like Rousseau who insist on putting their names on their books ruin the fun.

The system of irresponsibility does in fact have consequences, however. In it, authors who have the frankness to own their works will suffer the consequences of irresponsible prosecution. Prosecutors will even regard putting one's name on a work as an aggravation of the offensiveness of the work and therefore be more likely to take steps against it (CW 9:220; Pl. 3:793). As a consequence, authors who wish to be at all bold will be forced to be guided by something other than the truth when they publish. As Rousseau says, "In order to be useful with impunity one lets one's Book loose among the public, and one ducks" (CW 9:219; Pl. 3:792). Truth will suffer in a system that rewards and even compels anonymity.

Two types of authors will thrive in such a system: approved authors who flatter the prejudices of the powerful who can injure or reward them and those who hide behind anonymity. Both types are marked by a profound hypocrisy when they claim to be disinterested. About the former Rousseau says, "Listening to the people who are allowed to speak in public, I understood that they dare or wish to say only what suits those who command; and being paid by the strong to preach to the weak, they only know how to speak to the latter about their duties and to the former about their rights" (*Beaumont*, CW 9:52; Pl. 4:967; see "Richesses," Pl. 5:478–79; and "State of War," Pl. 3:608). Even very intelligent writers, Grotius, for example, find themselves entangled in sophistry when they try to reconcile their desire for "embassies, professorships, or pensions" with their desire to be truthful (*Social Contract*, CW 4:146–47; Pl. 3:370–71).[34] Such writers undermine both the few restraints that exist for the powerful and the few consolations that exist for the poor ("Letter to Voltaire," CW 3:108–12; Pl. 4:1059–65; and "Richesses," Pl. 5:481).

Some might endorse anonymous publishing because it is evidence that a writer is unconcerned with self-promotion and because it would allow for boldness without fear,[35] but Rousseau is no more hopeful about writers who resort to anonymity for protection than he is about the named writers who simply flatter the great. The sort of boldness that issues from a concern for protection of oneself is no more disinterested than the sort of restraint imposed by a desire to curry favor with the powerful. In the section of *Letters Written from the Mountain* that contains the explicit identification of Voltaire as the author of the *Oath of the Fifty*, Rousseau refers to those who use anonymity to give vent to "the poison of calumny and satire" as cowards (*Mountain*, CW 9:219; Pl. 3:792). Rather than inspiring them to be bold in expressing the truth, the shield provided by anonymity gives them freedom to pursue personal vendettas with impunity. For both officially approved and anonymous writers, the system of censorship causes the predominance of self-seeking, bad faith, venom, and irresponsibility.

While Voltaire justifies his resort to anonymity as an attempt to combine maximum effectiveness with safety, Rousseau names himself as the author of his works in an attempt to combine effectiveness with responsibility. Voltaire could object that such a project is doomed to failure because it makes the censors more diligent and gives them an easy target. Thus, he could attack Rousseau alternately for imprudently endangering the cause of philosophy and for hypocritically making too many concessions to established religion in order to see his name in print. Rousseau would certainly concede that safety was not his aim, although he could also point to his concern for scrupulously following all legal forms. He could defend himself against the charge that he made too many concessions by pointing to both his successful opposition to censors and to his persecution.

Finally, Rousseau does argue that the success of his books proves his effectiveness and that this success is linked with his persona as an author. As Foucault has pointed out, "A name can group together a number of texts and thus differentiate them from others."[36] In Rousseau's case, his name on a book guaranteed its success because this name embodied boldness in defying injustice, openness, and responsibility for what he wrote.[37] This connection between his name and his books is a major part of the reason why Rousseau wrote so much explaining his own personality. The intimate connection he establishes between his name and his books makes it imperative that he protect his good name in order to protect the reputation of his books and make them affect their readers in the right way. The *Dialogues* is the key example of this attempt. In the three dialogues that make up this work, Rousseau first confronts the bad reputation given to him by his enemies that makes it impossible for readers to grasp his intention in his books; second, presents a more accurate account of the author of these books; and, third, shows the sort of reading that results from this better appreciation of the author.[38] In sum, Rousseau self-consciously set out on a mission both to be a new sort of writer and to make himself into a conspicuous model of behavior. This is the reason he set out to become famous as a champion of openness and transparency.

The discussion up to this point has focused on the issue of naming oneself as the author of one's books. In making the argument for the importance of naming oneself, Rousseau is making an argument for taking responsibility. As important as this issue is, it is not as important as the contents of those books. Indeed, a crucial part of Rousseau's argument about naming names is that the lack of responsibility characteristic of anonymous authors will make them write different books from the ones that will be written by named authors. Thus, the question of who is speaking leads quite directly to the question of what is being said. Rousseau's consideration of what should and—just as important—what should not be said will be the subject of the next chapter.

CHAPTER TWO

THE CASE FOR (AND AGAINST) CENSORSHIP

A consideration of what Rousseau says in his books reveals a side of him that, at first glance, looks very different from the one sketched in the preceding chapter. His attack on the irresponsibility promoted by the eighteenth-century European system of censorship is not an attack on all possible forms of censorship. In fact, support of various forms of censorship is not at all inconsistent with his claim that authors should boldly take responsibility for what they write. Indeed, taking responsibility as an author requires giving serious thought to the content of books whose publication one is authorizing. Boldness in asserting one's identity as an author may even require some reserve once one moves beyond the title page. Thus, caution and willingness to endorse censorship (or at least self-censorship) can be logical consequences of unusual openness in naming oneself. In sum, Rousseau's insistence on taking responsibility for what he publishes is quite compatible with acknowledging restraints upon what he should publish, and he frequently endorsed such restraints. The work that launched his literary career contains a note praising the Caliph Omar for urging the burning of the library of Alexandria. The note goes on to predict that the sovereigns of Europe would soon be obliged to make efforts to rid their states of the "terrible art" of printing (*First Discourse*, CW 2:20; Pl. 3:28). Several years later Rousseau attacked d'Alembert's proposal for the establishment of a theater in Geneva. In the *Social Contract* he praises the Roman office of censor and endorses an exclusive civil religion. Finally, in *Emile* he condemns popular children's literature because of its corrupting effects. In short, throughout his career Rousseau supported a variety of types of censorship, and it is not surprising that some regard him as one of its most important modern supporters, if not simply as a systematic enemy of liberty in any genuine sense of the word.[1] Those who support censorship today because they lament the hostility of intellectuals to community standards, the debasing effects of popular entertainment, assaults on religious belief, and trends in the education of children can approach him as a potential ally.

The more closely we look at the details of Rousseau's position, however, unsettling features begin to emerge. For example, he is less worried about the lowest end of popular culture and the seamier sides of entertainment than he is about the highest of high culture. As d'Alembert was quick to point out in their dispute over the establishment of a theater in Geneva, Rousseau attacks the most respectable forms of literature and ignores the prevalence of disreputable forms of popular entertainment. His targets are Molière, Racine, Corneille, La Fontaine, Hobbes, and Spinoza, figures who cannot be regarded as the gangsta rappers or their work as the *Hustler* magazines of his day. One might well think that any criticism of these writers could also apply to Rousseau himself and that his endorsement of censorship would be an invitation to those who wished to censor his works. How can Rousseau exempt himself from the attack he makes on other writers?

The principles underlying Rousseau's position on censorship are found in the sharp critique of the sciences, arts, and literature in his *First Discourse* and subsequent defenses against opponents of his argument. The outlines of this critique are fairly generally agreed upon among scholars who approach Rousseau from a variety of perspectives and disciplines.[2] Some of the details and nuances of this critique will emerge at various points in this book. For now it will be sufficient to summarize Rousseau's conclusions in order to see how they affect his treatment of censorship. Briefly, Rousseau's critique of the sciences and the arts claims that philosophy in particular and intellectual life in general undermine the best parts of society, the beliefs that hold it together, while the arts enhance the worst parts of society, the luxury, inequality, and sense of isolation that divide it. While he condemns the "condition worse than ignorance" that preceded the restoration of the sciences and arts to Europe, he also insists that the immediately premodern moral situation might have been better than the modern one (*First Discourse*, CW 2:5; Pl. 3:6–7; and *Raynal*, CW 2:25; Pl. 3:31).

It might seem that this sweeping condemnation of the sciences and arts calls for the most complete censorship possible. It is not unlikely that Rousseau would approve of a statesman in some remote corner of the world who had a gallows especially prepared for the first European to arrive with a book or the knowledge to make a printing press (*Final Reply*, CW 2:125; Pl. 3:90–91). Nevertheless, this conclusion is only of limited use for understanding his position. After all, speech remains after printing has been eliminated. Once it is conceded that censorship cannot and perhaps even should not be total, the question of what sorts of speeches and writings should not be suppressed comes to the fore. Moreover, Rousseau did not live in anything resembling what he regarded as optimum circumstances. What, beyond making oneself into a martyr of resistance, should be done in a situation that is already corrupted?

Although it is not always possible to make the separation between categories perfectly clear, for convenience the consideration of Rousseau's discussions of censorship can be divided into three different areas. These areas are (1) the moral consensus underlying any community; (2) a community's fundamental principles, laws, and particular policies; and, finally, (3) purely speculative philosophic doctrines. Each of these will be discussed in general terms here, and the relation between them and Rousseau's understanding of his authorship will be treated in the subsequent chapters.

I. Moral Consensus

For political purposes, the shared moral opinions of a society are most crucial. The term Rousseau uses most commonly to designate this crucial component of social life is *moeurs*, a term that has caused considerable perplexity for translators. It has been translated variously as "morals," "customs," "morals [manners]," and "ways of life." The problem is not that Rousseau does not use the term with precision, but rather that there is no single modern English term that corresponds to the French. It is particularly important to give a satisfactory explanation of this term because the translation I favor, "morals," can easily suggest good or bad behavior, a meaning that is somewhat too narrow. The word "moral" used to have a broader meaning in English applying to character in general, and early translators of Rousseau had no qualms about using "morals" as an equivalent for *moeurs*. I persist in this choice because I can think of none that is better.

Rousseau's use of the term is close to that of his contemporaries. His friend Charles Duclos defined it as "natural or acquired habits for good or for bad," but the term was also used by naturalists like Buffon to indicate characteristic modes of behavior of animal species. Rousseau himself gives an excellent idea of the range covered by *moeurs* in a human context by explaining that they are concerned with decency, suitability, and seemliness.[3] Each of these terms is connected with morality but covers a range of issues that cannot be reduced to simple principles of right and wrong. Finally, in a passage that is very pertinent to this theme, he says, "There is no use distinguishing between the morals of a nation and the objects of its esteem" (*Social Contract*, CW 4:214; Pl. 3:458). One could say that morals are the beliefs, customs, and ways of life that follow from opinions about what is worthy of respect. They involve matters such as respect for the elderly or belief in the sanctity of marriage. In Rousseau's view, morals are in a certain sense what constitute any particular community and give it an identity. These "sentiments of sociability," as he refers to them sometimes, differ from the fundamental principles that will be discussed in the next section because their ultimate rational grounding is obscure or because they are not consciously examined by most members of the community. Because they are the product of unexamined prejudices, they are particularly vulnerable to the sort of rational scrutiny made by philosophers.

The significance of sentiments of sociability or morals for Rousseau can be seen by situating his position within the debate between "liberals" and "communitarians" in contemporary political thought. Most of the important recent attempts to justify liberal democracy—those associated with names such as Rawls, Dworkin, and Ackerman—have been characterized by legal formalism in their content and their method. In content, these justifications emphasize a liberalism that is neutral to competing claims about the best way of life. In method, they employ formal or abstract theories of justice. Both elements of formality have encountered criticism. The neutrality espoused by these theories has been attacked for being an inadequate justification for the way of life found in liberal democracies or as hiding an unconscious appeal to a particular view of the good life.[4] The formal method has been attacked from an equal variety of perspectives as being blind to the complexities of the political world and as ignoring the connection between moral reasoning and concrete ways of life.[5]

With some qualified exceptions, both sides in this debate link Rousseau with the formalists at least as far as his method is concerned.[6] Rawls, for example, claims the *Social Contract* as a notable ancestor of his own work.[7] On the other side, Habermas agrees, "The procedural type of legitimacy was first worked out by Rousseau."[8] Rousseau's subtitle for the *Social Contract*, *Principles of Political Right*, indicates an element of kinship with books such as *A Theory of Justice*, although it also reveals an emphasis on the political aspect of justice not always found among contemporary liberal theorists. It is impossible for any reader of the *Social Contract* to deny its kinship with the formal theories of justice that follow it. Nevertheless, it would be a mistake to make too much of this undeniable kinship. In fact, Rousseau's political thought, in the *Social Contract* and elsewhere, represents an attempt to combine a Rawlsian *esprit de géométrie* in the derivation of principles with an *esprit de finesse* in the discussion of the relation between these principles and concrete political life. This focus on morals or sentiments of sociability is one of the primary indications of the need to supplement formalism with something substantive.

Rousseau considered one of the hallmarks of his thought to be his insistence on putting morals at the center of the discussion in political philosophy. He allies himself with ancient political thinkers who "incessantly talked about morals and virtue" as opposed to modern thinkers who "talk only of business and money" (*First Discourse*, CW 1:14; Pl. 3:19). He argues that morals, customs, and opinions constitute the most important laws: more important than fundamental political laws, civil laws, or criminal laws. This type of law "is the genuine constitution of the state" (*Social Contract*, CW 4:164–65; Pl. 3:394). Morals, then, are a sort of unwritten law having a deeper hold on behavior than those that are written.

The relation between morals and laws more narrowly defined is a very complex one. Without the support of morals, laws can have no effect, but morals themselves can be very dependent on support from the laws. The most perfect subordination of morals to laws took place in Sparta, where, in fact, laws were concerned almost exclusively with morals (*Political Fragments*, CW 4:26; Pl. 3:488; and *Second Discourse*, CW 3:62; Pl. 3:187). In spite of his admiration for the wholehearted devotion of Spartan citizens for their community that was the consequence of this subordination, Rousseau did not waver in his judgment that it was Rome, not Sparta, that was the "model of all free peoples" (*Second Discourse*, CW 3:4; Pl. 3:113). This judgment is based on his view that Roman laws proceeded from good morals rather than producing them. One of the consequences of this was that while Rome subordinated private life to public life, it did not destroy the private altogether. In fact, "the Romans stood out over all the peoples of the earth for the deference of the government toward private individuals and for the scrupulous attention to respecting the inviolable rights of all members of the state" (*Political Economy*, CW 3:153; Pl. 3:257). Rousseau's ultimate claim of the superiority of Rome to Sparta is an indication of his view of the futility of attempting to bring all human affairs under the sort of control that legislation appears to offer. Only at the founding of a community can the laws do much to shape morals for the better, and even then a people with bad morals is incapable of accepting good laws. Defective laws can do a great deal to corrupt morals, and good laws can do little to support them. This lack of confidence in the ability of laws to reverse corruption is one of the reasons for Rousseau's view of the inevitable decline of even the best communities.

Perhaps the most important aspect of Rousseau's treatment of the sentiments of sociability is his insistence that a community can demand conformity to these sentiments in the form of adherence to a civil religion. Rousseau's treatments of religion show his attempt to combine this desirable conformity with toleration. The distinctiveness of his position can be seen by comparing it with the alternative positions on toleration that he explicitly rejected. While it is impossible to do even a satisfactory survey of these alternatives here, it is possible to examine one of the most significant of Rousseau's encounters with an opponent. This encounter occurred in his response to d'Alembert's article on Geneva for the *Encyclopédie*.

In this article d'Alembert held up the Genevan clergy as models on the grounds that many of them had abandoned the intolerance that had plagued Geneva because of the influence of Calvin. He found the source of their new toleration in their disbelief in doctrines such as the existence of Hell, the divinity of Jesus, and other doctrines depending on revelation. In fact, d'Alembert asserts that these ministers "have no religion other than a complete Socinianism" (*d'Alembert* 146–47). Geneva surpasses other communities in toleration because it is unusually open to philosophic inquiry, as shown by its acclaim for Voltaire's works, which extends even to the ones that attacked Calvin, the founder of Geneva's religion. D'Alembert contrasts the enlightenment of Geneva with other countries "in which pusillanimous writers, who are called prudent, respect prejudices which they could combat with as much propriety as security" (*d'Alembert* 146). Thus, d'Alembert's standard of praise is the extent to which a society encourages attacks upon prejudices and is willing to abandon those prejudices that have been successfully attacked. Moreover, he makes it clear that all doctrines based on revelation are to be numbered among these prejudices.

By making public the extent to which the clergy were dissenters from orthodox Calvinism, d'Alembert hoped to further the cause of enlightenment by destroying what he regarded as a few lingering prejudices. The publication of his description of the beliefs of the Genevan clergy did indeed cause a public stir, but not the sort he had been hoping for. Although d'Alembert meant his characterization as praise, its implication that Calvinism (the official religion of Geneva) had been secretly replaced by its long-standing opponent Socinianism opened the clergy to the charge of treason.[9] In response to this danger, the body of clergy issued a statement denying d'Alembert's claim and reaffirming their commitment to Calvinism.

In the *Letter to d'Alembert on the Theatre*, Rousseau joined the clergy in their opposition to d'Alembert, but his defense of the clergy against d'Alembert's claim is rather surprising. He points out that the clergy publicly claim to be good Calvinists and argues that d'Alembert could have solid knowledge about their departures from orthodoxy only through private conversations that he would be honor-bound to keep secret. In short, he suggests that d'Alembert's crime consists of making assertions he had no right to make (*d'Alembert* 9–15; Pl. 5:9–14). In his reply d'Alembert insisted that he had derived his characterization only from well-attested public statements. This reply captures the peculiarity of Rousseau's defense of the clergy. D'Alembert responded to it by saying, "I do not know whether the Genevan ecclesiastics whom you wished to justify concerning their belief will be much more satisfied with you than they have been with me, and whether your laxity in defending them will please them more than my frankness. You seem to accuse me almost solely of *imprudence* with regard to them."[10] In other words, d'Alembert insists that Rousseau's "defense" of the clergy tacitly agrees with his own characterization of their views. Rousseau in no way denies the truth of d'Alembert's claim concerning the clergy's lack of orthodoxy. Because of Rousseau's tacit acceptance of his description of the clergy, d'Alembert considered their difference to be a trivial one and praised Rousseau's defense of freedom of conscience.

Rousseau, however, presents their difference as more than merely prudential in that it concerns the desirability of maintaining a separation between private belief and public avowal in certain matters. He speculates about the possibility that the clergy might have told d'Alembert that they were Socinians but concludes that they would have done this only "in secret, in the decent and frank expansiveness of philosophic intercourse; they would have said it to the philosopher and not to the author" (*d'Alembert* 11; Pl. 5:10). D'Alembert's error is to confuse the private activity of philosophy with the public activity of authorship and to make them both political in a partisan manner. He fails to see that when certain theological issues are made subject to public discussion, they cease to be subject to the rules of private, philosophic conversation and threaten morals. Rousseau objects to d'Alembert's campaign of publicity on two grounds. First, he argues that rather than furthering toleration, d'Alembert is stirring up theological conflicts that cannot be settled. Second, he claims that rather than having genuine toleration as his goal, d'Alembert is seeking to end conflict by promoting the victory of a sectarian dogma: that of enlightenment. He dogmatically sets up his own skepticism on matters of revelation as the measure of what should be publicly accepted.

In Rousseau's view, d'Alembert's attempt to combat prejudices and thereby to make politics more philosophic is dangerous because it threatens to make theological issues into matters of public dispute. While writers like d'Alembert and Voltaire attempt to combat prejudices and replace them with what they consider to be reason, Rousseau argues that they, in fact, are merely seeking to replace a relatively tolerant dogmatism with an intolerant one. Rousseau and the Genevan ministers as he portrays them respect prejudices about which they have private reservations because (unlike d'Alembert) they understand the role of such prejudices as sentiments of sociability that hold the community together. Rousseau's own solution to the problem of intolerance proceeds very differently from d'Alembert's. His various treatments of the civil religion show his attempt to keep the issues that divided Enlightenment orthodoxy from religious orthodoxy from emerging into the public arena. The key to Rousseau's solution is his division of religious matters into several discrete areas: ceremonies, moral teachings, dogmas that serve as the basis of moral teachings, and speculative dogmas having nothing to do with morals (*Mountain*, CW 9:139–40; Pl. 3:694).

Rousseau's position on the first area is very clear. He quite simply insists that ceremonies have nothing to do with what is essential to religion, and hence to religious freedom. Consequently, they can be regarded as matters of purely public significance and therefore as subject to public control for the sake of social cohesiveness. As he says in the *Confessions*, "I also judged that everything that is form and discipline in each country fell within the competence of the laws" (*Confessions*, CW 5:329; Pl. 1:392). On this issue Rousseau appears to be no friend of toleration except for his insistence that once the ceremonies of a minority religion have gained legal toleration, it would be tyrannical to withdraw that status (*Geneva Manuscript*, CW 4:123–24; Pl. 3:343–44).

In spite of the compulsion of uniform worship entailed by this position, Rousseau claims that, in fact, it requires no violation of toleration. Because he has argued that these ceremonies are essentially civil, having nothing to do with the essence of religion, he concludes that nonbelievers can cheerfully participate in the ceremonies required by a national church without feeling that their religious freedom has been infringed. He even argues that one can serve as a clergyman in a church whose speculative dogmas one does not share as long as those doctrines are not contrary to morality (*Emile* 308–10; Pl. 4:627–29). As is indicated by the form of his defense of the Genevan clergy against d'Alembert, he insists only that ministers faithfully execute their public duties as clergy and urges that their private beliefs should not be matter for public speculation. In short, toleration is served by making ceremonies into nonreligious, civil duties. While Rousseau's position is compatible with a far wider range of actual religions than d'Alembert's position is, it should be noted that it offers grave problems for anyone (Jews or Muslims, for example) who believes that ceremonies and other observances are of the essence of religion. Within Rousseau's framework the only satisfactory situation for such people is to live in a community in which their religion is the civil religion.[11]

With regard to the moral teachings that form part of the civil religion, Rousseau's position is equally clear. It is this part of the civil religion that can be considered as constituting the "sentiments of sociability" that give a society its unity and identity. With respect to this area, he claims that open skepticism about these doctrines can be understood as at best a declaration of independence from the community and at worst a declaration of war against it. On this score, Rousseau is clearly no friend of toleration, and likewise he is no friend of open skepticism.

With regard to the dogmas that serve as the foundation of these moral teachings, dogmas such as the existence of God, freedom of will, and the immortality of the soul, Rousseau's position is more complex. In part, the difficulty in establishing his position stems from his very different statements when writing to different audiences. On the one hand, when writing to religious skeptics, he implies that any civil profession of faith must be purely negative once it goes beyond statements of principles of morality. In other words, it must explicitly exclude only intolerance ("Franquières," CW 8:266–67; Pl. 4:1142; and "Letter to Voltaire," CW 3:119; Pl. 4:1073). For example, in a draft to the "Letter to Voltaire," Rousseau says that "a reckless examination" into the beliefs of certain friends of his who were accused of skepticism on religious matters was of no significance for society "because they are decent people" ("Fragment," Pl. 4:1077). On the other hand, when addressing the Catholic archbishop of Paris, he asserts, "In society, everyone has the right to find out whether another person believes himself obligated to be just, and the Sovereign has the right to examine the reasons on which each person bases this obligation" (*Beaumont*, CW 9:57; Pl. 4:973). This position leads to a more affirmative profession of faith such as the one in the *Social Contract*, requiring a statement of belief in "a powerful, intelligent, beneficent, foresighted, and providential Divinity; the afterlife; the happiness of the just; the punishment of the wicked; the sanctity of the social Contract and the Laws" (*Social Contract*, CW 4:223; Pl. 3:468). Finally, when writing to Genevan citizens who were neither skeptics nor dogmatic Catholics, Rousseau stakes out a more neutral position, saying, "Magistrates, Kings have no authority over souls, and as long as one is faithful to the Laws of society in this world, it is not at all up to them to meddle with what will happen to one in the other" (*Mountain*, CW 9:153; Pl. 3:711). This statement leaves the positive content of the civil profession of faith open depending on what one sees as being required as a sufficient guarantor of justice; it is quite consistent with the view that behavior alone, independent of faith, is enough.

The tensions among these statements are a consequence of Rousseau's effort in each case to find a common ground with his addressee, an effort that leads him either to overstate or understate his own position. These positions, which seem irreconcilable in principle, can be very close in practice, amounting to a policy of "don't ask, don't tell" with regard to these dogmas. The major point of each is to exclude a wide range of religious issues from both governmental control and open public debate. Even when he insists that a government can form a national church, codifying positions on rather speculative matters, he leaves considerable room for purely private dissent. Although he stops short of counseling dissenters from publicly affirming belief in doctrines that they hold to be absurd, he urges them to keep their genuine beliefs to themselves (*Mountain*, CW 9:145; Pl. 3:702; Leigh 20:315).

Rousseau's position can be appreciated best through an examination of the extreme cases of dissent from these doctrines involving radical skeptics or atheists. Several of his works contain assertions about the danger of skepticism and the impossibility of virtue in atheists (*d'Alembert* 97; Pl. 5:89; and "Franquières," CW 8:266–67; Pl. 4:1142). He praises Cicero and Cato for attacking Caesar as a bad citizen when he attempted to establish the mortality of the soul (*Social Contract*, CW 4:222–23; Pl. 3:468). Such passages suggest that dissent from the doctrines that ground morality cannot be tolerated in a society endorsing a civil religion, but the broader contexts make this less clear. For example, when Rousseau attacks atheism in the "Letter to Franquières," he argues only that atheists do not possess the sort of virtue that can make them stand against extreme adversity or rise above great temptation. He explicitly concedes that they can be excellent rulers and just citizens in less extreme circumstances. In the case of Cicero's condemnation of Caesar, the objection is only to the public teaching of mortality of the soul, and Rousseau indicates elsewhere that Cicero's private views were not far removed from Caesar's (*Observations*, CW 2:45–46; Pl. 3:46). In the final analysis, Rousseau's reservations concern the solidity, as opposed to the mere existence, of the virtue of atheists or others who denied the doctrines that support morality.

The most prominent example of a radical skeptic in Rousseau's works is the character Wolmar in *Julie*, whom Rousseau presents as a moral man even though he is in no way a believer. Wolmar is not, however, a proselytizing atheist; publicly he cannot be distinguished from believers. Although he is a "sincere and true man," he is "discreet." He attends church, although he never says he believes anything he does not and "does with respect to worship regulated by laws all that the State can exact of a Citizen" (*Julie*, CW 6:484–85; Pl. 2:592–93). Wolmar is not a simple hypocrite because his public acknowledgment of religion is based on his recognition of the respectability of the sentiments of sociability supported by the religion. This example shows Rousseau's wish to avoid prying into consciences.

Rousseau's attempt to combine support for religion and toleration in his civil religion has been called a failure because it makes it "impossible for a good citizen to profess atheism openly."[12] Rousseau would seem to consider it a success for precisely this reason. The atmosphere he seeks to promote is not far removed from the one Tocqueville claimed to find in America. In discussing the causes that tend to maintain a democratic republic, Tocqueville gives an important place to religion and says, "Among the Anglo-Americans there are some who profess Christian dogmas because they believe them and others who do so because they are afraid to look as though they did not believe in them."[13] The consequence of this is not the active suppression of disbelief, but a necessity for nonbelievers "to profess a certain respect for Christian morality and equity." Similarly, Rousseau's primary concern is that citizens show respect for certain doctrines. He is less concerned about whether every single citizen actually believes them.[14]

The final discrete area of religion concerns purely speculative dogmas among which Rousseau counts such issues as creation versus eternity of matter, the divinity of Jesus, and transubstantiation. His position on these combines complete skepticism, toleration, and social uniformity. To begin with, he regards these topics as outside of the area of rational discussion because they are simply unintelligible (*Confessions*, CW 5:329; Pl. 1:392). In this respect, his position resembles that of d'Alembert, who praised the Genevan clergy for abandoning positions that could not be upheld under rational critique. Unlike d'Alembert, however, Rousseau insists that the unintelligibility of these issues makes them impossible to reject. The very attempt to resolve them on the basis of reason alone involves one in attempting to explain what one cannot understand. In the end, d'Alembert's skepticism leads him to the dogmatic assertion of possessing the truth on these matters and therefore makes him intolerant of those who disagree. Rousseau's skepticism, on the other hand, makes him unwilling to meddle in these matters.

The consequence of Rousseau's position is not simply to let the different sides freely argue for their own position. Precisely because the argument cannot be won, it threatens to erupt into violent conflict and intolerance. Therefore, he says he concluded that "in each country it was up to the Sovereign alone to settle both the worship and this unintelligible dogma, and that consequently it was part of the Citizen's duty to accept the dogma and to follow the worship prescribed by the law" (*Confessions*, CW

5:329; Pl. 1:392). Acceptance of the dogma means only public acceptance; it need not imply belief. Once again Rousseau insists that legal restrictions and toleration are not only compatible, but mutually supportive.

In short, Rousseau consistently argues that a community must make salutary beliefs immune to questioning, but at the same time he tries to preserve room for private unorthodoxy on any point of religious dogma. As he says in *Letters Written from the Mountain*, his goal is "to establish philosophic liberty and religious piety at the same time" (*Mountain*, CW 9:227; Pl. 3:802). Thus, Rousseau is prepared to encourage the unorthodox not to advance their dissenting opinions publicly and to speak and act as if they accept all the sentiments of sociability. He claims that freedom of private belief can coexist with public acceptance of sentiments of sociability and, therefore, that philosophy does not require a public war against all prejudices in the way that some of his contemporaries thought.

II. Policies and Principles

Rousseau's insistence on consensus about the sentiments of sociability has led some commentators to the conclusion that however zealous his ideal citizens might be in defending their community against foreign enemies, they are passive to the point of not engaging in genuine debate over domestic policy. Their consensus about morals seems to preclude any serious differences of opinion on political issues. Rather than arguing over perspectives on the general good, these commentators conclude, Rousseau's citizens simply recognize or discover a preexisting consensus caused by their homogeneity.[15] Evidence for this view is found in Rousseau's hostility to factions that push for their own interests in public debate and his claim that in a good society citizens will regard the laws as sacred and will be very resistant to change. Nevertheless, while the sentiments of sociability make up an unquestionable public consensus, with regard to both specific laws and policies, on the one hand, and fundamental political principles (as opposed to religious dogmas), on the other, Rousseau consistently argues for a wide latitude for freedom of speech and press.

Perhaps the best illustration of Rousseau's commitment to open discussion of particular policies can be found in his own activity in the dispute over establishing a theater in Geneva. Although his understanding of how an author can be a citizen will be the theme of chapter 4, here we can take a brief view of this in relation to the issues of censorship and self-restraint. Rousseau did not hesitate to leap into the debate caused by d'Alembert's article on Geneva suggesting the establishment of a theater. In fact, in the *Let-*

ter to d'Alembert, he also discusses some of the defects of French attempts to outlaw dueling. When he was subsequently criticized for undermining society by publicly objecting to existing laws rather than discreetly enlightening the government minister responsible for the relevant matter, Rousseau reacted strongly (Leigh 5:177–81). Refusing to rely solely on the defense that as a citizen of Geneva he was under only limited obligation to the French laws under which he was living, he also argued that French citizens such as Bodin, Fénelon, and Montesquieu had also criticized specific laws in their writings. He boldly added that he suspected that government ministers were the people least capable of being enlightened by a discreet warning. Most significantly, he argued that in a republic it would be an act of treason even to suggest such a need for restraint, only very grudgingly conceding that there may be rare situations in which the preservation of a community depends on leaving bad laws untouched by criticism. In sum, citizens must always be free to discuss not only proposed new policies, but also the defects of existing laws.

This raises the question of how unfettered debate over particular policies or pieces of legislation can avoid opening the sentiments of sociability to criticism. In fact, Rousseau's views bear some resemblance to those of communitarians today that effective social criticism depends on respect for these beliefs, that one can successfully improve a community only by appealing to and clarifying standards that it already accepts.[16] This explains some of the peculiar character of the *Letter to d'Alembert*. Throughout this work Rousseau goes out of his way to emphasize that he is writing as an ordinary Genevan citizen and not as one of d'Alembert's fellow intellectuals. He discusses the theater from the standpoint of beliefs that are widely shared by Genevans. When he discusses dueling, he does so by appealing to the French conception of honor. As readers often find to their frustration, he does not openly subject these beliefs to rational scrutiny and his arguments are not always easy to reconcile with those of his theoretical works.[17]

These theoretical works, such as the two *Discourses* and the *Social Contract*, are very different. They are concerned directly with fundamental principles rather than specific policies of existing communities. The issues of precisely what laws should be used to abolish dueling or of whether public funds should be used to establish a theater can be discussed within the horizon set by the sentiments of sociability. Is this the case, however, for theoretical issues such as whether consent is the only basis for the establishment of government, whether sovereignty is alienable, and so on? A case could be made that these fundamental principles of politics bear a resemblance to the religious dogmas (existence of God, freedom of will, immortality of the soul) that serve as the basis of the sentiments of sociability.

Rousseau, however, claims that the *Social Contract*, a work devoted to expounding principles of political right, was written precisely with a view to Geneva, "where on the trip I had just made I had not found them forming what I thought to be sufficiently precise and clear concepts about the laws and freedom" (*Confessions*, CW 5:340; Pl. 1:405).[18] Far from indicating that Geneva should be protected from open presentation of such principles, he argues that such a presentation is precisely what his native city needs. The most that he concedes is that he gave the *Social Contract* a very abstract form with no direct reference to existing governments in order to avoid inflaming political passions in Geneva.

What is true of the *Social Contract* might not be true of the more radical presentation of the *Second Discourse*. Terence Marshall has pointed out that in the *Social Contract* Rousseau mutes the radically unsocial presentation of human nature given in the *Second Discourse*.[19] Because the *Discourse* argues that humans are not naturally social and consequently implies that their allegiance to a particular community is an arbitrary accident, it might appear that this work could undermine the sentiments of sociability that tie citizens to their community. In fact, this is very similar to the charge that Rousseau levels against the works of other philosophers, few of whom deny the naturalness of social life as radically as he does (*Narcissus*, CW 2:191–93; Pl. 4:966–69). This would seem to lead to the conclusion that at least this theoretical writing would be banned from exactly the sorts of communities Rousseau favors.

Rousseau, however, does not reach this conclusion. There is no reason to believe that he ever came to regret the publication of the *Second Discourse* or that he thought it was unsuitable reading for citizens. In fact, in the *Confessions* he says that it is this work that earned him the nickname of "Citizen" and speaks approvingly of the suggestion that the government of Geneva should give him an award based on its contents (*Confessions*, CW 5:332; Pl. 1:395). His dedication of this work to Geneva seems to indicate that a properly informed Geneva is precisely the sort of community most consistent with the principles developed in the *Discourse*.

Rousseau's attentiveness to the question of the suitability of his various works to different sorts of societies is indicated by his remark that he wished he lived in an age in which his novel *Julie* deserved to be thrown into the fire rather than published (*Julie*, CW 6:3; Pl. 2:5). In the "Second Preface" to the novel, he says that he identifies himself as "Citizen of Geneva" only on the title pages of those of his books that would do honor to his fatherland (*Julie*, CW 6:20; Pl. 2:27). In each of these books, he writes as a citizen and, presumably, says things suitable for citizens in a good community to hear. All of his major theoretical works identify Rousseau as a citizen on the title page. Thus, the establishment of a clear understanding of the fundamental political principles of the sort that is undertaken in Rousseau's boldest works is compatible with the needs of a good community. What is required is only that these works maintain a proper reserve about other matters that would threaten such a community.

In his argument against the censorship of books such as the *Social Contract*, Rousseau endorses one sweeping principle. He says, "I am not the only one who, discussing questions of politics by abstraction, might have treated them with some boldness; not everyone has done it, but every man has the right to do it" (*Mountain*, CW 9:235; Pl. 3:812). He cites Althusius, the abbé de Saint-Pierre, Montesquieu, and Algernon Sydney as examples of others who have written this way. Above all, he cites Locke, who, he says, "treated [the same matters] exactly in the same principles as I did." This statement is sometimes taken as an indication that Rousseau thought that the principles of his political thought agreed with those of Locke, a claim that is hard to justify on anything but the most general level.[20] In fact, the context indicates that Rousseau is in fact claiming that the way in which he expressed his political thought is identical to the way Locke expressed his. He is claiming that both of them accepted the principle that discussions of general and fundamental principles of politics that do not explicitly attack particular governments should not be censored. This principle is based on a distinction between abstract reasoning and arguments directly inciting action (*Mountain*, CW 9:191, 210–11; Pl. 3:758, 782–83). On the one hand, authors who aim at undermining a particular government (rather than objecting to individual policies or laws) fall under the same category as those who act against the government. On the other hand, those who write on a sufficient level of generality cannot justly be punished for their works.

Rousseau made a similar argument when he settled on Prussian territory in 1762 and explained his "rules" about publishing to Frederick the Great's representative. He says, "I engage myself, and very wholeheartedly with respect to [His Majesty] and Your Excellency to respect—as I have always done in my writings and in my conduct—the laws, the Prince, decent people, and all the duties of hospitality." He goes on to state the limits of this respect to the community in which he is living by saying, "But as to my manner of thinking in general on whatever matter it might be, it belongs to me, born republican and free. And as long as I do not divulge it in the state in which I am living I do not owe any account of it to the sovereign, for he is not a competent judge of what is done outside of his territory by a man who is not born his subject" (Leigh 12:205). Thus, while Rousseau feels obliged to refrain from particular criticisms of Frederick and agrees not to publish inside his domain, he insists on his freedom to write on general issues (including the relative merits of monarchies and republics) as long as he publishes elsewhere.

Embedded in Rousseau's distinction between free expression of opinions on general issues and refraining from attacking particular governments is political dynamite. Critical examination of the principles on which a government claims to be based can be as threatening as direct attacks on the government. Rousseau's response to this is twofold. First, a government can be stable only if it is founded on correct principles. Second, the correct principles are compatible with an indefinite variety of forms of government (*Social Contract*, CW 4:172–73; Pl. 3:403–4). The first part of this response indicates that governments that cannot stand inquiry into their principles are already on shaky ground, and the second indicates that the proper mode of political reform is to correct the society's understanding of principles rather than to change its form of government. Precisely when Rousseau's thought appears to inspire revolutions, it can present itself as a conservative return to founding principles.[21] Depending on how one looks at Rousseau, he can appear as a revolutionary, a progressive, or even a conservative.[22] From any perspective, however, it should be acknowledged that he is a proponent of open discussion of both fundamental principles and particular policies, however much he opposes open discussion of religious and moral matters.

III. Philosophy

The topic of purely speculative opinions on philosophic issues other than fundamental political principles remains to be discussed. Here Rousseau tries to combine freedom of intellect with restraint on the expression of opinion much as he does with religious belief. As mentioned above, when writing to d'Alembert, he distinguishes between "the frank expansiveness of philosophic intercourse" conducted in private and the discretion necessary in public discussion (*d'Alembert* 11; Pl. 5:10). He condemns those contemporary philosophers who wish to erase the line between public and private, or politics and philosophy.

As part of his attack on the sciences and learning, Rousseau consistently argues that philosophy has always tended to make its adherents into bad citizens. First, within his discussions of the sciences or what he also calls learned activities, Rousseau accuses all philosophers past and present—with virtually no exceptions—of holding opinions contrary to popular beliefs in such things as the existence of God, the immortality of the soul, the conscience, friendship, patriotism, and the sanctity of marriage. He grants that there have been a few philosophers who have not been vicious in spite of their unorthodox views, although even most of these have been useless rather than virtuous (*Observations*, CW 2:40, 42; Pl. 3:39, 41; *Final Reply*, CW 2:111, 115; Pl. 3:73, 79; *Second Discourse*, CW 3:38; Pl. 3:156; *Political Economy*, CW 3:151; Pl. 3:255; *Hero*, CW 4:2–3; Pl. 2:1263–64; and *Confessions*, CW 5:312; Pl. 1:371). Even so, he argues that even in the best cases, philosophy tends to form bad citizens by either making its adherents indifferent to social life by attracting them to solitary contemplation or by making them disgusted with social life by teaching them to despise nonphilosophers. In short, philosophy tends to be an antisocial, misanthropic activity (*Observations*, CW 2:45–46; Pl. 3:46; and *Narcissus*, CW 2:193; Pl. 2:968).

Second, even philosophers who do not let their departures from orthodoxy affect their own moral behavior have a bad effect by inspiring imitation from less discreet and less intelligent men of letters or intellectuals. Behind a mask of impartial reason, such people form an interest group devoted to gaining status at the expense of the rest of society (*First Discourse*, CW 2:13–14; Pl. 3:19; and *Dialogues*, CW 1:238–39; Pl. 1:967–68). As Rousseau said about d'Alembert and Voltaire, such philosophers "always [have] some private interest as a motive, and always the public good as a pretext" (Leigh 5:664).[23] These are precisely the writers who thrive in the atmosphere of irresponsibility created by the prevailing publishing practices. They spread pernicious doctrines less because they believe them than because they desire to gain distinction among fellow intellectuals as the enemies of vulgar opinion. This desire for distinction makes them oppose any opinion that they believe is held by the majority. In Rousseau's view, the most dangerous intellectuals are those who attempt to transform political life by subjecting the sentiments of sociability to critical scrutiny. Individuals of this sort have always existed, but the danger from the dissemination of their doctrines is particularly acute in modern times because of both the development of printing and the extreme boldness of modern thinkers (*First Discourse*, CW 2:20; Pl. 3:27–28; and *Narcissus*, CW 2:191–93; Pl. 2:966–69).[24] In effect, Rousseau turns a favorite tactic of these writers back against them: they try to strip the veil of disinterestedness and benevolence away from political and religious authorities, and Rousseau strips this same veil away from them.[25]

It is clear, however, that Rousseau regarded his own philosophic activity as compatible with his devotion to justice. Rousseau claims that he uses philosophy to destroy the evils that were caused by philosophy. Moreover, his boldness in defying authority in declaring the truth in his writings was restricted to telling the truth "in every useful thing," rather than with regard to any truth whatsoever (*Beaumont*, CW 9:52; Pl. 4:967).[26] Thus, Rousseau's uniqueness with regard to telling the truth stems both from his willingness to live up to his motto of consecrating his life to the truth and from his ability to know when the truth should be told. To the extent that Rousseau made his philosophizing public, he did so by always linking it with an attack on the pride characteristic of philosophers who think they have the right to tell others what to do and think.[27] He tries to cure philosophers and their imitators of this pride by making them more sensitive to the concerns of nonphilosophers and to their own nonphilosophic concerns. He insists that philosophers behave as good citizens first and philosophers second. This means that a good community might justly censor some philosophic works. More significantly, it indicates Rousseau's opinion that philosophers should engage in self-censorship out of public-spirited motives. That this self-censorship usually need not extend to discussions of particular policies or to the fundamental principles of politics does not make it any less real or important.

Rousseau argues against those who would make politics submit to the rule of either religion or philosophy. Because of his insistence that philosophy is an essentially private activity, he can also argue that the public submission of philosophy to politics helps rather than harms philosophy. In general, however, he makes this argument speaking as a good citizen rather than as a philosopher. In chapter 6, I will open the question of whether the perspective of the citizen is the ultimate perspective for Rousseau.

IV. Conclusion

In sum, censorship in a good society will be guided by the need both to protect sentiments of sociability (and the religious dogmas that support them) and to stimulate public debate over laws guided by a correct understanding of the fundamental principles of political right. Both religious dissenters and philosophers can live in such a society, but only if they are willing to pay the price of self-censorship.

At the basis of this understanding is a well-considered view of the role of prejudices in society and the way these prejudices should be dealt with by authors. The issue is to determine what sort of prejudices should be attacked and what sort supported. Rousseau had occasion to address the questions posed for a writer by the prejudices of his readers shortly before the publication of *Emile* and, again, shortly after it. While the first of his statements points in the direction of reserve and the second in the direction of boldness, together they cover the range of possibilities addressed in this chapter and the preceding one.

In April 1762 a Swiss correspondent wrote to Rousseau wishing to enlist him in the establishment of a new literary society. On the basis of Rousseau's early writings, the correspondent identified him as one of the contemporary authors whose works indicate that the present age will succeed in "completely dethroning several prejudices that tyrannize over either the whole human race or at least particular nations and Societies, at the expense of their happiness" (Leigh 10:184). The new literary society (whose members, interesting enough, will remain anonymous) will propose topics for writings each year that will further this noble goal. Among the topics meant to inspire Rousseau's participation was the question "Are there respectable prejudices that a good Citizen ought to have qualms about combatting publicly?" (Leigh 10:186). Everything said in the letter indicates that the correspondent thought that the only possible answer to this question is a resounding "No."

Rousseau answered by warning his correspondent that by putting the issue in the form of a question, he was inviting unwelcome responses. His argument is that the replacement of prejudice by truth cannot be counted on to improve morality. Even people who know and approve of the good act badly because of their passions. Attacking prejudices while leaving the passions alone is insufficient for creating a disposition toward the lessons of truth and virtue.

This does not imply that passions and prejudices have no relation to each other. While the truth by itself cannot destroy unwholesome passions, some prejudices can restrain or redirect them. For example, belief in divine retribution does not cure anyone of the passion of fear, but it can direct fear in a wholesome direction. Questioning this belief in the name of the truth would harm rather than improve morality. As a result of reasoning like this, when Rousseau turns to a discussion of the specific essay topic mentioned above, he says, "If I had to treat your second question, I will not dissimulate to you that I would declare for the affirmative along with Plato" (Leigh 10:227). There are, then, respectable prejudices that should not be publicly attacked. Writers should therefore exercise the greatest possible reserve in dealing with prejudices.

In the *Letter to Beaumont*, dated seven months after his reply to the Swiss correspondent and also after the condemnation of *Emile*, Rousseau admitted that his writings left him open to the charge of violating his own maxim. He says that he must consider "whether when I had the courage to publish [my sentiments] and name myself, I attacked the Laws and disturbed public order" (*Beaumont*, CW 9:48; Pl. 4:962). He goes on to imagine himself engaged in private conversation with the archbishop of Paris, who, Rousseau suggests, secretly agrees with him on religious matters. Rousseau puts into the archbishop's mouth the speech "But this frankness is misplaced with the public! But not every truth is good to state! But although all sensible men think as you do, it is not good for the rabble to think so also" (*Beaumont*, CW 9:51; Pl. 4:966). Rousseau, in effect, makes Beaumont the spokesman for the position he had taken himself in the letter of seven months earlier.

Now, however, Rousseau attacks this position. He says that it would be taken only by a deceiver and imposter who persecutes honest people even against his own conscience. He answers the archbishop's question with the counterquestion "But is that principle really correct that not every truth is good to state?" The posing of this rhetorical question seems to imply that its proper answer is "No," but Rousseau does not give such an answer. Instead, he concedes the possibility that the principle in question may be correct. He then shifts to the different issues of whether it follows that "no error is good to destroy" and that "all of men's follies [are] so sacred that there is not one that should not be respected." With this shift he replaces the question of the goodness of stating the truth with the question of the respectability of prejudices. This leads him, at last, to raise the precise question posed by his Swiss correspondent. He does so by asking, "There are prejudices that must be respected?" (*Beaumont*, CW 9:52; Pl. 4:967).

Having arrived at this point, he gives an answer that is a qualified version of his original one. He says, "That may be, but it is when everything else is in order, and it is impossible to remove these prejudices without also removing what compensates for them." In other cases, including the present one in which "there can be no change that is not for the better," the truth must be used to counter harmful prejudices (*Beaumont*, CW 9:52; Pl. 4:967). The pernicious prejudices of corrupt communities should be undermined for exactly the same reasons that the wholesome ones of good communities should remain immune from attack.

That Rousseau thought the situation in France in 1762–63 justified boldness in attacking prejudices does not mean that he felt no need for restraint in his manner of attacking them. Books attacking prejudices can be read in healthier places and better times. Consequently, he felt himself to be under an obligation to write so that even his boldest writings would be, at worst, useless for readers free from the prejudices of his contemporaries (*Political Fragments*, CW 4:45; Pl. 3:516–17).[28] As we will see in the next two chapters, he also attempted to find a way to oppose corrupt prejudices by redirecting their root passion rather than simply countering them with the truth.

In sum, Rousseauian authorship requires the ability to distinguish between respectable and unrespectable prejudices. It is when dealing with the latter that Rousseau says he has promised to speak the truth "in every useful thing as long as it is in me." This means that Rousseauian authorship also requires the ability to distinguish between useful and other truths.[29] As we have seen, the domain of useful truths extends to the areas of general political principles and particular policies. Truth as such, as distinguished from useful truth, belongs to "the decent and frank expansiveness of philosophic intercourse" that necessarily takes place in secret (*d'Alembert* 11; Pl. 5:10). These considerations lead to what could be said to be the central thesis of this book, namely, that for Rousseau, while the activity of authorship is in its essence public, the activity of philosophy is private. In the following chapters, we will see how this understanding guided Rousseau's career as an author.

Rousseau's account of authorship contains both an insistence on openness in the sense of publicly taking responsibility for what one writes and an insistence on reserve in the sense of writing responsibly. His frequent attacks on other writers share the common charge that these writers are bold when they should be cautious and are cautious when they should be bold. They hide behind the shield of anonymity when they should be willing to take responsibility for what they say, and they boldly challenge all prejudices without considering the necessary role that prejudice plays in political life. For all his concern with openness or sincerity, the key word characterizing Rousseau's policy as a writer is "responsibility."[30] Rousseauian responsibility has two parts. First, writers must take responsibility for their works by openly proclaiming themselves to be their authors or editors. Anonymous authors are all too prone to use their anonymity as a screen for private agendas and purely personal attacks. Thus, Rousseau rejects Voltaire's motto, "Strike and conceal your hand." Second, writers must exercise responsibility by practicing discretion on certain issues. Even a writer who enjoys the relative freedom allowed by living in corrupt times must write with the idea that his books will last beyond his age to more wholesome times. Taken together, these two parts of Rousseauian responsibility explain the combination of boldness and caution characteristic of his works. Both his principles and practice consistently reveal his commitment to this view of responsible social criticism. The allure of Rousseauian responsibility stems in large part from Rousseau's intransigent and largely successful efforts to embody this image.

It now remains for us to examine the consequences of Rousseau's view of authorial responsibility for his published works. In doing so, we will continue to follow the order used in this chapter, focusing first on morals (chapters 3 and 4), then principles and policies (chapter 5), and, finally, philosophy (chapter 6).

CHAPTER THREE

The Case against (and for) the Arts

This chapter and the next one will be concerned with the relation between the arts and morals or the sentiments of sociability that Rousseau insists are the precondition of healthy social life. This chapter will develop the general understanding of the arts as a crucial component of morals that underlies Rousseau's practice as a writer, and the next chapter will deal with the application of this understanding with reference to his analysis of the importance of real and fictional heroes for good citizenship.

A brief sketch of Rousseau's critique of the arts was given in the preceding chapter to show the grounds of his position on censorship for the preservation of morals. In that context the arts were presented in an almost entirely negative light, and this is the way Rousseau's position appeared to his earliest readers. From its publication in 1751, the *Discourse on the Sciences and the Arts* drew the attention of a host of critics in several countries who focused on the apparent contradiction between the "Citizen of Geneva's" denunciation of the moral effects of the arts and sciences and his own efforts to gain fame as an artist and thinker.[1] The critics asserted that his authorship of poems, pamphlets outlining a new system of musical notation, and musical compositions contradicted his avowed principles of austere republicanism. Fuel was added to these attacks by the almost simultaneous publication of the first volume of the *Encyclopédie*, in which Rousseau appeared as the author of the articles on music. As d'Alembert points out in the "Preliminary Discourse" of the *Encyclopédie*, the "eloquent and philosophic writer" who attacked the sciences and arts was also a contributor to the grandest effort to further the sciences and arts.[2]

As years went by, critics continued to raise the charge of inconsistency because Rousseau steadily appeared to give new causes for raising it. In the year after the publication of the *First Discourse*, he enjoyed an immense popularity as the result of performances of his opera *The Village Soothsayer*.[3] Shortly thereafter he became embroiled in the pamphlet "*guerre des bouffons*" over the relative merits of French and Italian music and also published *Narcissus*, a play he had written in his youth. Finally, even while renewing his attacks on the moral consequences of the arts in the *Letter to d'Alembert on the Theatre*, he was arranging for the publication of *Julie*, which became the most popular novel of the eighteenth century.

In the *Letter to Pansophe*, a pamphlet published in 1766, Voltaire summarized many critics' view of Rousseau's career. He wrote:

> Judicious admirer of the stupidity and brutality of savages, you have cried out against the sciences, and cultivated the sciences. You have treated authors and philosophers as charlatans, and to prove this by means of an example you have been an author. You have written against the theater with the devotion of a capuchin monk, and you have composed bad plays.[4]

Although Voltaire painted his picture with characteristic immoderation and ill will, its outlines accurately portray Rousseau's career. In short, over a period of less than a dozen years, he criticized the arts and sciences in the *First Discourse*, several defenses of the *Discourse*, and the *Letter to d'Alembert* and also repeatedly engaged in artistic and literary activity. Over and over again he flaunted the apparent inconsistency between his principles and his practice.

In the face of this continued criticism, Rousseau insisted on the consistency of his position. In fact, the complexity of Rousseau's view bears a strong resemblance to the complexity seen today in debate over the social importance of the arts. Anyone who pays attention to these debates cannot avoid being struck by the widely divergent claims raised by the participants. Critics of public support for the arts frequently argue that the artists who receive such support represent an elite, anti-American privileged group whose artistic activities strike a blow at political life by undermining the traditional values that hold our community together. Other critics, who are concerned with the effect of the arts on popular culture, claim that they undermine personal autonomy by fostering a slavish conformism and concern for social approval. On the other side, defenders of the arts claim that artistic activity is the highest expression of our communal life, that it is our culture rather than our uninspiring political principles that gives us a deep and genuine sense of community. Other defenders argue that the arts are the vehicle for the development and expression of our unique individuality and that this is far more important than any mere political or social concern. In short, either the arts are bad because they promote individuality at the expense of society or because they promote society at the expense of individuality, or they are good for precisely the same reasons. Because we usually see these different claims raised by people who have very little in common, it can be unsettling to find them all raised by the same person. Nevertheless, Rousseau makes every one of these claims, and he does so not because he is a singularly incoherent thinker, but because he is a coherent one. In his view, the truth of each of these claims depends on the sort of society and sort of individual one is considering. In different circumstances the arts can foster either dependence or independence, and from different perspectives either of these can appear as worthwhile goals.

I. The Arts and Imitation

Before elaborating on Rousseau's cases for and against the arts, it will be useful to identify what he considers to be their essential character. Rousseau belongs to a tradition that views the arts in terms of the imitation of nature, but his use of traditional terminology conceals an important departure from this tradition. The distinctive character of his understanding can be shown by means of a comparison with one contemporary presentation with which he was well acquainted, the one given by Jean Le Rond d'Alembert in the "Preliminary Discourse" to the *Encyclopédie*, the work referred to above in which Rousseau's participation in this enterprise is cited against his attack on the sciences and arts.

D'Alembert's account of the arts indicates some of the dilemma of understandings of the fine arts in the eighteenth century. He embraces both a traditional doctrine that understands the arts to be imitative of nature[5] and a modern natural science whose account of nature provides little support for beauty. D'Alembert ranks the fine arts according to two criteria: how closely the imitation resembles the original, and how directly it appeals to the senses.[6] According to these criteria, painting and sculpture rank highest: they present accurate resemblances directly to vision. D'Alembert ranks poetry lower because it "speaks more to the imagination than to the senses." At the bottom of his hierarchy is music, which can imitate relatively few things when it tries to appeal to the senses with an exact imitation, for example, drums imitating thunder or trumpets the neighing of horses. To d'Alembert's contemporary readers, the precise order of this hierarchy would have been very familiar;[7] it is his explanation of the hierarchy that offered something novel.

The novelty of d'Alembert's view is derived from a certain tension between his accounts of poetry and music. While the criteria of exactness of imitation and directness of appeal to the senses force him to place these at the bottom of the hierarchy, he nonetheless expresses a great admiration for these two arts. For example, he says that poetry "seems to create rather than to depict" its objects. As for music, he argues that it increases the range of objects it can imitate to the extent that it abandons direct imitation. Most of his very brief discussion of music consists of an exhortation to composers and critics to perfect the previously poorly cultivated resource of music that can reproduce passions and even sensations in the absence of the objects that usually produce them. Thus, although he does not develop it, he introduces a new goal for music, one that is potentially sharply at odds with the criteria that serve as the basis of his hierarchy.

After reading this discussion, Rousseau wrote d'Alembert a letter in which he praised this new goal. His comments indicate both his appreciation of d'Alembert's novelty and his endorsement of this new perspective. He says, "I find your idea about musical imitation very accurate and very new. In fact, and with the exception of a very small number of things, the art of the musician does not at all consist in depicting objects without mediation, but in putting the soul into a disposition similar to the one into which their presence puts it. Upon reading you everyone will feel this, and without you perhaps no one would have taken it into his head to think it" (Leigh 2:160).[8] In his own writings on music, Rousseau develops this position in a way that completely reverses the traditional hierarchy to which d'Alembert had conformed. Rousseau does this by arguing that appeal to the imagination, rather than to the senses, is what makes all art genuinely imitative. This can be seen very clearly in his account of music. Rousseau agrees with d'Alembert that there are two types of music, one of which appeals directly to the senses and another that appeals to the imagination. He calls the former "natural" music and suggests that its appeal comes less from the accuracy of its imitation than from the physical pleasantness of sounds (*Dictionary*, CW 7:439; Pl. 5:918).[9] Only this type of music can be understood in relation to the principles of natural science. Rousseau calls the other type of music, which cannot be understood in relation to these principles, "imitative music." But if imitative music does not exactly imitate the sounds of the things it represents, what does it imitate? According to Rousseau, what music imitates is human emotion rather than things. He says that music "will not represent these things directly, but will arouse the same movements in the soul that are experienced in seeing them" (*Dictionary*, CW 7:414; Pl. 5:861). Thus, music does not so much imitate things as cause an imitation to take place in the listener's imagination. The purpose of music is not direct imitation, but excitement.

This power to stimulate the imagination through "an almost inconceivable magic trick" gives music an extraordinary range and depth, making it the foremost rather than the least of the arts and offering a new scope for the aspirations of musicians. As Rousseau says, "Not only will it agitate the sea, animate the flame of a blaze, make rivers flow, rain fall, and torrents swell, but it will paint the horror of a frightful desert, darken the walls of a subterranean prison, calm the tempest, make the air tranquil and serene, and spread from the orchestra a new freshness over the groves" (*Dictionary*, CW 7:414; Pl. 5:861). Rather than arguing that music should be measured by a standard of imitation set by the visual arts, Rousseau claims that the visual arts can rival music only to the extent that they use their ability to strike the eye as a means toward expressiveness, force, and vigor in their appeal to the imagination. In making this claim, he obviously gives an impetus to an understanding of the visual arts that ultimately abandons realistic representation of the external world for the sake of expressiveness. Both the excitement of emotion in music and the forcefulness of visual images will turn out to have significance in his political thought.

In sum, in Rousseau's understanding, the arts should strive to be imitative, but not of nature. Rather they should imitate human emotion, and they do this by inspiring emotion in members of the audience. The way Rousseau links the experience of all the fine arts to this expressive idea of imitation derived from music causes him to strain the link between the arts and nature still adhered to by d'Alembert. Therefore, he says, "It is seen from this that painting is closer to nature and that music depends more on human art," and in saying this, he is praising music over painting (*Essay*, CW 7:326; Pl. 5:421).[10] Both Rousseau's attacks upon and his support of the social role of the arts depend on this understanding of the imitative nature of artistic experience. As we shall see, this understanding is the key to the unity of his position.

II. The Political Case against the Arts

The best known part of Rousseau's evaluation of the arts is what could be called his political critique. This critique is an important part of his attack on modern culture that suddenly made him famous upon the publication of his *Discourse on the Sciences and the Arts* in 1751. This political critique—developed mainly in the *First Discourse*, Rousseau's defenses of that work, and the *Letter to d'Alembert on the Theatre*—has two basic elements. First, Rousseau argues that the fact that the arts are esteemed in a society is the symptom of an unhealthy political and social inequality. Second, he claims that the arts are incapable of lending support to morality in the ways that their proponents think they can. The first of these attacks concerns the indirect effects of artistic activity, while the second more directly concerns the nature of the experience of the arts.

In the first place, Rousseau argues that, from the standpoint of society as a whole and as a practical matter, there is little that distinguishes artistic works from luxury goods such as jewelry, designer clothing, or wigs. When discussing the purveyors of such goods, Rousseau refers to "these important fellows who are called artists instead of artisans, and who work solely for the idle and the rich" (*Emile* 186; Pl. 4:457). Since eighteenth-century French does not always distinguish between artists and artisans, both of whom can be referred to as artists, it is clear that Rousseau is going out of his way to ridicule the blurring of the distinction here. What hairstylists and jewelers share with painters, sculptors, and the like is that their clientele is made up of people who want to distinguish themselves from the crowd and are willing to pay to do so. This clientele is less interested in beauty than in distinction. For them, and for the societies in which they live, the arts are merely tokens of inequality based on money or status.

Of course, artists can be embarrassed by, or even disdain, the link between their world and the world of luxury even as they attempt to profit from it. No doubt artists who have had to seek patronage have always resented the lack of artistic sensibility of their prospective patrons. Rousseau himself was very well aware from personal experience that financial independence is a rather rare outcome of the pursuit of the artistic life. Accordingly, he acknowledges that artists are likely to be motivated by something other than the desire for wealth. As he says, "Every Artist wants to be applauded. The praises of his contemporaries are the most precious part of his reward" (*First Discourse*, CW 2:15; Pl. 3:21). The interest of artists in praise suggests that they can be flexible, adapting themselves to the various tastes of different audiences. From a political or moral perspective, one might try to take advantage of this by distinguishing those artists who ignobly pander to depraved tastes from those who assist in the cultivation of a more wholesome taste. Rousseau insists, however, that even the most public-spirited artist contributes to the depreciation of civic virtue. This is so because even the most rigorous moralist will prefer an interesting and beautiful depiction of morality in a work of art to an equally moral, but dull and homely depiction. Thus, even when artists produce morally praiseworthy works, the praise they receive results more from their talents than from their morality. Because of this, even a society characterized by a wholesome taste encourages what Rousseau calls "the disastrous inequality introduced among men by the distinction of talents and the debasement of virtue"

(*First Discourse*, CW 2:18; Pl. 3:25). In short, any praise given to artistic talents is subtracted from the amount that might be given to moral actions.

Rousseau does not stop here. The rewards given to those with a talent for pleasing an audience stimulate everyone to learn how to please. The high status of the arts tends to go along with a general concern for elegance and polished manners. Although defenders of politeness and elegance from the opponents of the *First Discourse* in 1751[11] to Miss Manners today argue that these things make life more pleasant, increase social harmony, and make people more humane, they must be prepared to admit that elegance and politeness are accompanied by a great deal of hypocrisy. Such people are fond of citing La Rochefoucauld's famous maxim "Hypocrisy is an homage that vice pays to virtue" (see *Observations*, CW 2:49; Pl. 3:51). While they admit that politeness is not identical to good morals, they insist that it is superior to openly bad morals and, furthermore, that it requires even immoral people to acknowledge a standard to which they should submit.[12] Rousseau, however, responds that mastering the rules of polite social interaction allows the vicious to succeed and, even worse, makes them respectable. Those who have not mastered these rules of deception may occasionally find themselves engaged in open hostility, but the appreciation of fine art and veneer of politeness characteristic of the more sophisticated merely cover this hostility rather than bringing it to a peaceful and humane conclusion. Rousseau describes the hidden reality behind polite exchanges, "One says to the other deep in his heart: *I treat you like a fool and I laugh at you*, the other replies deep in his heart: *I know you lie shamelessly, but I return the favor as best I can*" (*Letter to Grimm*, CW 2:84; Pl. 3:60). Even the thin veneer of sociability provided by conventional politeness applies only among social equals. In the mouths of the socially superior, the vain formulas of politeness are accompanied by the harshness of command. "The fancy education of the rich never fails to leave them politely imperious, by prescribing to them the terms they are to use in order that no one dare resist them" (*Emile* 86; Pl. 4:312). The politeness accompanying sophisticated cultivation of the arts replaces a state of occasional war based on force with a state of constant war or domination based on fraud or barely concealing underlying force. In Rousseau's view, this substitution is a poor masquerade of a genuine sociability.[13]

This part of the case against the arts attacks their more or less indirect consequences, and Rousseau is quite ready to admit that the arts are the symptoms rather than the causes of these forms of corruption. He addresses himself to the more direct moral effects of the arts most explicitly when he considers one particular art, namely, the theater. This case is particularly important because defenders of the theater can draw on a long tradition dating back to Aristotle that claimed that theater is the clearest case of a type of art that can have a good moral effect. The most common assertion of Rousseau's contemporary defenders of the theater was derived from Aristotle's claim that it can support morality by purging the passions. To this they added that it could provide models of good behavior for imitation. These proponents of the theater knew that particular plays can have bad effects: they can stimulate the wrong passions and inspire the imitation of bad behavior. Consequently, they tended not to oppose censorship in principle. They merely argued that a properly purified drama—like the French drama from the classical age on—could satisfy the most rigorous standards of any reasonable censorship.[14] Significantly, in the debate over the establishment of a theater in Geneva, it is Rousseau, not d'Alembert, who argues against censorship on the grounds that it is an inadequate solution to the problems caused by the theater. Although in other cases he does not regret censorship, with regard to the theater, Rousseau's position is more radical than any traditional pro-censorship position because he insists that censorship is not an adequate solution to the dangers posed by the theater. He insists that even a rigorously purified drama could not bring about the good effects its proponents claimed for it.

Rousseau does not deny that plays can have a moral content, although he is rather skeptical about the likelihood of this. Morality is not attained simply by giving villains an unhappy end. The ending of a drama is the least important contribution to its morality. A play in which a wicked man is presented as attractive and clever for four acts is not redeemed by the fact that he arbitrarily commits an implausible act of stupidity that leads to his undoing in the final scene (see *d'Alembert* 28–29; Pl. 5:26–27). When plays of a more genuinely moral character are written, they are likely to be less interesting and therefore less successful than immoral ones because their authors have sacrificed the goal of pleasing an audience for the sake of a tedious preaching.

To be sure, Rousseau does not deny that unusually gifted dramatists can combine the goals of entertainment and moral content. In fact, he concedes that contemporary French dramatists, and Voltaire in particular, were as successful as possible in achieving this combination. Nevertheless, the essence of his political critique is that even a genuine moral content does not guarantee a moral effect. The heart of his criticism of the theater is found in his analysis of the fact that plays really do sometimes inspire the audience to identify with good characters (although it will more commonly admire brilliance rather than goodness).[15] It is in this experience of identification in which Rousseau's account of theatricality joins his account of musicality that we can see a part of the significance of his general analysis of artistic imitation as the ability to stimulate passions in an audience.

Rousseau is so far from denying the reality of this experience of identification that he insists that even the most notorious tyrants and coldhearted villains are frequently moved to tears at the sight of the misfortunes of good people portrayed in plays (*d'Alembert* 24–25; Pl. 5:23). In fact, Rousseau goes beyond many of his contemporaries by arguing that the experience of identification in the theater is more powerful than similar experiences in ordinary life. He claims that we identify with the characters in plays so strongly because our identification with them is pure, that is, untainted by the selfish concerns that adulterate our ordinary experiences of identification. When we enter the theater, we leave our own concerns at the door and are free to give vent to our most generous impulses. Nevertheless, precisely because Rousseau insists on the reality, strength, and purity of theatrical identification, he denies that it makes us better people.

The very purity of the theatrical experience of identification makes it sterile. One of the critics of the *Second Discourse* raised the question of why the populace "enjoys with such avidity the spectacle of an unfortunate dying on the rack" ("Letter from Philopolis," CW 3:125; Pl. 3:1386). Rousseau responded with the same argument he gives in the *Letter to d'Alembert*, "For the same reason you go to the theater to weep and to see Seide kill his Father or Thyeste drink the blood of his son. Pity is such a delightful feeling that it is not surprising that we seek to experience it" ("Letter to Philopolis," CW 3:131; Pl. 3:131) In both cases Rousseau is far from denying the reality of the feeling of pity. Furthermore, he does seem to be implying that the populace feels no impulse to assist the victim of a public execution any more than it feels an impulse to assist a victim in the theater. Because of this their feeling of pity is so pure that it brings about no result other than an intense pleasure at a spectacle. A theatrical performance demands nothing of its spectators except that they abandon themselves to their pure and unadulterated emotion, an experience that is far more pleasant than that of actually working for the benefit of others. This is why more tears are shed over plays about suffering than over solicitations from charities. Similarly, people frequently feel stronger feelings of admiration for theatrical accounts of heroes' lives than they do for living heroes.

To the extent that it is not merely sterile, the strength and purity of theatrical identification encourages an easygoing moral smugness, a false sense of having done one's duty simply by having sympathized with the suffering of someone who is innocent. Because the members of the audience feel so purely in the theater, they congratulate themselves for possessing an exquisite sensitivity that is, in fact, acquired without any cost beyond the price of admission. Rousseau's political critique of the arts can be summed up in his remark "People think they come together in the theater and it is there that they are isolated" (*d'Alembert* 16–17; Pl. 5:16). In short, the theater creates only an illusory sociability.[16] Rather than leading the audience to reenter the world seeking to do good, it leads them to shun the world in favor of the purity of theatrical enjoyment. If this is true for the most defensible of the arts, it is so for the others as well.

III. The Natural Case against the Arts

Rousseau's insistence that the basis of artistic experience is intense identification with emotions is also at the heart of his second critique of the arts. In this criticism he attacks the arts not because they make us unsocial, as he said about theater, but because they make us dependent and too social.

Even though it is not simply natural, artistic imitation clearly does have a natural root, according to Rousseau. In a passage added to the 1782 edition of the *Second Discourse*, he literally repeats his claim in the *Letter to d'Alembert* that cruel tyrants have been observed to weep at tragedies on the stage (*Second Discourse*, CW 3:36; Pl. 3:155). In this context he cites this as evidence of the remnants of natural commiseration in the most depraved of civilized men. Rousseau identifies commiseration as one of the two fundamental principles of the human soul and calls it "a sentiment that puts us in the position of him who suffers" (*Second Discourse*, CW 3:37; Pl. 3:155). Humans, then, naturally possess the capacity to identify with feelings, the capacity that is the distinctive characteristic of artistic experience. However, although this capacity is natural, it requires development. In its primitive form, it is simply "a natural repugnance to see any sensitive being perish or suffer" (*Second Discourse*, CW 3:15; Pl. 3:126). Because natural humans can understand only physical suffering, they are unable to conceive of the suffering of, for example, Oedipus when he discovers that he has killed his father and slept with his mother. They certainly cannot understand Othello's jealousy or Macbeth's ambition. While natural humans would be unmoved by Sophocles or Shakespeare, they would be affected by works that show purely physical suffering in graphic terms and would flee from the spectacle rather than enjoy it. Such works, however, would barely qualify as imitative art in Rousseau's terms. Any genuinely imitative art that wishes to stimulate emotions beyond physical pain depends on the acquisition of such emotions in its audience.

In sum, the imitative arts depend on two things: the ability to identify with others and the imagination to experience and recognize a complex range of emotions. The first of these may be natural, but the second is certainly not. Furthermore, Rousseau presents the development of what we can call theatrical emotions such as ambition, vanity, desire for vengeance, jealousy, et cetera, as a threat to natural personal independence. These dramatic passions are passions that involve us with other people and tend to make us dependent on them. These are the passions that make us social beings.

Rousseau's description of an education meant to preserve natural independence in the first half of *Emile* illustrates this point. In this part of the education, all of the fine arts appear as threats to independence. For example, Emile does learn to draw, but Rousseau says that he does so "not precisely for the art itself, but for making his eyes expert and his hand flexible" (*Emile* 143; Pl. 4:397). He will never draw without having the original in front of him and will never substitute "bizarre and fantastic shapes for the truth of things." Every effort is made to suppress the development of what would today be called "creativity." Similarly, Emile is taught to sing in order to make his voice "exact, even, flexible, resonant," but, Rousseau says, "above all, never a bizarre song, never a passionate one, and never an expressive one" (*Emile* 149; Pl. 4:405). Here the "natural" criterion of exactness excludes the imitative criterion of emotional expressiveness. The young Emile is a natural artist, and therefore not a genuine imitative artist in the full sense of the term.

The reasons for this restriction of the arts become more apparent in the context of Rousseau's attack on poetry in *Emile*. One aspect of his criticism of La Fontaine's fables is connected with the tendency of the reader to identify with the character who takes advantage of others rather than the one who is the recipient of the lesson. On a deeper level, Rousseau's argument attacks identification altogether. Later, when he gives a qualified endorsement to the study of history and of Plutarch's *Lives* in particular, Rousseau says, "As for my Emile, if in these parallels he just once prefers to be someone other than himself—were this other Socrates, were it Cato—everything has failed. He who begins to become alien to himself does not take long to forget himself entirely" (*Emile* 243; Pl. 4:535). Clearly, novels, plays, and fables are at least as likely to cause this alienation as history is. As we shall see, Rousseau discusses the complexity of this alienation in his own experience of reading.[17] Rousseau's political attack on the arts claims that they make us forget our neighbors and our duties and become too self-indulgent. Now it appears that his natural attack on the arts claims that they make us forget about ourselves and become involved with other people and their feelings and opinions. The political attack claims that the arts do not make us social enough; the natural attack claims that they make us too social.

IV. THE POLITICAL CASE FOR THE ARTS

In spite of their appearances, these very different critiques from the perspectives of politics and nature are complementary rather than contradictory. They simply move in opposite directions from a common beginning point. Naturally, humans are both radically independent and completely immune to the appeal of the arts, and, moreover, their independence depends on their immunity to the "theatrical" emotions appealed to by the arts. At the same time, however, their independence keeps them from being citizens. The problem with the arts in the form criticized by Rousseau is that they help to destroy independence and substitute for it only the worst sort of dependence. Finding the right place for the arts depends on establishing their proper relation to the sentiments of sociability or morals that hold a society together. The arts can have a positive function if they can be made to contribute to a better form of social dependence. Within Rousseau's political thought, the establishment of this sort of dependence is the function of the legislator.

A. The Legislator as Artist

As is well known, the figure in Rousseau's works responsible for finding the proper relation between morals and laws is the legislator. This figure, who appears not only in the *Social Contract* but also in *Considerations on the Government of Poland* and elsewhere, stands at the center of Rousseau's account of the relation between his abstract principles and their application. It seems odd to appeal to such an authoritative figure in a theory based on the consent of equal individuals. Neither Rousseau's predecessors in the social contract tradition, such as Hobbes and Locke, nor his successors among liberal political theorists today make such an appeal. Accordingly, Rousseau's use of the legislator has struck commentators as a puzzle that needs to be explained, and some have considered the legislator as one of Rousseau's least successful portraits.[18] Even the scholars who regard his account as more plausible can conclude that the legislator's "function has no status, strictly speaking, in political right."[19]

If the legislator stands outside of the theoretical discussion of political right, then where does he stand? Rousseau's presentation reveals at least three parts to the legislator's task. First, he must understand the principles of political right. Second, he must discover or invent institutions that embody these principles in a manner that suits the conditions of a particular society. Finally, he must find a way to make his people consent to follow these institutions.[20] The precise way in which Rousseau conceives the relations among these three functions distinguishes him from other social contract theorists.

The latter two parts of the legislator's function are concerned with political practice and therefore stand outside of pure political right. In fact, these parts are not concerned so much with political practice in the ordinary sense as with establishing conditions in which politics can take place.[21] The legislator must create an environment made up of sentiments of sociability that can serve as the precondition of political life. The legislator begins by facing a situation in which he understands the principles of political right and the institutions that embody these principles, but his people, "a blind multitude," lack knowledge of either. Rousseau says that "the true political thinker" will admire a legislator's institutions, but a blind multitude is not made up of true political thinkers (*Social Contract*, CW 4:154, 157; Pl. 3:380, 384). From this statement of the beginning point, it might seem that the legislator's function is to enlighten his people in a more or less straightforward manner, and some commentators have interpreted the legislator in this way;[22] however, the political nature of his situation suggests that the legislator is all too likely to lack both the proper audience and the necessary time for this sort of enlightenment.

There is a second, equally serious obstacle to understanding the legislator as simply a bringer of enlightenment. Not only is enlightenment impossible in the circumstances faced by legislators, it would be insufficient even if it were possible. Rousseau denies that there is any necessary connection between possessing a clear understanding of what justice is and having a disposition to be just. "Private individuals see the good they reject" (*Social Contract*, CW 4:154; Pl. 3:380), or as Rousseau's "independent man" says in the first version of the *Social Contract*, "It is not a matter of teaching me what justice is, but of showing me what interest I have in being just" (*Geneva Manuscript*, CW 4:80; Pl. 3:286). Rousseau's doctrine of the general will requires both an ability to generalize and a disposition to will generally. The formation of this disposition is an essential task and one that cannot be reduced to presenting a correct "theory of justice."[23]

Thus, it is not enough for a legislator to make his people "see objects as they are"; he must also sometimes make them see objects "as they should appear to be" (*Social Contract*, CW 4:154; Pl. 3:380). There are passages outside of the *Social Contract* in which Rousseau elaborates on the differences between the communication of a theoretical doctrine to philosophers and a variety of popular presentations to an unenlightened multitude. This elaboration can lead us to the reconsideration of a possible positive political function of the arts.

Rousseau's most general account of the difference between the different sorts of authority appropriate for philosophers and others occurs in his essay "On Theatrical Imitation," which he composed while writing the *Letter to d'Alembert*. In this context he distinguishes the activity of a philosopher from that of an imitative artist. On the one hand, the "philosopher who reasons submits his reasonings to our judgment." Rousseau compares the reasoning of philosophers to a painstaking act of measuring. Philosophy is like measurement, which, "giving us successively one dimension and then the other, instructs us slowly about the truth of things" (*Theatrical Imitation*, CW 7:344, 339; Pl. 5:1204, 1199). Thus, philosophy requires both an audience capable of judging and the time necessary to perform a laborious demonstration. As the *Social Contract* says, the language of the wise is not the language of the people (*Social Contract*, CW 4:156; Pl. 3:383). On the other hand, the imitative artist can be successful without depending upon either of the requirements of philosophic demonstration. Instead of giving one dimension and then another, he "offers us the whole at one time." Instead of submitting to judgment, the imitator "puts himself forward as judge" (*Theatrical Imitation*, CW 7:339, 344; Pl. 5:1199, 1204). He does so without recourse to force, however. His audience accepts his judgment willingly. In short, the consideration of imitation shows a way to gain consent without using either reason or force. This account of consent is reinforced in the *Reveries*, where Rousseau describes the method necessary for teaching what he calls "moral truths." This method is akin to that employed by the imitative poet. Rousseau says that moral truths will be perceived and accepted only if they are wrapped in "easily perceived and pleasing forms" (*Reveries*, CW 8:32; Pl. 1:1029). A blind multitude must be made to sense the things it cannot see, and these things must be made agreeable to win consent.

The requirements for teaching moral truths are identical to those faced by a legislator if he is to gain an immediate willing consent. He needs an ability that would allow him to show his people things as they should appear to be. While the art of the "true political thinker" may be philosophic, that of the legislator must also be, in Rousseau's terms, "imitative" or artistic. Because Rousseau sees no essential connection between an understanding of justice and a disposition to be just, he is forced to conclude in the *Social Contract* that the legislator must not depend on reason alone. Instead, he "must necessarily have recourse to another order of authority, which can win over without violence and persuade without convincing [persuader sans convaincre]" (*Social Contract*, CW 4:156; Pl. 3:383).[24] Persuasion, then, involves an appeal to something other than reason, while convincing involves rational demonstration.

The most common explanation of the legislator's ability to persuade focuses on the use of religion. Rousseau's references to Moses and Mohammed as legislators, as well as his phrase "another order of authority," show that he sees religion as the major tool of the legislator's persuasion. Commentators on this section of the *Social Contract* almost invariably refer to the legislator's use of religion, but they fail to discuss in any detail the way he uses it. Rousseau's discussion of this question requires examination, however, because it is more complex than it might appear at first glance. It is necessary to understand how religion can help a legislator to portray things as they should appear to be or to present useful truths in an agreeable form. Moreover, it is necessary to understand how a legislator can inspire (as well as make use of) religious belief.

The legislator's use of religion cannot be reduced to the reliance on contrived miracles. Rousseau does refer to miracles, but he does so only to argue that they are inadequate for the legislator's purpose. He says that "any man" can temporarily impress the people with a false miracle. However, "not every man . . . can make the Gods speak" (*Social Contract*, CW 4:157; Pl. 3:384). When he discusses the success of the nonpolitical founding of Christianity in *Letters Written from the Mountain* (written in defense of the *Social Contract*), Rousseau elaborates on this attack on the importance of miracles by saying that miracles impress those who are "incapable of coherent reasoning, slow and reliable observation, and in all things the slave of its senses" (*Mountain*, CW 9:167; Pl. 3:729). The multitude may well be the slave of its senses when the legislator finds it, but a reliance on miracles is too likely to leave it in this condition, that is, ready to be the dupe of the first impostor to appear with a talking bird. Talking birds are much more common than talking gods. The use of miracles is like the use of force in that only the most recent application is effective. The legislator requires a more enduring effect if he wishes to preserve his institutions.

While the legislator may be obliged to begin with people who are slaves of their senses, he seeks to turn them into what Rousseau calls "good and upright people." Such people are won over less by miracles than by the character of those who preach, by their "sanctity, their veracity, their justice, their pure and spotless morals, their virtues inaccessible to human passions" (*Mountain*, CW 9:167; Pl. 3:728). Similarly, in the *Social Contract* Rousseau concludes, "The legislator's great soul is the *true* miracle that should prove his mission" (*Social Contract*, CW 4:157; Pl. 3:384; emphasis added). Although a great legislator cannot convince a blind multitude with the reasons justifying a set of institutions, he can make the multitude feel rather than see his soul. Rousseau's account of how this takes place will be discussed in the next chapter. For now it is sufficient to note that the perception of the legislator's soul secures consent for his institutions and a disposition to follow them. As Judith Shklar has said, "The altering of public opinion, the revolution in attitudes that impinge on behavior can only be done by an example so impressive that it imposes the will to imitate."[25] It is this desire to imitate the great soul of the legislator that will make the people "good and upright" citizens, just as it was the desire to imitate Jesus and the saints that made good and upright Christians.

In sum, the legislator's use of religion has two components, neither of which depends decisively on the fabrication of miracles. First, he indeed must "make the Gods speak," and he must make them speak in "the language of the people" (*Social Contract*, CW 4:156–57; Pl. 3:383–84). Second, he can win acceptance for himself as the mediator between the gods and the people through his true miracle of making his great soul felt by the people. This indicates that the real skill of the legislator is shown in the way he makes use of religion, not in the mere fact of using it.

The discussion above indicates Rousseau's judgment about the mistake of relying on rational argument alone. We must still identify the nonrational means by which the legislator can make the gods speak. As Rousseau says, the legislator must "persuade without convincing." It is precisely "persuasion" that must be explained. The next chapter will focus on the significance of the greatness of soul of the legislator. At present we will treat the more general issue of the arts as means of persuasion.

B. The Imitative Basis of Social Life

While it is true that Rousseau does not explain the real miracle of the legislator's persuasion in this context, it is not completely true, as Shklar once contended, that he "never really explained it."[26] Considered in very broad terms, the legislator's project is to move an asocial multitude into the specific condition of citizenship. It is this project that requires the "miracle" of persuading the people to accept good institutions whose workings they do not understand. In other words, the people must already be open to some form of persuasion. For example, they must already be capable of understanding language. As this example indicates, it is necessary to understand the place of the formation of citizens within the major concerns of Rousseau's system as a whole, namely, the delineation of the distinction between natural and social humans. As Rousseau makes clear in the *Second Discourse*, the acquisition of language is the most fundamental and puzzling step in the transformation of asocial, natural humans into social beings of any sort. The "language" of the pure state of nature is only the "cry of Nature" that existed "before it was necessary to *persuade* assembled men" (*Second Discourse*, CW 3: 29–33, 31; Pl. 3: 146–50, 148; emphasis added). In the pure state of nature, persuasion is both unnecessary and impossible, and (aside from sexual relations and the care of mothers for children) the few relations that exist among humans are characterized by force (*Second Discourse*, CW 3:65; Pl. 3:191). The existence of a conventional language that can persuade must be regarded as the absolute precondition for the legislator's "miracle." The inventor of language, if there could have been one, could be considered as a meta-legislator. The key to an explanation of the persuasive power of the legislator's soul must be an explanation of the conditions of persuasion in language as such.

According to Rousseau, the first language beyond the cry of nature stands at the dividing point between the asocial independence of the state of nature and the social dependence of civilized life. He calls speech "the first social institution" (*Essay*, CW 7:289; Pl. 5:375). The earliest language incarnates persuasive ability to the ultimate, or at least penultimate, degree.[27] Precisely what distinguishes this first conventional language from the simple cry of nature is that it partakes of the social character of persuasion. In his account of the characteristics of this language in the *Essay on the Origin of Languages*, Rousseau makes use of his formulation from the *Social Contract*. He says that the earliest language "would *persuade without convincing* and depict without reasoning" (*Essay*, CW 7:296; Pl. 5:383; emphasis added). In effect, the first language did exactly what the legislator must do. An explanation of how this language persuades without convincing can help to reveal how the legislator can perform his miracle.

Rousseau is quite clear about the essential precondition of human language. He says, "As soon as one man was recognized by another as a sentient, thinking Being and similar to himself, the desire or the need to communicate his feelings and thoughts to him made him seek the means for doing so" (*Essay*, CW 7:289–90; Pl. 5:375). Notice the peculiarity of this formulation. Rousseau does not say, "As soon as one man recognized another, he desired to communicate." What he says is "As soon as one man was recognized by another, he desired to communicate." The desire to communicate apparently depends on the awareness that someone else recognizes us as similar, rather than simply on our recognition of the other person as similar to us. We must be aware of other people as being aware of us. This entails a more developed and complex identification with others than is the case with the natural form of commiseration.

The relation between this sort of consciousness of someone else's consciousness and musical or artistic imitation is made clear in Rousseau's discussion of the dependence of music upon melody and melody upon voice later in the *Essay*. In refuting a supposed analogy between colors and sounds, he says, "Colors are the finery of inanimate beings; all matter is colored; but sounds proclaim movement, the voice proclaims a sensitive being; only animated bodies sing. It is not the automated flautist that plays the flute, it is the mechanic who measured the air flow and made the fingers move" (*Essay*, CW 7:325; Pl. 5:420). The ability to appreciate music corresponds to the ability to be aware of another living being. The fact that music stimulates in us the passions we attribute to its living source makes us aware of this source as directing itself outward. In short, social life begins with the institution of the communication of feelings through what we have identified as artistic, musical, or theatrical imitation. Genuine social life is coextensive with artistic life.

Of course, Rousseau is far from claiming the existence of a meta-legislator who stood outside of language in order to invent it. The function of his discussion of language in the *Second Discourse* is to show that such an invention of language is not susceptible to rational understanding. He most assuredly does not posit even the possible existence of the sort of meta-legislator referred to here.[28] How this first institution originated is ultimately mysterious. The issue here is how a physical phenomenon such as sound can have more than merely physical effects. There are a few contexts in which Rousseau gives a sort of attempt at a causal explanation of such phenomena (*Dialogues*, CW 1:9–10; Pl. 1:669). More commonly, however, he rejects any attempt to explain them by dismissing them as metaphysical issues that he neither can nor needs to explain (*Emile* 488–89 n. 2; and *Dictionary*, Pl. 5:1026). It is enough for his purposes to have identified the emotional effect that language, music, and the arts in general have on us.

Note that Rousseau identifies two different aims of language: the communication of thoughts and the communication of feelings. His definition of language as "the institution of perceptible signs to express thought" applies more to written than to spoken language (*Essay*, CW 7:290, 296; Pl. 5:375, 389) because written language corresponds to the substitution of ideas for feelings. As the first social institution, spoken language is much more bound up with communicating feelings as a means of identification with others than it is with the communication of thoughts. Unlike Aristotle, for example, who presents the connection between language and rational deliberation as essential to the political nature of humans, Rousseau regards language as a means for communicating thoughts (as opposed to feelings) as secondary and also as inadequate to the demands of political life.

Rousseau's treatment of language establishes a continuum moving from feeling/persuading to reason/convincing. The most persuasive is the first spoken language; the least persuasive would be a purely written language, for example, a language of mathematical symbols. The *Essay* subtly adds to this spectrum by dividing each of these categories into several others. For our purpose here, it will be sufficient to note that there is one further step that can be added to the extreme end of the spectrum in the direction of persuasion. While the first spoken language is very expressive of feelings, it also partakes of the nature of all language, which is to express thoughts or ideas as much as feelings. The first language is a mixture of ideas and feelings; it uses sounds to represent "the idea that the passion presents to us" (*Essay*, CW 7:294; Pl. 5:381). The most powerful, or purest, medium of persuasion would be one that intensifies the expression of feelings even more than the first language does. Such a "language" would be an example of pure persuasion or imitation of feelings even beyond what is the case in the original language. It would be a standard according to which all other means of persuasion could be measured. As we have seen, Rousseau identifies this standard as imitative, as opposed to natural, music.

If imitative music is the most effective means for transporting people outside of themselves and inspiring them with appropriate feelings, it seems as if it should be the favored medium for the legislator's persuasion. In fact, there are some indications that Rousseau took the idea of a musical legislator seriously. In an article in his *Dictionary of Music*, Rousseau makes an explicit connection between ancient music and laws. He approvingly cites Athenaeus, who "assures us that in the past all the divine and human laws, the exhortations to virtue, the knowledge of what concerned the Gods and Heroes, the lives and actions of illustrious men were written in verse and sung publicly by Choruses to the sound of instruments." Thus, not only the laws, but also exemplary lives and religious doctrines were conveyed through music. Rousseau reinforces the testimony of Athenaeus by observing in his own name that "we see by our sacred Books that such were, from the first times, the customs of the Israelites" (*Dictionary*, CW 7:442; Pl. 5:921). Thus, Moses' founding, the model of successful legislation, was a musical one.[29] Rousseau goes on to assert that the connection between music and great feelings is so natural that it would arise spontaneously even in those communities that lacked individual legislators. All early political communities, even those without great legislators, relied on music to transmit and support laws.

In his article "Song" Rousseau goes so far in asserting the connection between music and laws as simply to identify the two, saying, "The Ancients did not yet have the art of writing, but they already had songs. Their Laws and their histories, the praises of their Gods and Heroes were sung before being written. And from this it happens, according to Aristotle, that the same Greek name was given to the Laws and Songs" (*Dictionary*, Pl. 5:690). In the *Social Contract* Rousseau connects the word "nomos" to Rome's second king, Numa, whom he calls "the true founder of Rome" (*Social Contract*, CW 4:203; Pl. 3:444). These claims reinforce the argument of the *Social Contract* discussed above in which Rousseau refers to the legislator's need for religious authority to support his laws and his use of persuasion and his own example to establish his religious authority. It is the existence of a persuasive medium of musical language, rather than any illusory miracles such as talking birds, that allows the legislator to make the gods speak.

There is an additional source of persuasive rhetoric available to a legislator beyond that of music. Rousseau does not believe that music alone is simply sufficient to inspire the sort of spirited devotion required by citizenship. He is far from denying the necessity of harsh exemplary actions to supplement song. For every peaceful Numa, there must be an accompanying Romulus, whose name according to Rousseau means "force." The sort of forcefulness used by a legislator must be distinguished, however, from the simple physical force of the state of nature and from the more sophisticated force of modern tyrants. In the *Essay* Rousseau refers both to the musical first language and to a different sort of ancient "language" that is unmusical. He claims that "the most energetic language is the one in which the sign has said everything before one speaks." He explicitly connects this sort of language of visible signs or actions to founders of countries. He says, "The Prophets of the Jews, the Legislators of the Greeks, by often presenting perceptible objects to the people, spoke to them more effectively through these objects than they could have done through long discourses" (*Essay*, CW 7:290, 291; Pl. 5:376, 377). Rousseau provides numerous politically important examples of such symbolic actions; for example, the Levite of Ephraim's call for vengeance by dividing his wife's body into twelve sections, Saul's dismemberment of his oxen, and elsewhere Marc Antony's appearance with Caesar's body (*Emile* 322–23; Pl. 4:648).

Perhaps the most notable of such examples is the first Brutus's execution of his sons (*Political Fragments*, CW 4:38–39; Pl. 3:506–7). After deposing the Tarquins, the Romans remained "a stupid mob" until examples like the one provided by Brutus gave them "that severity of morals and that pride of courage which eventually made them the most respectable of all peoples" (*Second Discourse*, CW 3:5; Pl. 3:113). Such examples are terrifying, but their use as symbols distinguishes them from direct use of force. They inspire awe by a sort of visible persuasion. Furthermore, in each instance cited by Rousseau, they inspire an active indignation against apparent injustice rather than the passive acceptance of injustice that would result from naked force. These examples suggest that a legislator's ability to inspire awe is a useful accompaniment to his persuasion through music. Rather than being mutually exclusive, the two methods can complement each other. The visible examples can endure by being incorporated into a story or song. Both methods illustrate persuasion without convincing.

The political importance Rousseau attributes to artistic imitation and to music in particular might well appear to be a Platonic element of his thought. After all, in the *Republic* the best city is founded on a musical education that looks like a prefiguration of Rousseau's principles in that it uses melody, harmonic modes, and rhythm to direct the souls of citizens in the proper way. Certainly Rousseau and Plato are the two philosophers who made the strongest arguments for a connection between music and good citizenship. There is, nonetheless, a very important difference in emphasis between the two of them. In the account in the *Republic*, the ability of melody, harmony, and rhythm to channel passions is clearly secondary in importance to the need to subordinate these elements of song to speech and, furthermore, to subordinate speech to the reasonable demands of the city.[30] Socrates suggests a hierarchy that descends from reason to speech to music. In modern music prior to Rousseau, one can trace a Platonic inspiration based on this hierarchy running from Monteverdi through Lully.[31]

Rousseau, on the other hand, places far more importance on melody than on reason or articulated speech. To be sure, he does try to restore a connection between music and speech that he claims had been severed in Rameau's music, or at least his theorizing about music.[32] Nevertheless, the connection he tries to restore is between music and the melodic accents of speech, not between music and the articulation of reasonable speech. While those inspired by Plato are interested in taming the power of music and submitting it to reason, Rousseau is interested in taking advantage of the untamed power of melody. Perhaps because he regards social life as unnatural, Rousseau thinks that the full power of music is needed to socialize people. This is not to say that he would be unwilling to use reasonable argument to discuss what sort of music would be best for civil purposes. He did write an interesting essay, "On Military Music," and composed a pleasant march in accord with his principles. On balance, however, Rousseau turns on its head the Platonic order, which urges giving primacy to reason over feeling.

Rousseau argued tirelessly against the predominant tradition of French music, which he saw as abandoning expressive power in the name of a purely technical expertise. In particular, he engaged in a lengthy and acrimonious debate with Rameau over the very nature of music.[33] One of the most interesting facets of Rousseau's treatments of music is his attempt to call attention to the music of other countries. This began with his championing of Italian music in France, and extended to his attempt to reproduce Chinese and South American music in his *Dictionary* and finally to his composition of a rather unusual tune, the "Chanson Negre," to suit lyrics written in Creole. There are at least two reasons for this interest on Rousseau's part. First, he wished to explore types of music that might recapture some of what had been lost in modern French music. Second, he attributed a great importance to the encouragement of unique cultures.

The emphases on what could be called primitivism and cultural diversity both stem from Rousseau's insistence that the artistic experience is not natural because the passions, feelings, and emotions with which we identify in our experience of art are unnatural ones. Precisely because these feelings are unnatural, they are susceptible to an indefinite number of variations. They will vary from individual to individual and even more from nation to nation because of variations of temperament, climate, diet, historical accidents, and any number of other causes either natural or artificial, some of which can be influenced by human activity and others that cannot.[34] As a result, different types of art will affect different cultures. To illustrate this point, Rousseau refers to the traditional story that songs can be used to cure tarantula bites. While provisionally accepting the fact of such cures, he denies that they have a directly physical cause. Rather, he asserts that the songs have an effect on the emotions, which in turn have an effect on the body. Because of this, he insists that each nation would require its own songs and concludes his account by saying, "Bernier's Cantatas have, it is said, cured the fever of a French musician; they would have given one to a musician of any other nation" (*Essay*, CW 7:324; Pl. 5:418). As even successive generations within a single nation often find to their dismay, what is mere noise to one audience is music filled with profoundly moving associations to another.

Legislators must be aware of this variability in the power of the arts. They are not free to use any means whatsoever. They must learn to diagnose the artistic or cultural temperament of their own people and then use the means suited to channeling this temperament in the right direction. In a sense, all happy political communities, like all happy families, are alike; that is, they are all founded on an artistic experience that makes citizens identify with one another because they share the same passions, but this formal similarity is compatible with—and indeed requires—the maximum possible distinctiveness for each community.

Rousseau's first critique of the arts can now be put into proper perspective. Beyond his attack on the link between the arts and luxury, his precise complaint against the theater concerns the sterility of theatrical identification. This sterility comes from the very purity of the theatrical experience in which the spectator forgets about his normal existence as a citizen. Where citizenship is concerned, Rousseau seeks a cure for the sterility of this form of identification, not for the identification as such. Genuine citizenship depends on finding a sort of identification that avoids this sterility and forgetfulness. Rousseau's two, apparently opposite, critiques of the theatrical and musical arts as they are cultivated by his contemporaries combine into the criticism that these arts are too imitative to preserve naturalness, but not imitative enough (or in the proper way) to support citizenship.

Rousseau's most concrete positive account of what a good community is occurs in *Considerations on the Government of Poland*. In this work he restates his criticism of the arts very briefly in a passage that calls to mind the arguments of the *First Discourse* and the *Letter to d'Alembert*. He says, "It is necessary to abolish, even at Court, because of the example, the ordinary amusements of courts, gambling, theaters, comedies, opera; everything that effeminates men, everything that distracts them, isolates them, everything that makes them forget their country and their duty" (*Poland*, Pl. 3:962). This is a restatement of the view that the tendency of the arts, and amusements in general, is to destroy social bonds. This time, however, Rousseau is very specific in presenting this argument against the amusements characteristic of Paris in the context of a more general praise of amusement.

The amusements Rousseau praises are very different from the sophisticated arts of Paris. He says, "By what then move hearts and make them love the fatherland and its laws? Do I dare to say it? By the games of children; by institutions that are idle in the eyes of superficial men, but which form cherished habits and invisible attachments" (*Poland*, Pl. 3:955). Here Rousseau gives amusements, although not the fine arts, a positive endorsement. What is it that distinguishes the amusements that develop citizenship from those that destroy it?

When Rousseau gives an example to illustrate the sort of amusement he advises the Poles to encourage, he seems to contradict his attack on the fine arts. He appeals to the practice of the ancient Greeks, and even to the Athenians, who in the *First Discourse* were examples of the corruption connected to the arts. He says, "It was the poems of Homer recited to the

Greeks solemnly assembled, not closed up in chests, on the stage and money in hand, but in the open air and as the body of the nation, it was the tragedies of Aeschylus, Sophocles, and Euripides represented often before them, it was the prizes with which to the acclamation of all Greece, were crowned the victors of their games, which set them aflame with emulation and glory" (*Poland*, Pl. 3:958). To some extent, this praise of Athens can be attributed to Rousseau's effort in this work to contrast ancient politics with modern politics. From this general perspective, even a corrupt ancient regime like Athens looks relatively good. Nevertheless, it remains the case that Rousseau praises the theater as the source of something positive in Athens.

In fact, this passage of praise for Athenian theater is far from an aberration. Strikingly similar language occurs in the *Letter to d'Alembert* in a similar contrast between the ancient and modern theaters as public institutions. In the *Letter* Rousseau concludes a list of the advantages of ancient theater over modern by saying,

> Finally, their performances had none of the meanness of today's; their theatres were not built by interest and avarice; they were not closed up in dark prisons; their actors had no need to make collections from the spectators or to count out of the corner of their eye the number of people whom they saw coming in the door to be sure of their supper.
>
> These great and proud entertainments, given under the sky before a whole nation, presented on all sides only combats, victories, prizes, objects capable of inspiring the Greeks with an ardent emulation and of warming their hearts with sentiments of honor and glory. (*d'Alembert* 78; Pl. 5:72)

This passage contains all the elements of the later passage in *Considerations on the Government of Poland*. The Athenian theater managed to escape the problems Rousseau presents as inevitable for the proposed Genevan theater. In particular, in being free and in the open air, it did not contribute to inegalitarian luxury. Thus, this example shows that the theater, considered simply as a public institution, can in certain circumstances escape from the particular corrupting form it has been given in modern France. In sum, while Rousseau's natural attack on the arts as destroying independence is absolute, his political attack is dependent on circumstances. Accompanying his political attack on the arts is a political defense of the arts.

The problems of the content of the drama and the experience of the spectators still remain, however. Rousseau insists that the body of the nation was genuinely assembled in the Greek theater, whereas when he attacks the modern theater, he argues that the physical assemblage of people in one place masks an actual isolation since the spectators become absorbed in the drama in order to forget about their neighbors and their duties. Beyond the physical characteristics of Greek theaters, Greek plays have a particular subject matter that allows Rousseau to give them a qualified endorsement. In the *Letter to d'Alembert*, he explains, "If the Greeks tolerated such theatre it was because it represented for them national traditions which were always common among the people, which they had reasons to recall constantly; and even its hateful aspects were part of its intention" (*d'Alembert* 33; Pl. 5:31). To the argument that contemporary dramatists could follow this example and write patriotic plays, Rousseau responds that in principle this may be true, but that in practice the modern depreciation of patriotism would undermine any such attempt (*d'Alembert* 120–21; Pl. 5:109–11). Once again, what is wholesome in certain circumstances is impossible in other circumstances.

What is crucial to Rousseau's acknowledgment of the beneficial effects of Greek drama is that it represented to the Greeks an image of themselves as citizens rather than of imaginary beings that had nothing to do with their lives or of corrupt versions of their own lives. As a result, when they attended the theater, they forgot not about their public responsibilities, but about their purely private life. Rousseau's claim is that this aspect of the Greek theater can serve as the model for other amusements.

One other problem with the theater remains: that is, the sterility of the pure identification that takes place in the experience of the theater. Even the experience of the most wholesome and patriotic of sentiments is likely to turn into self-congratulatory vanity that has no positive consequences once the performance has ended. It is this aspect of theatrical identification that is at the core of Rousseau's attack on the theater. The solution he proposes to this problem is twofold. First, it is necessary to end the passivity of the spectators. Second, it is necessary to keep the performance from ending. In effect, Rousseau's final argument is not that theatricality should be simply banished from political life, but that it should be pushed to a new extreme. Thus, instead of attacking the dangers of the predominance of amusement in Poland, Rousseau says, "It is necessary that one be amused more in Poland than in other countries, but not in the same way" (*Poland*, Pl. 3:963).

These new forms of amusement will counter passivity by making spectators into participants. Thus, Rousseau recommends public competitions in skills like horsemanship. In the *Letter to d'Alembert*, he similarly recommends large-scale public balls to the Genevans (*d'Alembert* 127–31; Pl. 5:115–20). Such activities, which should provide a stimulus for all citizens, will encourage a healthy spirit of competition or emulation. Rousseau goes much further than recommending many public games and competitions. In effect, he argues that the entire life of the community should be turned into a never-ending public spectacle filled with emulation and identification. In the *Letter to d'Alembert*, he discusses the fine spectacle provided by the life of the city of Geneva and thereby implicitly contrasts it with the theatrical and musical spectacles of France (*d'Alembert* 93; Pl. 5:85). In an absolute monarchy, citizens are kept passive and isolated by being provided with spectacles.[35] In republican Geneva, citizens are kept active and united by being made participants in a spectacle.

Rousseau argues that virtually all aspects of service to the community can and should be turned into competition for rewards and that these rewards should be visible honors rather than concealable money (*Poland*, Pl. 3:1007). Each citizen should be presented with regular opportunities to advance upon an ascending ladder of public responsibility and esteem even to the point that each should regard it as possible to advance to the position of monarch (*Poland*, Pl. 3:967, 1020–36). Thus, all citizens will be presented with constant examples of success to which they can aspire and will, in turn, serve as such an example for others.

The effect of this constant stimulation of identification with fellow citizens is that all citizens will come to identify with the nation as a whole because their whole life will be wrapped up in acts of citizenship. This will be true even though, or because, the nation places constant demands upon them. This, Rousseau claims, was the secret of the success of Sparta at inspiring an unprecedented devotion to the community. He says of Lycurgus, "He imposed on them a yoke of iron, the like of which no other people has ever borne; but he attached them to, identified them so to speak, with the yoke by always occupying them with it" (*Poland*, Pl. 3:957). The curtain never falls, the citizens ceaselessly experience theatrical identification, and the object with which they identify is themselves.

One might object to Rousseau by suggesting that nonrational persuasion can be used to inspire an unwholesome fanaticism instead of salutary citizenship. Alternatively, one could also object that persuasion can be used as a fraud by an apparent legislator who lacks the virtues that a true legislator must have and has the passions that a true legislator must lack. Rousseau acknowledges these possibilities, but in spite of his hatred of fanaticism and of tyrants who dupe the people, he claims that persuasion is the only method to ensure political liberty and opposition to tyrants. A social human is, in his essence, a being open to imitation and, hence, to persuasion. Only a few philosophers, if anyone, can substitute reason for persuasion, and they can do so only when alone or when dealing with other philosophers. According to Rousseau, to ignore this would be to ignore the soul of political life.

What conclusion can be drawn from this survey of Rousseau's complex views that consider art as the source of both human dependence and independence, of healthy and unhealthy social life? Perhaps the most significant practical outcomes of Rousseau's thought are the profound dissatisfaction it inspires with the current state of both the arts and politics and what enormous hopes it inspires about their possible future improvement. It is easy for Rousseau's readers to conclude that the arts as they are cultivated now destroy our autonomy and make us exploiters of one another, but the arts as they could be cultivated would fulfill us as individuals and unite us as fellow members of a community. This strange view raises artistic aspiration very high, but it is also easily fragmented into the different contentions about the arts that we see around us today. In sum, Rousseau's political critique of the arts as they were cultivated by his contemporaries ultimately leads him to a claim that, far from being in contradiction with the arts, healthy political life must be founded on an artistic basis. Chapter 5 will turn to the question of whether his critique of the arts from the perspective of independence undergoes a similar sort of reversal.

V. Rousseau's Artistic Project

It is very tempting to regard Rousseau's analysis of the failure of the arts to accomplish in modern society what they accomplished in ancient societies as a call to restore them to their proper importance. His recommendations for Poland indicate he believed that at least in certain circumstances such a restoration was possible. Certainly one of Rousseau's effects on the artists who followed him was to inspire them to attempt to recover the ancient connection between the arts and political life. He inspires them to see themselves as the genuine founders of communities rather than as the servants of the rich. Schiller found the inspiration for his *Letters on the Aesthetic Education of Man* in *Emile*, and one hears the echo of Rousseau in Shelley's assertion "But poets, or those who imagine and express this indestructible order, are not only the authors of language and of music, of the dance and architecture, and statuary, and painting; they are the institutors of laws, and the founders of civil society."[36] It is no wonder that Rousseau's name figures prominently in the poems of not only Shelley, but also Byron, Schiller, Hölderlin, and other Romantic poets who aspired to the goal of using art to construct a new culture.[37]

Rousseau's position on the crucial importance of the arts for political life indicates that the arts must be of great concern to legislators, and given the great importance Rousseau attributed to legislators, it is tempting to think that Rousseau saw his literary and artistic career as contributing to an act of legislation. It has frequently been argued that the legislator is a sort of stand-in for Rousseau himself, who hopes to accomplish through his writing something akin to what the ancient legislators he admired accomplished. Nevertheless, if it is understood too simply, such a conclusion should be resisted for two reasons.

First, as we have seen, and as Rousseau asserted specifically on numerous occasions, he was very pessimistic about the possibility of a successful legislator in contemporary circumstances. What is crucial about the persuasion required for legislation is its appeal to feelings that Rousseau presents as a middle road between coercion and rational argument. It is the abandonment of this middle road that Rousseau regards as a decisive mark of the defects of modern politics. "I observe that in the modern age men no longer have a hold on one another except by force or by self-interest; the ancients by contrast, acted much more by *persuasion* and by affections of the soul" (*Emile* 321; Pl. 4:645; emphasis added).

Rousseau's depiction of the unique persuasive ability found in the first language and in music illustrates his contention in the *Social Contract* that founding or legislating can take place only under certain conditions. Some languages are well suited for persuasion; others are not. In the *Essay* Rousseau mentions Chinese, ancient Greek, and Arabic as sharing some of the characteristics of the earliest language. The modern European languages are much further removed from this original persuasive power. A developed language "substitutes ideas for feelings, it no longer speaks to the heart but to reason" (*Essay*, CW 7:296; Pl. 5:384). This formulation implies that "the heart" is the canvas on which the persuasive speaker paints and that sentiments or feelings are the subjects that he portrays. This difference between European languages and the earlier languages gives an indication of the limited possibility for persuasion in the communities that speak these languages.

Rousseau elaborates on this characterization of the European languages and applies it specifically to French in his *Letter on French Music*. There, after arguing that French is not conducive to either music or poetry, he says, "On the other hand, the French language seems to me that of Philosophers and the Wise: it seems made for being the organ of truth and reason" (*French Music*, CW 7:142; Pl. 5:289). Rousseau's appraisal of the unmusical character of French and the other modern European languages kept him from being as hopeful as Nietzsche later became (at least for a while) about the possibilities for a rebirth of a healthy culture through music. Nevertheless, Rousseau's role as a champion of melodic, imitative music is part of his attempt to form a place for some degree of persuasion in modern life.

The language in which the *Social Contract* is written is appropriate for philosophic discussion of legislators, but it is one of the languages least suitable for the persuasion of a legislator. Elsewhere Rousseau extends this account of the difference between a purely rational language and one suitable for legislation, by describing the progress of Greek. In its origin, Greek resembled the first language in its persuasive power. Then, however, philosophers attempted to make the language more suitable for reasoning. "By cultivating the art of convincing, that of moving the emotions was lost" (*Essay*, CW 7:329; Pl. 5:425). Again, convincing and reasoning are placed on one side in opposition to a nonrational persuading or moving.

The analysis of language builds upon and confirms the argument of the *First Discourse*, in which Rousseau insists upon the negative effects of direct intrusion of philosophy into public life. In the *Essay* as well as the *First Discourse*, Athens is the preeminent example of these destructive consequences. With regard to the philosophic attempt to purge Greek of its persuasive power, Rousseau argues that tyrants were quick to take advantage of the lack of "fire" that came from the rational, enfeebled language. What happened in Greece prefigures the pattern of the relations among the French language, philosophy, and tyranny. According to Rousseau, in political life persuasion, even with all its dangers, is the only alternative to coercion. As will be shown in chapter 5, this is not to say that Rousseau thinks rational deliberation has no role in politics. Instead, he argues that its role is only within a horizon set by persuasion rather than as a replacement for persuasion.

At the end of the *Essay*, Rousseau explicitly addresses himself to the modern political predicament by contrasting ancient languages with "our" modern languages. He says, "In ancient times, when persuasion took the place of public force, eloquence was necessary. What use could it serve today, when public force substitutes for persuasion?" (*Essay*, CW 7:331; Pl. 5:428). Having earlier argued that reliance on force is the result of the loss of persuasion in language, Rousseau now claims that once the effect has been brought about, it becomes a sustaining cause. Just as the absence of persuasion makes reliance on force possible, reliance on force makes persuasion unnecessary for oppressive rulers. The loss of persuasiveness in a language, whether caused by philosophers or tyrants, makes exclusive reliance on force both possible and necessary. Whichever factor was the initial cause in a particular case, the result hinders or prevents new legislation. If a legislator needs persuasion to be successful and modern languages have been rendered unsuitable for persuasion, force is the only tool left for politics. In such circumstances there is no political life properly speaking, only despotism. To resort to the formulation of the *Social Contract*, one could say that Rousseau's picture of modern politics is of a situation in which persuasion is impossible and rulers win over only *with* violence. "And as there is no longer anything to say to the people but, *give money*, it is said to them with placards at street corners or with soldiers in their homes" (*Essay*, CW 7:332; Pl. 5:428). An act of legislation comparable to those of Numa, Lycurgus, or Moses is extremely unlikely in such circumstances.[38]

In the *Social Contract* Rousseau declares, "In Europe there is still one country capable of legislation; it is the Island of Corsica" (*Social Contract*, CW 4:162; Pl. 3:391). After reading this passage, Corsican patriots approached Rousseau about acting as their legislator, and he briefly entertained the idea of moving to Corsica and playing at least an indirect role in its politics, but for a number of reasons failed to follow through on this plan (*Confessions*, CW 5:543–46; Pl. 1:648–51). Thus, Rousseau gave up the single promising opportunity available in contemporary circumstances to be a legislator. As we shall see in the following chapter, Rousseau also considered and rejected a more literary restoration of ancient politics in his attempt to write a play based on the Roman heroine Lucretia.

The second reason one should hesitate to consider Rousseau as a legislator follows from the qualities he regards as necessary for a legislator and those he saw in himself. As will be shown below, Rousseau regarded greatness or strength of soul to be the single most important characteristic for any sort of heroic activity, including founding a community, but he consistently presents himself as a good but weak man who only occasionally can rise above his weakness. In sum, modern circumstances are not right for legislation, and Rousseau himself is not a potential legislator. Nonetheless, the temptation to look at Rousseau as a legislator is not entirely misleading. In the "Letter to Franquières," Rousseau discusses someone who found himself in circumstances similar to those in which Rousseau found himself. Rousseau suggests that the proper way to understand Jesus is as a potential legislator who had to face the facts that he lived in political circumstances that made legislation impossible and that he himself was too gentle for the harsh task of legislation. Rousseau says that rather than leading to a simple abandonment of the project of legislation, this realization led Jesus to an extension of the project. He says that "unable by himself to make a revolution among his people, he wanted to make one, through his disciples in the Universe" ("Franquières," CW 8:270; Pl. 4:1146).[39]

Rousseau seems to have understood Jesus as the author of a moral rather than political founding, and whatever one might think of this understanding of Jesus, it is a plausible account of Rousseau's understanding of his own project as a writer. While Rousseau was interested in preserving healthy morals in the few places they continued to exist, his broader project must be viewed in different terms. As one of his characters in the *Dialogues* says about him, "If his doctrine could be of some utility to others, it was in changing the objects of their esteem and perhaps thus slowing down their decadence which they accelerate with their false appreciations" (*Dialogues*, CW 1:213; Pl. 1:935). His goal as a writer, then, involved the promotion of "objects of esteem" suitable for his corrupt contemporaries. The next chapter will discuss his analysis, creation, and use of such objects of esteem in the context of his treatment of heroes. In many respects, the argument will directly parallel the one of this chapter because the treatment of heroes is a particular application of the principles developed here.

CHAPTER FOUR

HEROIC AND ANTIHEROIC CITIZENS

"The Legislator's great soul is the true miracle that should prove his mission" (*Social Contract*, CW 4:157; Pl. 3:384). This statement, discussed in the preceding chapter, testifies to Rousseau's belief that there is such a thing as a great soul and that such souls have political consequences. This chapter will attempt to explain the significance of greatness of soul by exploring Rousseau's understanding of heroism, to see how important he regards hero worship to be for citizenship, and to examine how sensitive he is to the presumed dangers to equality and independence involved in a politics of heroism. Finally, it will show how the same line of reasoning that led him to a theoretical understanding of heroism affected his literary practice, leading him to the novel *Julie* and to the *Confessions*, both of which attempt to provide models of a new sort of hero for an age that had rejected the traditional understanding of heroism.

Rousseau's defense of equality and attack on personal dependency are sufficient to establish his credentials as a champion of democratic politics.[1] Nevertheless, he has frequently been a troublesome figure to liberals, not least because his works abound with heroic figures whose presence is required to rescue ordinary people who are simply incapable of taking care of themselves. Emile has his tutor, Julie and St. Preux have their Wolmar, the people have their legislator, and so on.[2] Rousseau's frequent praises of the heroes of antiquity are among the most distinctive features of his writing. He admits that he goes out of his way to present a favorable picture of these heroes by mitigating their flaws as much as possible (*Final Reply*, CW 2:121; Pl. 3:86). Liberal democrats tend to be suspicious of hero worship, fearing that it encourages inequality and dependency on those who are, or claim to be, superior. While they can be generous in their praise of heroic action, in their ordinary speech they frequently replace heroes with "role models," for whom the part played or the function fulfilled predominates over intrinsic admirable qualities. It is easier to consider oneself as equal to one's role model than to one's hero. The importance of heroes for Rousseau, then, requires explanation.

In spite of his defense of traditional heroes, many of the features of Rousseau's account of heroism are very untraditional. Moreover, the importance of his account comes from its complexity as well as its novelty. He shows how admiration of heroes can help to form a civic identity that fosters a strong sense of active citizenship, but he also acknowledges that the hero's pursuit of greatness can be dangerously destructive to communities. He explores the possibility of a form of citizenship not dependent on heroic models, but he does so with an acute sense of what will be missing from a community that bases itself on this possibility. In short, just as he did with regard to the arts, Rousseau gives us both a case for heroes and a case against them. The distinctiveness of Rousseau's understanding becomes most apparent in his answers to two questions: First, what makes someone a hero? And, second, what does it mean to have a hero? These answers provide the context for his account of the advantages and disadvantages of heroism to citizenship.

I. What Is a Hero?

Rousseau's most extensive treatment of heroism occurs in his *Discourse on the Virtue Most Necessary for a Hero*, written as a response to the topic posed in 1751 by the Academy of Corsica: "Which is the virtue most necessary for a hero and which are the heroes who lacked this virtue?" Rousseau did not submit the discourse, and it was first published (without his permission) in 1768. Even prior to this, however, he had planned to publish it in the definitive edition of his works.

Because neither the Academy nor Rousseau gives a definition of a hero, one must look to Rousseau's examples to discover what he thinks a hero is. He discusses three different types of hero: conquerors, legislators, and people who make supreme sacrifices for their community. The preeminent examples of each type are Alexander, Lycurgus, and Regulus. Rousseau explicitly distinguishes heroes from other praiseworthy types such as statesmen and citizens (*Hero*, CW 4:9; Pl. 2:1272). What distinguishes the hero from these seems to be simply the ability to compel admiration from most people rather than any necessary prudence or devotion to the common good. In effect, Rousseau seems to suggest that we need not define heroism because we cannot help but recognize it when we see it.

Rousseau indicates a strong kinship between heroes and legislators by saying that the "occupation and talents" of the hero involve constraining men "to bear the yoke of laws" (*Hero*, CW 4:2; Pl. 2:1264). In one of the few studies of the *Hero*, David R. Cameron argues that Rousseau distinguishes between heroes and legislators in that the former can use force while the latter cannot, and Rousseau certainly does not identify legislators with conquerors.[3] Nevertheless, since heroes need not use force, this means only that not all heroes can be legislators, but not that one can be a legislator without also being a hero. Thus, a better understanding of the enigmatic figure of the legislator is one of the things we can hope to learn from examining Rousseau's treatment of heroism. In particular, the inclusion of the legislator in the category of hero reveals a moral ambiguity not visible in Rousseau's other discussions.

Both the Academy's question and Rousseau's list of types of heroes point to a tension within the traditional understanding of heroism. On the one hand, our admiration for heroes seems to indicate that they must have some sort of moral excellence or virtue. On the other hand, when we consider the range of people who are called heroes, it is not clear that they share any particular virtue. While the Academy stops short of implying that there can be a hero who is totally lacking in all virtues, its questions acknowledge that heroes are not simply identical to virtuous people. Traditional attempts to resolve this ambiguity move in one of two directions. Either—taking their cue from Socrates in book 2 of *The Republic*—they insist that heroism must be redefined to encompass a wide range of virtues such as wisdom, courage, and moderation and to exclude a series of vices commonly attributed to traditional heroes, or—following Machiavelli in *The Prince*—they argue that imposing moral notions of virtue undermines heroism. In short, heroes are either made more moral and perhaps less heroic, or their heroism is preserved at the expense of their morality.

Cameron argues that Rousseau's treatment in *Hero* falls victim to this tension by seeking but failing to establish a link between heroism and "personal virtue" and similarly seeking but failing to connect heroism to the "public good."[4] Cameron is correct to point out that Rousseau does not prove that moral virtue necessarily accompanies heroism, but it is less clear whether his treatment should be understood as a failure or as a successful diagnosis of a problem intrinsic to virtually any notion of heroism.

Rousseau begins his discussion by comparing heroes to wise men or philosophers. He asserts that from the standpoint of virtue, the wise man is superior because he possesses all the virtues while the hero may lack some of them. Nevertheless, from the standpoint of the public good, the hero is the clear winner. We have seen earlier Rousseau's insistence that reason alone is an insufficient basis for virtue. Here he says, "The Philosopher can give the Universe some salutary instructions, but his lessons will never correct either the nobles who scorn them or the People which does not hear them at all. Men are not governed in that way by abstract views" (*Hero*, CW 4:2; Pl. 2:1263). With this attack Rousseau joins a long line of enemies of philosophy and, indeed, even many philosophers who regard philosophy as politically impotent. Having established the political superiority of heroes, Rousseau turns to the question of their virtues. At first he seems to define heroism as "the collection of a large number of sublime virtues" and provisionally attributes an almost complete public-spiritedness to heroes. As he proceeds, however, this easy harmony between heroism and the community disappears. Implicitly admitting that his first account did not reveal the essence of heroism, Rousseau says, "Let us not conceal anything; public felicity is far less the end of the Hero's actions than it is a means to reach the one he sets for himself, and that end is almost always his personal glory" (*Hero*, CW 4:3; Pl. 2:1265). In their pursuit of glory, heroes must frequently mix vices with their sublime virtues. In sum, Rousseau's clear position is that pursuit of the public good is a means to the end of heroes, but it is less clear that pursuit of the public good is always the sole necessary or even appropriate means to this end. When other methods are more promising, the hero might well use them at the expense of the public good. Accordingly, while in certain circumstances heroes may be useful, and even indispensable, to "public felicity," they are always dangerous.

Rousseau does not stop at this recognition of the tension acknowledged in the traditional understanding. He continues by examining the cardinal virtues of courage, justice, prudence, and temperance, showing that each in turn is unnecessary for heroism. Even courage, which might seem to be the strongest candidate to answer the Academy's question, sometimes abandons heroes without them becoming unheroic. Finally, claiming to take his inspiration from Francis Bacon, Rousseau concludes that the sole virtue necessary for heroes is "strength of soul" (*Hero*, CW 4:9; Pl. 2:1273).[5] The case for this virtue is based on its ability to keep its possessor from being dominated by fortune. In other words, it is more connected with effectiveness than with morality. Rousseau severs heroism from moral virtue much more radically than the traditional account implicit in the Academy's questions. Taking note of the Machiavellian inspiration for this understanding, Cameron calls Rousseau's inspiration "perhaps Florentine, rather than Greek."[6]

Rousseau's departure from expectations is reflected in his professed inability to answer the Academy's second question, "Which are the heroes who lacked this virtue?" No virtue other than strength of soul is required for heroism, but that one is indispensable. Given its difference from other virtues and its ready alliance with the pursuit of personal glory at the expense of the public good, one might wonder whether strength of soul should be considered a virtue at all.

In the *First Discourse* Rousseau seems to provide the clearest possible positive answer by saying, "It is in the rustic clothes of a Farmer and not beneath the gilt of a Courtier that strength and vigor of the body will be found. Ornamentation is no less foreign to virtue, which is the strength and vigor of the soul" (*First Discourse*, CW 2:6; Pl. 3:7; see also "Franquières," CW 8:267; Pl. 4:1143). Strength of soul appears to be not simply one out of several virtues; it is identified as the unifying principle of all of them. What this means is indicated in the *Hero* when Rousseau says that strength "is the source or the supplement of the virtues that constitute [heroism]" (*Hero*, CW 4:9; Pl. 2:1272). Similarly, in *Emile* he calls strength the "foundation of all virtues" (*Emile* 444; Pl. 4:817). In sum, strength of soul appears to underlie the other virtues in that it brings them into being or makes them effective. Its morality will depend on circumstances, but it clearly benefits its possessor. It is like what Rousseau calls a natural or physical virtue rather than a moral or social virtue (*Second Discourse*, CW 2:34; Pl. 3:152).[7]

That strength of soul forms a sort of substratum on which other admirable characteristics are built indicates its primacy for Rousseau. Arthur M. Melzer has argued convincingly that the true novelty of Rousseau's understanding of human nature is missed if one tries to understand him as primarily interested in virtue, which can easily be shown to have an ambiguous status in his thought. Melzer suggests that what is fundamental for Rousseau is the experience of feeling one's own existence and that he endorses other things such as virtue, compassion, or freedom to the extent that they enhance this feeling.[8] Building on Melzer's argument, one can say that for Rousseau strength of soul is what allows its possessors to maximize the feeling of existence by allowing them to extend it to the maximum degree without falling into the weakness of dependence (*Emile* 78–82; Pl. 4:299–302). Strength of soul, it might be said, yields a greater quality and quantity of existence to its possessor. This formulation should be qualified by the importance of sensitivity for Rousseau. Sensitivity, which we will see is a quality possessed by some of Rousseau's unheroic characters, certainly increases the ability to feel existence, but it usually comes with the cost of a greater weakness, or vulnerability.

What Rousseau means in saying that strength of soul is the source or foundation of moral virtues can be seen from his treatment of its opposite, weakness of soul. He consistently maintains, "All wickedness comes from weakness" (*Emile* 67; Pl. 4:288).⁹ Weakness causes wickedness because weak souls are easily deflected from the naturally good goals of preservation and happiness, and because they are unable to resist temptations. Being frustrated in their desires, the weak are subject to passions such as hatred and resentment and to the vices that accompany these passions. This sort of weakness is a purely relative term: someone with great strength in absolute terms who has even greater desires must be considered to be weak because of this disproportion (*Emile* 80–81; Pl. 4:304). In such a case, this relative weakness will lead to vices such as greed. In some sense, all moral vices can be traced back to weakness of soul or to circumstances that produce weakness.

Weakness ultimately tends toward vice, but strength of soul does not invariably lead to moral virtue. The Savoyard Vicar, apparently with Rousseau's endorsement, does argue that goodness is the necessary consequence of omnipotence (*Emile* 282 and note; Pl. 4:581). In the case of less-than-omnipotent humans, however, strength can be linked with or severed from any number of moral virtues. The number of potential variations makes it impossible to talk about types of heroes. To exaggerate only slightly, aside from having strength, each hero is different from every other one. Rousseau is even far from denying that there are people with very robust souls who are virtually completely lacking in moral virtue. Because he sees weakness as the primary source of vice, he frequently displays toleration for those vices that give some sign of a residual strength of soul. In the *First Discourse*, for example, he shocked some of his readers by attacking the gentleness or softness that came with the spread of the sciences and the arts. He says that he would gladly trade modern urbanity for rusticity even with its characteristic vices of profanity, boasting, insults, national hatreds, and ignorance (*First Discourse*, CW 2:6; Pl. 3:7). In responding to one of the offended readers, he states his preference for "lofty characters who bring even to crime an indefinable quality of pride and generosity" over "the vile and groveling soul of the hypocrite" (*Observations*, CW 2:50; Pl. 3:51; see also *Final Reply*, CW 2:116; Pl. 3:79; and *Emile* 335; Pl. 4:664–65). Even when it does go astray, strength remains more capable of turning into virtue than weakness is. There is no escaping the fact that the severing of moral virtue from heroism leaves Rousseau open to a certain admiration for what could be called heroic criminals.¹⁰ In this he paves the way for the establishment of a distaste for "bourgeois" vices such as avarice and petty vanity and a taste for those who rebel against these qualities.

It is true, as Cameron argues, that in the *Hero* Rousseau tries to bring heroism and morality together as much as possible. The key to the attempted reconciliation is the claim that strength of soul is produced by mastery over oneself (*Hero*, CW 4:10; Pl. 2:1273). Accordingly, in spite of his inclusion of conquerors among his list of heroes, Rousseau can argue that in its highest form, heroism is incompatible with the desire to dominate, a desire that comes only from weakness. The self-mastery characteristic of the strongest souls excludes at least certain forms of wickedness. In spite of this partial reconciliation of heroism and morality, however, it remains the case that Rousseau does not attribute any moral motive to heroes. Whatever morality they may possess remains in the service of their desire for glory. Although heroes lack the specific desire to dominate others, they will do so to reach their predominant end.

In sum, Rousseau indicates that the public good and moral virtue are by-products of heroism rather than its necessary accompaniments. The political problem posed by heroism is to make these by-products more likely, to show heroes that they can obtain glory by cultivating virtue and serving the public good. His entire account shows that he has no illusions about how difficult it is to accomplish this goal.

II. What Does It Mean to Have a Hero?

It is clear that in Rousseau's view heroes are strong and effective, but (or therefore) dangerous. In itself this would seem to lead the unheroic to regard them with respect coupled with wariness, much as they would look upon unstable explosives: indispensable on certain occasions, but to be avoided whenever possible and kept under lock and key when not in use. Part of what is distinctive about heroism, however, is that most people regard it with virtually unmixed admiration. How, then, does one explain hero worship? What, exactly, is the effect that the mere proximity of a strong soul has on others?

Strength of soul is politically effective because it gives the ability to dazzle or impress other people. Rousseau refers to the "brilliance" that strength gives to heroism (*Hero*, CW 4:9; Pl. 2:1272). Elsewhere he discusses how this brilliance affects those who encounter it even when they are only reading about it in works of ancient history. He says:

> The soul is raised up in its turn and courage is inflamed by wandering through these respectable monuments; in some way one participates in the heroic actions of these great men, it seems that meditation about their greatness communicates a part of it to us, and one could say about their person and their speeches what Pythagoras said about the simulacra of the

Gods, that they give a new soul to those who draw near them to obtain their oracles. (*Political Fragments*, CW 4:60; Pl. 3:538–39)

In some way, heroic actions instill strength into the souls of their observers, and this is the source of the hold that heroes have over others who need such support for their own strength. In the terms of the preceding chapter, the imitation inspired by heroes entails an imitation of their strength as well.

Rousseau discusses his own experience of this effect in his *Confessions* when he describes his first encounter with heroes. In one of the most vivid passages of his autobiography, he indicates the power of this experience by saying that when he read about "the illustrious men of Plutarch," "I believed myself to be Greek or Roman; I became the character whose life I read" (*Confessions*, CW 5:8; Pl. 1:9). The identification with heroes caused an acute loss of self. The young Jean-Jacques was conscious of himself only as being someone else: he felt himself to be Brutus and Aristides before he knew what it meant to be Jean-Jacques Rousseau.[11] He experienced in an extreme way the peculiar form of self-consciousness of hero worship: a loss of oneself coupled with a feeling of strength.

Is this transformation of oneself into someone else, this living outside of oneself, good or bad, natural or unnatural? Is it an experience to be sought or shunned? The answers to these questions closely parallel the comparable ones given with regard to the arts in general in the preceding chapter.

III. The Political Need for Heroes

Heroes have a natural strength of soul that they use in the service of their own goals, which may or may not be social goals. Those who are influenced by heroes could be said to have an artificial or derivative strength of soul. The artificial strength differs from the natural in being a social acquisition. Its social character comes both from its requiring at least two people—a hero and an imitator—to arise and from the possibility that many people can have the same hero and undergo the same transformation through his or her influence. While each hero is a unique individual, his or her many imitators will share a large part of their identity.

Rousseau shows the civic importance of the imitation of heroes in his *Considerations on the Government of Poland*. In this work the terms "imitation" and "emulation" are presented as the key to good politics.[12] Like the young Jean-Jacques, good citizens do become someone else; they identify with great citizens from the past and with legislators. Citizens can be made to engage in a constant striving to live up to these great examples. As Rousseau says, "From the effervescence excited by this shared emulation will be born that patriotic intoxication which alone can raise men above themselves, and without which freedom is only a vain name and legislation only a chimera" (*Poland*, Pl. 3:1018). While most people are dominated by the weakness that leads to vice, emulation of heroes gives them the strength that is the foundation of virtue. Good citizens must think of themselves in terms of a civic identity rather than exclusively in terms of themselves. Because humans are not naturally social, community can come only from something like a common identification with the same heroes.

Rousseau calls the sort of community that succeeds in cultivating this sort of shared identity a fatherland (*patrie*), which he distinguishes from a country (*pays*) or a nation. A country is merely a geographical area under a single political rule, but lacks the strong sense of unity characteristic of a fatherland.[13] A nation possesses unity from shared language, traditions, and customs, but need not have any political identity. Only members of a fatherland deserve the title of citizens in the full sense of the term.

The task of founding a fatherland belongs to the legislator. We are now in a position to see the significance of the manifestation of the legislator's great soul in this founding. Rousseau's treatments of citizenship in a republican fatherland are filled with praise of striking examples at foundings or turning points of regimes such as Brutus's execution of his sons, the suicides of Cato and Lucretia, the endurance of torture by Scaevola and Regulus (*Emile* 40; Pl. 4:249; *Political Fragments*, CW 4:58–59; Pl. 3:556–57; and *Final Reply*, CW 2:111; Pl. 3:73). Given that these examples involve being tortured, suicide, execution of one's children, and martyrdom, it might seem strange that Rousseau would regard them as inspiring a desire to imitate or a sense of identification. Nevertheless, these extreme examples represent the ultimate forms of self-mastery, which (as we have seen) Rousseau identifies as a key manifestation of the strength of soul characteristic of heroes. In *Julie* two of his characters engage in a debate over suicide, the turning point of which hinges on the distinction between committing suicide for purely selfish reasons and doing so in accordance with the duties of a good citizen (*Julie*, CW 6:310–23; Pl. 2:377–93). In these latter cases, rather than merely pitying the suffering of these heroes, we admire their fortitude. In identifying with such heroes, we imagine ourselves to possess the strength of soul that makes their extreme sacrifices possible. In this process we gain some of the strength of soul we normally lack. The emulation of heroes provides artificial enhancement of natural strength of soul.

It is obvious that the ability of legislators and other heroes to inspire emulation gives them enormous opportunities for developing personal authority. Rousseau's recourse to a legislator who persuades without convincing and who is characterized by strength of soul has led some readers to claim that he is in favor of an authoritarian or totalitarian politics.[14] While the beginning of the *Hero* shows that Rousseau is well aware of the dangers posed by the personal authority heroes can gain, he is unwilling to renounce the benefits that come from them. It is his argument that the dangers to democracy posed by heroes can be avoided and that the advantages they bring are indispensable. The dangers can be avoided if heroes are not given any personal authority; for example, the heroic legislator must not be a part of the community he founds. The advantages are indispensable because sound politics depends on the strength of soul imparted by the emulation of heroes.

As was mentioned in chapter 1, other critics persuasively make the lesser, but still serious charge that Rousseau's emphasis on shared cultural identity including the reliance on heroes produces a certain passivity among citizens. The active side of citizenship in Rousseau is easy to miss because proponents of pluralism look for signs of activity in opposition among citizens, each side bargaining, pushing for its own interest or view of the public good. Rousseau, however, sees conflict among interest groups as a sign of corruption rather than political health. While he does not exclude the possibility of citizens honestly debating the public good, a point that will be established more firmly in the following chapter, he also sees extremes in such debate as a sign of absence of community. What Rousseau looks for in such debate is the defense of the community against the government rather than the promotion of diversity of opinion in the community. He sees the fundamental danger to an established good community as the tendency of the government to assert its own identity against that of the broader community. The need for diligence in the face of this tendency is the major theme not only of much of the *Social Contract* but also of *Letters Written from the Mountain* (see especially *Mountain*, CW 9:256–58; Pl. 3:836–68). Rousseau's goal is to form citizens who agree with one another and oversee the government with suspicion.

Thus, while the strength of soul that Rousseau looks for in citizens does depend on a certain social conformity, it does not imply complete passivity. Strong-souled citizens are capable of self-assertion on behalf of the community not only against outsiders, but also against a usurping government. In fact, among Rousseau's favorite examples of heroic figures, those like Lucretia, Brutus, and Cato, who support republicanism against tyranny, predominate over those like Regulus, who acts against a foreign enemy. In fact, then, in its strongest sense, citizenship for most people depends on the strength of soul that is imparted by the emulation of such heroes.

IV. The Unnaturalness of Hero Worship

Rousseau's insistence on something as artificial and dangerous as emulation of heroes to support political life follows from his radical claim—which we have encountered in his account of the unnaturalness of the arts—that there is nothing natural that can serve as such a support. Rousseau claims that natural independence and freedom are so absolute that natural humans have virtually no need for one another once they are no longer infants. He does concede that some common interest such as the need for food can bring them together, but he concludes that an association formed on this basis "obligated no one and lasted only as long as the passing need that had formed it" (*Second Discourse*, CW 3:45; Pl. 3:166–67). Without some development of needs beyond the natural ones, humans will have almost nothing to do with one another.

Just as no one is less appreciative of artistic imitation than the natural man in the pure state of nature described in the *Second Discourse*, similarly, no one is less subject to imagining himself to be someone he is not. Such an individual has no need for heroes: "His desires do not exceed his Physical needs" (*Second Discourse*, CW 3:27; Pl. 3:143). Furthermore, his "imagination portrays nothing to him; his heart asks nothing of him. . . . His soul, agitated by nothing, is given over to the sole sentiment of its present existence" (*Second Discourse*, CW 3:28; see also 43; Pl. 3:144, 164). His limited imagination gives the natural man no awareness of the future and no knowledge of the inner characteristics of other humans. He might imitate their actions as he imitates those of other animals, but he will certainly have no heroes (*Second Discourse*, CW 3:21; Pl. 3:135). He is as thoroughly absorbed in himself as the citizen of a fatherland or the young Jean-Jacques is in his heroes. In short, natural humans have limited imagination and no need for, or capacity to appreciate, heroes. Furthermore, these deficiencies are the source only of good because it is precisely the absence of imagination and the awareness of others that ensure natural independence and freedom. They guarantee that the natural man will not be plagued by shame, pride, desire to dominate, or willingness to be dominated, and someone with limited imagination can form few needs that exceed his strength. Viewed in the light of what is natural, hero worship appears as a curse. Of course, the same can be said of virtually all characteristics of social life.

If the natural condition is one of freedom and independence supported by the absence of the imagination necessary to appreciate heroes, it is not surprising that when Rousseau turns to the education intended to preserve that freedom and independence in a civilized human, he attempts to regulate the imagination very carefully. In particular, imitation and emulation, which figure so strongly in Rousseau's accounts of citizenship in a fatherland, have a very low status in Emile's education. Near the end of the education, Rousseau asks rhetorically, "But who in the world is less of an imitator than Emile?" (*Emile* 331; Pl. 4:659). To be sure, he does learn to imitate things accurately, but rarely if ever does he imitate other people (*Emile* 70, 98, 130, 140–45; but cf. 95; Pl. 4:293, 330–31, 377, 390–98, 325–26). The one time he self-consciously does so—when he attempts to gain praise by imitating a magician—he learns that such imitation leads to disastrous consequences for himself (*Emile* 173–75; Pl. 4:437–39).[15] If Emile is ultimately intended to be a citizen, he cannot become one in the strong sense of a citizen of a fatherland.

Rousseau does argue, as he did in the *Second Discourse*, that humans have a natural and wholesome capacity for imitation, but he emphasizes that this capacity is easily transformed into something dangerous. He says, "Man is an imitator. Even animals are. The taste for imitation belongs to well-ordered nature, but in society it degenerates into vice" (*Emile* 104; Pl. 4:339–40). This degenerate form of imitation "comes from the desire always to be transported out of ourselves," exactly the experience of the young Jean-Jacques in his reading of Plutarch and novels. The experience of becoming someone else that forms the very origin of Jean-Jacques's consciousness is delayed as long as possible for Emile, who is meant to remain self-absorbed and consequently independent until an advanced stage of his education.

When Emile finally learns to read, he does experience an identification with a character and is even said to have a hero. His first book is *Robinson Crusoe*, and Rousseau says, "I want him to think he is Robinson himself" (*Emile* 185; Pl. 4:455). Nevertheless, even while encouraging and making use of this imitation, Emile's tutor lessens its force. In two respects Robinson Crusoe, as he is understood by Emile, is very different from ordinary heroes, especially those heroes of Plutarch imitated by Jean-Jacques. First, Robinson lives in isolation from other people. Even Friday is apparently left out of the version of the story read by Emile. Thus, Emile's identification with Robinson will increase his sense of independence rather than socialize him. Emile's identification with such a hero will inoculate him against dependence on anyone else. In effect, in imagining himself to be Robinson, he imagines himself to be precisely what he already is: a natural man who judges the world in terms of his natural needs. He emulates someone whose distinctive characteristic is that he has no one to emulate.

The second respect in which Robinson is an atypical hero stems from the way Emile is encouraged to look at him. Immediately after saying that Emile will think he is Robinson, Rousseau indicates that the boy will constantly be made "to examine his hero's conduct; to investigate whether he omitted anything, whether there was nothing to do better; to note Robinson's failings attentively; and to profit from them so as not to fall into them himself in such a situation" (*Emile* 185; Pl. 4:455). In other words, the intensity of Emile's identification with his hero is considerably diluted by an actively critical spirit. In the end, it is Robinson's situation with which he identifies more than his personality. He judges things less as Robinson does in fact than as someone in his position should. Emile might relish the thought of taking Robinson's place on the island, as he apparently was going to do had Rousseau finished his sequel, but in doing so he would avoid imitating Robinson's many mistakes and would remain immune to Robinson's constant desire to escape and rejoin civilization.

The independence and critical distance that characterize Emile's reading of *Robinson Crusoe* continue when he later turns to Jean-Jacques's favorite author, Plutarch. He will not be infected by the desire to be like those great heroes whose weaknesses and failings will be constantly in his mind (*Emile* 243; Pl. 4:535).[16] Any identification will be sufficient only to allow him to pity them. Anything beyond this would entail the loss of psychological independence and self-sufficiency. In sum, the goal of at least the first three books of *Emile* is the attainment or preservation of independence by means of an extreme regulation of the imagination, including the imaginative identification that constitutes hero worship.

With respect to virtue, at this stage of his education, "Emile has all that relates to himself," but he has no social or moral virtues (*Emile* 208; Pl. 4:488). At numerous points Rousseau explicitly identifies the development of strength of soul as one of the prime goals of the education (*Emile* 119, 232, 446; Pl. 4:362, 518–19, 820); but instead of relying on the artificial enhancement that comes from emulation, Emile's natural strength of soul is carefully nurtured. The man raised according to nature has all the strength of soul necessary to be a hero, and he is favorably compared to such traditional heroic figures as David, Ulysses, and Alexander the Great (*Emile* 137, 163; Pl. 4:388, 425). Rousseau even says, "He is made for guiding, for governing his equals" (*Emile* 162; Pl. 4:424). There is no question that Emile has the virtue most necessary for a hero. What keeps him from becoming one is his lack of concern for glory (*Emile* 119; Pl. 4:362). He has no desire to affect other people beyond a willingness to contract with them for the few things he cannot provide for himself. If he is to be considered a hero, he is a hero of independence and self-sufficiency, not a hero of political accomplishment.

V. Citizenship without Heroes?

Rousseau's radical split between natural independence and citizenship based on emulation of heroes is bound to disappoint modern democrats who look to him as a potential ally. Their suspicion of personal authority and their desire for political community makes them want to find a type of citizenship that does not run the risks that accompany emulation. There is reason to believe that Rousseau is willing to provide an alternative model of citizenship that can partially satisfy these competing demands. Nevertheless, this alternative model must always be measured against the standard set by heroic citizenship.

From Rousseau's standpoint, the drawback, if there is one, of the heroic model of citizenship is the harshness that accompanies fanatical devotion to the community.[17] Although Rousseau frequently defends fanaticism in the face of the moral laxness that he detected in his contemporaries, he also argues that its energy must be directed very carefully (*Emile* 312–13; 633–34). In the first draft of the *Social Contract*, he suggests that he would be willing to sacrifice some of the advantages of fanaticism to avoid its harshness. When discussing the civil religion, he argues that the zealousness of Roman citizens was inseparable from their cruelty and says, "It is better, then, to bind the citizens to the state by weaker and gentler ties, and to have neither heroes nor fanatics" (*Geneva Manuscript*, CW 4:119; Pl. 3:338). What sort of citizenship can dispense with heroes and hero worship?

Rousseau explores the possibility of citizenship without heroes when he turns to Emile's participation in a community. He began *Emile* by deploring attempts to combine citizenship with independence, but when he announces his own goal, he says it is to judge whether this double goal can be achieved within the context of an education devoted to independence (*Emile* 39–41; Pl. 4:249–52). The question is what sort of citizen Emile is at the end of his education. To this can be added the second question of whether Emile's education could be extended to an entire citizen body.

Rousseau's answer to the first question is complicated because Emile does not live in a good community. As his tutor tells him at the end of his political education, "If I were speaking to you of the duties of the citizen, you would perhaps ask me where the fatherland is" (*Emile* 473; Pl. 4:858).

Because Emile has no genuine fatherland, he does not have the full duties of a citizen. If he did have a fatherland, however, he would have not only a complete set of duties, but also a need to share in the social identity of the community, including emulation of its heroes. Citizenship within a fatherland requires heroes.

The independent Emile could not be this sort of citizen, but his tutor hastens to add that the absence of a fatherland does not completely absolve one from civic duties. Even someone "who does not have a fatherland at least has a country."[18] Unlike a fatherland, a country allows a degree of independence, including independence from the influence of heroes; nonetheless, citizenship in a country implies real, if reduced, responsibilities. While Rousseau might have an ultimate preference for "heroic citizenship," he does hold up citizenship of a country, or unheroic citizenship, as an alternative that is both less harsh and more readily achievable in an age devoted more to debunking than to praising heroes. Such citizens do not run to participate in political assemblies the way heroic citizens do. Instead, they exercise their beneficence in local communities and do so more for the sake of their families than out of concern for the general good. When called to more strenuous civil duties, they comply but are glad to return to private life. They are poor candidates for the sort of heroism exemplified by Cato, Regulus, or Lucretia.

The looseness of Emile's bonds to his community is shown in the unfinished sequel, *Emile and Sophie*. Cruelly betrayed in his domestic life, Emile begins a wandering existence. He leaves his country with little regret, explaining, "Bursting the bonds that attached me to my country I spread it out over the whole earth, and from that I became all the more a man in ceasing to be a Citizen" (*Emile and Sophie*, Pl. 4:912). Eventually he is captured by Barbary pirates and finds himself being worked to death as a slave. Along with a young knight, he undertakes an act of political leadership by organizing a revolt. Only desperation leads him to this political act.

These two leaders show the contrast between traditional heroism and the new heroism of self-sufficiency. The knight is guided by a desire for vengeance and extreme pride and is also said to have "heroic virtues." He wins over many supporters because "he inflames their courage so much through admiration of the strength of soul that can brave torments" (*Emile and Sophie*, Pl. 4:920, 921). In contrast, Emile appeals to a cool calculation of the best chances for success. Like his own actions, his rhetoric is based on self-interest. His coolness yields only four or five recruits. As it happens, neither approach is sufficient for a successful revolt: the knight's numerous followers prove to be unreliable, and Emile's prove to be too few. The revolt succeeds only because of the sudden inspiration of national spirit among different groups of slaves who wish to outdo one another in their revolutionary zeal. In this account Rousseau shows both the advantages and limitations of both heroism and independence. In situations of complete despotism, neither is sufficient to bring about a radical change, but both can be useful. Those who look to Rousseau for an alternative to heroic citizenship must be prepared to accept the limits of Emile's civic-mindedness. While in normal circumstances it may be possible to ask more from citizens of countries with greater legitimacy than the absolute monarchy of France or the slave system of Algeria, these citizens without heroes may not feel enough of a sense of community to meet the demands of a crisis.

Even if we accept the limits of unheroic citizenship, we are left with the dependence of this alternative on the very special education given to Emile. Without this education, strength of soul will evaporate and inevitable vices will sap even limited civil allegiance. *Emile*, however, is not a practical plan for education (*Mountain*, CW 9:211; Pl. 3:783). Practical barriers make a complete success impossible, and a partial success in such an enterprise cannot be distinguished from a complete failure. Tempted though they may be to do so, readers of Rousseau's treatise on education in novel form should not try to raise their children to be Emiles. Thus, while a community of citizens who do their duty even though they are attached to their individual independence is imaginable, it is not clear how practical its realization is.

In a way, however, *Emile* can help to approximate this sort of citizenship. Rousseau's novel can make its readers more like Emile by using their un-Emilian tendency to identify with characters in books, that is, by making Emile their hero to a greater degree than Robinson Crusoe is Emile's hero. Such people need an imaginative support for a life of independence. They must be able to imagine themselves to be someone like Emile in order to keep from imagining themselves to be someone who is less independent. By seeing themselves in Emile's situation, they will gain a healthier perspective on their own. By wishing to be more like Emile, they may approximate his strength of soul. Although such imitators of Emile cannot be expected to have a strength of soul equal to his or to that of heroic citizens, they may have enough to meet the reduced demands of the new type of unheroic citizenship of a country rather than heroic citizenship of a fatherland. They will be citizens in the same sense that Emile could be, for the sake of their private lives with their families, out of what Tocqueville later called self-interest rightly understood.

Heroic citizenship of a fatherland and the unheroic citizenship of a country share the need for strength of soul. This strength depends on either a civic education or an education that aims at sustaining natural strength. Rousseau argues that one or the other is necessary for any kind of meaningful citizenship, but he is very pessimistic about the possibility of either in the modern world, which is plagued by weakness of soul. This leads him to consider alternatives that do not attain even the lower standards of citizenship met by Emile but palliate the vices caused by weakness.

As argued above, strength of soul is necessary to support virtues when they come under attack by temptation. This means that weak-souled people who have been kept out of the way of temptation can have virtues, although they cannot be counted upon to maintain them. An example of such a person is Rousseau as he describes himself in the *Confessions*. He lives a life of basic goodness intermittently overwhelmed by vices stemming from weakness. As he says, the one virtue he most lacks is the heroic virtue of strength (*Confessions*, CW 5:233; Pl. 1:277). Certainly a complete account of exemplary figures in Rousseau requires a treatment of Rousseau's account of himself.[19] In fact, the *Confessions* contains a roster of secondary characters who illustrate the range of both strength of soul (the comtesse de Vercellis and Marshal Keith) and weakness of soul (Mme. de Warens and the duc de Luxembourg, as well as Jean-Jacques himself).

Within the context of this chapter, however, it will be more useful to complement the discussion of Emile above with an analysis of his other great fictional figure, Julie. This is particularly true because, as will be argued below, Julie represents a new sort of heroine suitable for an antiheroic age, and Rousseau arrived at this new image of a heroine only after setting out on and abandoning an attempt to resurrect an appreciation of a more traditional heroine. The importance of Julie as a sort of heroic figure for Rousseau's understanding of women and his attempt to influence female readers are of obvious importance, but the exploration of this theme would expand the scope of this book excessively. Even limited reflection on the genesis of *Julie* will give insight into what Rousseau considered the social function of the novel to be and why he chose this literary genre over others. In order to retrace this genesis, it will be necessary to revisit some of the themes of this and the preceding chapter, this time from a chronological perspective.

VI. From Discourse to Novel

Perhaps more than most others of his contemporaries who were known for fiction and political writings, Rousseau turned into a novelist and political thinker rather than setting out to be either. When he arrived in Paris at the age of twenty-nine, he was equipped with two arms to aid him in the struggle for success in the intellectual world: his newly invented system of musical notation and his play *Narcissus*. It was only nine years later that he published his first work of political philosophy and an additional ten years afterward that he published *Julie*. One might well ask about the relation between these mature phases in Rousseau's career, whether there might be a connection between his analysis of politics and his authorship of novels.

Rousseau tells the story of his composition of *Julie* in book 9 of the *Confessions*. The general context of this discussion is his account of his move away from Paris in April 1756. When he arrived in the country, his mind was full of plans for books: his great *Political Institutions*, an edition of the works of the abbé de Saint-Pierre, the *Sensitive Morality or the Wise Man's Materialism*, a system of education, and a *Dictionary of Music*. While social obligations made sustained work difficult at times, on the whole he was in an excellent position to execute these grand projects. Nevertheless, the only ones he finished were the *Dictionary* and the work on education. His novel *Julie*, which he presents as the unplanned outcome of flights of the imagination undertaken out of dissatisfaction with his personal life, came to take precedence over the other literary projects. If one considers that the treatise on education also turned into a novel, one must conclude that between 1756 and 1762 Rousseau turned himself from a writer of academic discourses into a novelist.

Rousseau attributes this shift in his literary enterprise in large part to the emotional change caused by his move to the country. Relative solitude returned him to himself from the period of "effervescence" he had experienced for several years beginning with his "illumination" on the road to Vincennes, which launched him to fame by inspiring the *First Discourse* (*Confessions*, CW 5:349–50; Pl. 1:416). During this period of intoxication with virtue, he had written the two *Discourses*, engaged in controversy against their critics, and participated in a pamphlet war over music. Rousseau suggests that at least the style of these early works was embittered by his constant exposure to the vices he was attacking. Once he left Paris, that stimulus was gone, and he lost the indignation that had fueled his efforts. In addition to these emotional changes, there were also factors inherent in his thought that had been leading him to a reconsideration of the style proper for its expression.

The planned edition of the abbé de Saint-Pierre's works was the first of his projects to which he turned. This edition appeared to offer a golden opportunity to use the abbé's name as a shield to protect Rousseau from persecution as he sharpened the criticisms of the French government found in these works. This would constitute no violation of the view of authorial responsibility developed in chapter 1, because Rousseau would be identified as the editor of the selections chosen from the abbé's works. As he proceeded, however, Rousseau realized that in fact he was putting himself into a vulnerable position. He says, "By taking it into my head to repeat his censures, even though under his name, I exposed myself to having myself asked, a little roughly, but without injustice, what I was meddling with" (*Confessions*, CW 5:356; Pl. 1:424). Consequently, he abandoned the edition after producing abridgments of and commentaries on two works.

Rousseau had other reservations about the abbé's works that clarify his understanding of what a writer can and cannot accomplish. While looking through the manuscripts, he found that while Saint-Pierre was more intelligent than he had presumed, his political schemes were impractical because of a single flaw. The abbé stubbornly persisted in the belief "that men were led by their enlightenment rather than by their passions." As a result, he made errors "out of having wished to make men similar to him, instead of taking them as they are and they will continue to be" (*Confessions*, CW 5:354–55; Pl. 1:422). From this it can be inferred that Rousseau's own opposing views are that passion is stronger than reason and that while one might aim at changing people, their transformation is subject to permanent constraints. This inference is supported by a fragment in which Rousseau refers specifically to the abbé's error, saying, "The mistake of most moralists has always been to consider man as an essentially reasonable being. Man is a sensitive being, who consults solely his passions in order to act, and for whom reason serves only to palliate the follies his passions lead him to commit" (*Political Fragments*, CW 4:70; Pl. 3:554). This reservation is closely related to the claims made earlier in this chapter and in the preceding one that social life is founded in the imitation of feelings rather than the calculation of reason and that, consequently, it depends on heroic figures whose example inspires emulation.

That Rousseau remained attentive to the limitations he saw in human nature can be seen from the beginning of the *Social Contract*, which announces, "I want to inquire whether there can be a legitimate and reliable rule of administration in the civil order, taking men as they are and laws as they can be" (*Social Contract*, CW 4:131; Pl. 3:351). While he also argues that good politics requires making men into what they should be (*Political Economy*, CW 3:148; Pl. 3:251), the necessary beginning point is to take them as they are. Even at his most optimistic moments, he does not suggest that they can be thoroughly transformed into the completely rational beings envisioned by the abbé de Saint-Pierre.

That reason is neither independent of nor superior to passion is a constant theme in Rousseau's early writings. We have already seen it in the case made for the superiority of the hero over the wise man in the *Discourse on the Virtue Most Necessary for a Hero*, but it is visible from the beginning of Rousseau's career. In the *First Discourse* he argues that all the accomplishments of reason upon which civilized humans pride themselves have their origin in vices fueled by selfish passions (*First Discourse*, CW 2:12–13; Pl. 3:17–18). In defending the *Discourse* against its critics, he observed that these self-proclaimed champions of reason verified his thesis by angrily rushing to the support of their own privileges as members of academies or professors (*Letter to Grimm*, CW 2:90; Pl. 3:67). Behind their superficial devotion to reason looms their deeper attachment to their own interest. The *Second Discourse* goes to the root of the abbé's error, saying, "Whatever the Moralists may say about it, human understanding owes much to the Passions, which by common agreement also owe much to it" (*Second Discourse*, CW 3:27; Pl. 3:143). Naturally humans have both little reason and few passions. Reason develops only when spurred by passions, which demand satisfaction. Each step in this development brings an awareness of new objects that serve as new stimuli for passion ad infinitum. In sum, rather than liberating from the passions or palliating their effects, reason usually increases their power. At the culmination of this process, when one looks at the souls of civilized humans, "one no longer finds anything except the deformed contrast of passion which believes it reasons and understanding in delirium" (*Second Discourse*, CW 3:12; Pl. 3:122). Even though the abbé de Saint-Pierre himself might have been genuinely ruled by reason, he was foolish to believe that the same is or can be true of others.

The discovery that civilization is rooted in and causes the stimulation of passions and the related discovery that reason reinforces the passions that it claims to control are at the heart of the "illumination" that began Rousseau's literary career. The natural outcome of this illumination might seem to be the philanthropic project of curing the erroneous judgments that make people rush headlong down the path to misery and injustice. Rousseau describes himself as having been inspired by precisely this project: "I no longer saw anything but error and folly in the doctrine of our wise men, anything but oppression and misery in our social order. In the illusion of my foolish pride I believed I was made to dispel all these illusions" (*Confessions*, CW 5:349; Pl. 1:416).[20] This goal inspired him to engage in several years of controversy with the opponents of his works.

If Rousseau had thought that academic discourses and disputations could transform corrupt humans who were led by their passions, he would have been making the same mistake he attributed to the abbé de Saint-Pierre, that is, he would have assumed that reason can rule over passion. The futility of this project is shown by the very diagnosis of the problem. A rational demonstration that people have been corrupted by the exercise of their reason is as likely to further the corruption as to cure it. Perhaps even more likely, if the development of reason and civilization has estranged them from their nature, these denatured beings will be incapable of acknowledging the truth when it is shown to them (*Second Discourse*, CW 3:12; Pl. 3:122–23). In short, precisely if Rousseau's analysis is true, his readers can respond to it only as they in fact did, with indignation or a refusal to take his argument seriously.

Even while he was attempting to dispel illusions, Rousseau was manifestly aware of this problem. In the *First Discourse* he predicts that anyone who exposes the effects of the sciences and arts will meet "insulting ridicule and scorn a hundred times worse than death" (*First Discourse*, CW 2:11; Pl. 3:15). In one of his last efforts at a defense of the *First Discourse*, he says, "I know very well that the trouble I am taking is useless, and in my exhortations I don't have the chimerical pleasure of hoping for the reformation of men." He explains that he continues in his efforts only out of a sense of duty and concludes, "It is for a more powerful voice to make them love it." In the end, all of his arguments benefit only a few readers, "those who know how to understand." ("Bordes," CW 2:183; Pl. 3:104). Rousseau's acute grasp of his dilemma shows both his theoretical consistency and a practical impasse. The issue for his literary project, then, becomes whether he can develop the "more powerful voice" that can change his readers.[21]

After settling in the country, Rousseau addressed himself to this impasse several times. In his so-called "Lettres morales," written to Sophie d'Houdetot a year and a half after his move, he says that writing to one intelligent woman is a better use of his time after he had "lost so many days pursuing a vain glory, by telling the public truths that it is in no condition to understand" ("Lettres morales," Pl. 4:1082). Nevertheless, the fact that he wrote these letters with an eye to eventual publication is ample proof that he was reluctant to reduce the scope of his project.[22] From this it would seem that writing in a more popular form than academic discourses and treatises should be Rousseau's own next step.

In very different ways, both *Julie* and the *Letter to d'Alembert on the Theatre* (which were both completed in the next several years) respond to this need. Near the beginning of the *Letter*, Rousseau announces this change by saying, "I am not dealing here with vain philosophical chatter but with a practical truth important to a whole people. I do not speak here to the few but to the public, nor do I attempt to make others think but rather to explain my thought clearly. Hence, I had to change my style" (*d'Alembert* 6; Pl. 5:6). In addressing a matter of immediate practical concern to a broad audience, one must speak its language and use its frame of reference.[23] He hopes to influence Genevan policy by taking his fellow citizens as they are, not by treating them as philosophers. Clarity and simplicity are more appropriate for this goal than abstract arguments are.

Rousseau addresses this issue in *Julie*, saying, "To make what you have to say useful, first you have to get the attention of those who ought to make use of it" (*Julie*, CW 6:12; Pl. 2:17). Although this is the same concern expressed in the *Letter to d'Alembert*, the two works are extremely different. Clarity and simplicity may be the right style for a discussion of a proposed change in legislation to an audience of republican citizens, but a different modification of style is called for in a novel. Rousseau distinguishes this work from his early writings by saying, "My means have changed, but not my purpose. When I tried to speak to men no one listened to me; perhaps by addressing children I shall be better listened to; and children do not relish the taste of naked reason any better than ill-disguised medicines" (*Julie*, CW 6:12; Pl. 2:17). He continues with a quotation from Tasso concerning the need to adorn the truth to make virtue appealing, which is comparable to the practice of concealing bitter medicine with something sweet.[24] Philosophers may require complex argument and citizens, clear and simple statements, but children and adults who are like them require stories that make use of their passions even while changing them for the better.

Rousseau had already made a version of this point in his first response to critics of the *First Discourse*. When the abbé Raynal urged him to expose his position more fully and clearly, saying, "It is impossible to shed too much light on truths which clash so very directly with the general taste," Rousseau responded, "I do not entirely share this opinion, and I believe that playthings should be left to children" (*Raynal*, CW 2:26; Pl. 3:33). The *Social Contract* (published in 1762) could be regarded as a reversion to "philosophic style" on Rousseau's part. He explains that this work was in fact written for the benefit of Geneva and that his effort was to be "precise and clear," but also indirect in order to avoid offending (*Confessions*, CW 5:340; Pl. 1:405).

In short, there is an extremely close correspondence between Rousseau's theoretical speculation and his literary practice. His account of the practical limits of reason in political life led him to tailor his mode of presentation to the specific audience he had in mind for a particular work, whether that be the academicians addressed in the *First Discourse*, the citizens addressed in the *Letter to d'Alembert*, or the broad audience addressed in *Julie*. It remains for us to see why Rousseau made the specific choice of the novel form and what sort of heroic image is transmitted by this particular novel.

VII. *The Death of Lucretia* and the Resurrection of Heroism

By itself, the need to adopt a popular form in order to have a practical effect does not explain Rousseau's choice of the novel. The popular form with which he was most experienced was dramatic. His opera *The Village Soothsayer* had already been a great success, his play *Narcissus* had been performed, and he had dabbled in writing plays for private performance. As was indicated in the preceding chapter, Rousseau certainly thought that, in principle, music could have an immense moral effect on its audience, but his view of the lack of expressiveness in modern languages caused him not to expect too much from composition. On the other hand, shortly before he moved to the country and only a few years before he undertook his criticism of the theater in the *Letter to d'Alembert*, he did briefly entertain the idea of using the theater to bring about moral reform and began a play based on the death of Lucretia. He says that he hoped to astound those who scoffed at characters like Lucretia in "daring to allow this unfortunate person appear again, when she could no longer do so in any French Theater" (*Confessions*, CW 5:331; Pl. 1:394). The themes of chastity and republicanism in this story would represent an enormous departure from the themes to which the Parisian audience was accustomed.

This abandoned play is worth examining because of its similarities to and differences from *Julie*. It has been observed that in general terms the two works deal with similar themes.[25] This resemblance can be extended to the situations described in the two works. The husband of a virtuous woman welcomes into their house a young man who is torn between virtue and passion, who loved the woman before her marriage, and whom she secretly (and perhaps unconsciously) still loves. This sentence equally well describes both the second half of Rousseau's novel and the whole of that part of his play he completed. From the fragments left of the rest of the play, it can also be said that in both works the young wife undergoes a struggle between love and virtue, that virtue wins, but that it does so only at the ultimate cost of her life. Rousseau never stated his reasons for abandoning his play, but they are certainly connected with the radical critique of the theater that he undertook in the *Letter to d'Alembert*. The facts that the *Letter* and the novel were written simultaneously and that they refer to each other suggest that in spite of their great differences and even apparent opposition, each was written with the other in mind. From this perspective, it could be said that *Julie* is *The Death of Lucretia* rewritten, although the changes involved in this rewriting exclude the possibility that Julie could be "la nouvelle Lucrèce."

To prepare for a comparison between the play and the novel, it will be useful to summarize Rousseau's distinctive use of the Lucretia story. Lucretia's death is the decisive event in the transformation of Rome into a republic. In the versions told by Livy and Ovid, Sextus (the son of the Roman king Tarquin) develops a passion for Lucretia, the virtuous wife of Collatinus. While paying a visit during her husband's absence, he is rebuffed by Lucretia but forces her submission to his rape by threatening to kill her and then to accuse her of having committed adultery with a slave. Subsequently, Lucretia proclaims what has happened, demands vengeance, and kills herself. Led by Brutus, the Romans rise against the monarchy, depose the king, and establish the Republic.[26]

Rousseau is far from the first author to adapt this story and to make numerous changes in it. The changes he makes from the original, such as addition of characters and invention of details, all contribute to the effect he wishes to accomplish. Three changes are particularly noteworthy. First, unlike the Roman sources that present Sextus's attempt on Lucretia as an unforeseen event, Rousseau makes it into the tragic consequence of a plot by Brutus (who in the Roman sources becomes involved only after Lucretia's suicide) to overthrow the Tarquin tyranny by exposing the prince's designs on a virtuous wife. The conspiracy goes awry and is saved only by the greatness of soul of Lucretia, who makes herself into a martyr. The portrait of Brutus in the play is intended to portray what Rousseau means by a legislator, but with the important difference that he acts behind the scenes, as it were. It is Lucretia's great soul rather than Brutus's that inspires others. Something similar could be said about the relation between Julie and her husband Wolmar.[27] Second, while in both Livy's and Ovid's versions, Sextus meets Lucretia only after her marriage, Rousseau transforms him into her unsuccessful suitor before her marriage. Moreover, she was and still is in love with him. Finally, Rousseau makes Lucretia's husband Collatinus into a weak and indecisive character, unlike the good husband in the Roman sources. Coupled with the background love story, this change makes Lucretia's virtue even more extreme: she resists a man she loves out of fidelity to a not very admirable husband. Each of these changes gives an indication of how Rousseau conceived his project and also may provide clues as to why he abandoned it for *Julie*.

In choosing to emphasize the republican conspiracy, Rousseau clearly wished to introduce a strongly political and antimonarchical theme to the French stage. In *Julie* St. Preux repeats the argument of the *Letter to d'Alembert* that such themes were the stock of ancient tragedy, "which offered the Greeks an instructive and agreeable spectacle taken from the woes of their enemies the Persians, from the crimes and follies of the Kings this people had rid itself of" (*Julie*, CW 6:206; Pl. 2:251). For an audience capable of appreciating them, such stories would be much more effective than the cold lessons of wisdom contained in academic discourses. The return of Lucretia to the French stage would run counter to two tendencies lamented by Rousseau: the Christian depreciation of political virtues based on honor and the modern depreciation of honor of any sort.

Lucretia's virtue had been called into question by Christians since Augustine, who had argued that the only conceivable justification for her suicide would be remorse over guilt for committing adultery. If she was guilty, she cannot be considered virtuous; and if she was innocent, she should be blamed for killing herself.[28] In this view, her innocence before God should have made her indifferent to the possibility that people might regard her as guilty and to the repercussions that might follow for reinforcing the Tarquin tyranny or disgracing her family. In one of a series of fragments in which he attacks Augustine for debunking Roman virtue, Rousseau contrasts contemporary views with Roman ones by saying, "A few women will perhaps die for that apparent honor which consists in the opinion of others, but show me one capable of dying for that genuine honor which consists in purity of actions" (*Political Fragments*, CW 4:39; Pl. 3:506). This indicates that he does not attribute Lucretia's suicide simply to concern for her reputation. Beyond the Christian attack on linking virtue to a genuine sense of honor is the modern irreligious tendency to scoff at any notion of virtue that demands the sacrifice of one's life. Rousseau's ambition in undertaking *The Death of Lucretia*, then, was the restoration of an appreciation of political virtue in the face of these attacks.

In *Julie* Rousseau argues, as we have seen he does in the *Letter to d'Alembert*, that a jaded audience from a modern monarchy is unlikely to be moved by themes suitable for ancient republicans (*Julie*, CW 6:206; Pl. 2:251). In effect, the modern audience is made up of people who agree with Rousseau's invented character Sulpicius that "duty and virtue are terms void of sense in which no one believes" (*Lucretia*, Pl. 2:1028). For them, Lucretia's sense of honor is unintelligible and her scruples about adultery are laughable. Thus, this play requires an audience that no longer exists; it does not take the audience as it is. Rather than causing a political and moral revolution, its success would depend on one having been accomplished in advance.

Rousseau's invention of the love between Sextus and Lucretia is a concession to the modern audience. As he says about modern drama in the *Letter to d'Alembert*, "No longer able to maintain the strength of comic situations and character, the love interest has been reinforced. The same has been done in tragedy to take the place of situations drawn from political concerns we no longer have, and of simple and natural sentiments which no longer move anyone" (*d'Alembert* 47; Pl. 5:43). The analysis of Racine's *Bérénice* in the *Letter* indicates why Rousseau came to be skeptical about using the modern interest in love to engender concern with politics. Racine makes virtue triumph over love but unwittingly induces in the audience a secret desire for the reverse (*d'Alembert* 52–54; Pl. 5:48–50). The better an actress is at portraying Bérénice, the more lovable the character becomes and the more the audience wishes love to triumph. Rousseau's decision not to finish his play could be seen as the logical consequence of this analysis. In spite of the attempt to use the modern interest in love to gain a hearing for republicanism, the romantic theme is sure to overwhelm the political theme it is meant to support.

Julie is written in recognition of these difficulties and tries to remedy or at least mitigate each of them. Five major differences between the novel and the play are particularly significant. First, Rousseau's novel contains no character as wicked as Sulpicius, the villain of the play. Second, the novel is set in an almost totally apolitical context in the provinces rather than in a politically charged atmosphere. Third, the first half of the novel focuses on the love story between the protagonists, which has already taken place by the time the play begins. Fourth, Julie lacks the heroic strength of soul of Lucretia. Finally, there is the difference in literary form of the two works. Each of these changes can be understood as a response to the difficulties that led Rousseau to abandon *The Death of Lucretia*.

In Rousseau's opinion, the greatest novelist was Richardson, and it is the key Richardsonian element of sensibility, or sentimentality, that Rousseau attempted to isolate and perfect. His one criticism of Richardson is that he does not place sufficient reliance on this element. In response to Diderot's praise of Richardson for his ability to portray a great variety of characters and situations (and the implicit suggestion that Rousseau failed in *Julie*), Rousseau argued that surprise twists and wicked characters are cheap tricks used by the least talented novelists. His own novel succeeds without such devices by focusing on a relatively simple story and the sensitive or beautiful souls of its protagonists (see *Confessions*, CW 5:456–57; Pl. 1:546–47).

Rousseau's response to the gulf separating ancient republicanism from modern corruption is the apolitical setting of *Julie*. He addresses this problem in his "Second Preface" to his novel, saying, "When it comes to morality, no reading, in my view, will do worldly people any good. First, because the abundance of new books they leaf through, and which state by turns the pros and cons, destroys the effect of the former by the latter and nullifies the whole. Select books which are reread are equally ineffectual: if they support worldly maxims, they are superfluous; and if they oppose them, they are useless" (*Julie*, CW 6:13; Pl. 2:18).²⁹ *The Death of Lucretia* falls into the category of books that are useless because they oppose worldly maxims too directly. *Julie*, however, would seem to be in the same category. This statement of the problem suggests that no book could accomplish anything more than to be part of the pro canceling out the con of all the corrupting books. Even the best possible book would only leave people no worse than when they started.³⁰

This is indeed Rousseau's answer for the "worldly people" who want to receive moral improvement from books. Nevertheless, there is a middle position between corrupt sophistication and austere virtue. This position is found in the provinces, where people are not Lucretias or Brutuses, but do not face the obstacles to moral reform that exist in a large city. As Rousseau says, "The further one gets from the bustle, from great cities, from large gatherings, the smaller the obstacles become. There is a point where these obstacles cease to be insurmountable, and that is where books can be of some use" (*Julie*, CW 6:13; Pl. 2:18). Although one should not underestimate Rousseau's seduction of sophisticated potential readers by charging them with the crime of being incapable of being affected by his book, the main audience intended for *Julie* is in the middle ground.

Like all readers, these readers must be taken as they are and not, at the beginning, as one would like them to be. Their situation requires protection against corruption more than positive reform. Even these provincial readers are deluged with novels that "heap derision on the simplicity of rustic morals" (*Julie*, CW 6:14; Pl. 2:20). Writing an outline for a novel by Balzac or Stendhal, Rousseau paints a grim picture of the fate of these readers. He sees the respectable provincial family leaving for Paris to seek out the exciting life they have read about only to "die in misery and dishonor" after being reduced to infamy.

Rousseau even agrees with critics who claim that novels can induce a sort of madness in their readers—what could be called Don Quixote's disease³¹—by making them long for an impossible way of life and then imagine that they can lead such a life. As pointed out above, in the *Confessions* Rousseau describes himself as having suffered from exactly this sort of malady, alternately seeing himself as a Roman hero and a pastoral lover (*Confessions*, CW 5:8; Pl. 1:8). The resulting dissatisfaction with his own condition as an apprentice contributed to his decision to seek adventure in the world beyond Geneva, where he was surprised to find no damsels to serenade and disappointed to find ironworkers where he had been hoping to find romantic heroes (*Confessions*, CW 5:38–40, 138; Pl. 1:45–48, 164).

His novel avoids this sort of madness by rooting its action firmly in experiences accessible to its readers.

The Death of Lucretia failed to do this. For provincial readers, the politics of ancient Rome would be only slightly less alien than it is to the corrupt readers of Paris. They might not scoff at Lucretia's heroism, but it is hard to see how they could apply it to their own situation. Like Claire in *Julie*, they might understand how precious political liberty is, but that awareness would have little effect on their lives (*Julie*, CW 6:540; Pl. 2:657). As Rousseau's interlocutor in the preface points out, novels that romanticize country life by turning shepherds into poets would be equally unsatisfactory. Both sorts of story would lead the readers to futile dissatisfaction with their own lives. By depicting an agreeable life in the provinces, *Julie* will make the provincial readers imagine themselves to be something not very far from what they already are. "They will fulfill the same functions; but they will fulfill them with a changed soul" (*Julie*, CW 6:17; Pl. 2:23). The novel will change them only by making them happier and more proud in being what they already are. This "revolution in daily life" mainly appears in the second half of *Julie*, which depicts the family life at Clarens.³²

The love story between Julie and St. Preux in the first half of the book also attempts to begin where the readers already are. As suggested above, the modern audience would be all too likely to reverse Lucretia's choice of marital fidelity over love. In the first half of *Julie*, on the other hand, the opposition is not between love and virtue, but between the love of two souls made for each other and arbitrary social conventions (in the form of the aristocratic pride of the baron d'Etange, who rejects his daughter's suitor because of his low birth). Love, which is constantly identified with nature in the first half of the novel, becomes the standard in accordance with which everything else is judged. An audience attached to social status can be turned into an audience attached to love more easily than it can be turned into one attached to virtue.

From the perspective of republican citizenship, this half of the novel is a struggle between two equally defective standards. In the dialogue preface Rousseau's interlocutor chides him for the inconsistency between *Julie* and the austere republicanism of the *Letter to d'Alembert* (*Julie*, CW 6:18; Pl. 2:25). Without denying that the tension exists, Rousseau responds by appealing to the text of the *Letter* where he concedes that, in spite of its dangers for a republic, using romantic heroines as preachers of morality "has its advantages" in some circumstances (*d'Alembert* 49; Pl. 5:45). Subsequently, he elaborates by arguing that while romantic love is a threat to love of humanity and country, it is morally superior to complete selfishness. He concludes, "On this principle, I say that there are countries where the morals are so bad that they would be only too happy to be able to raise themselves back up to the level of love; and there are others where it would be unfortunate to descend to it" (*d'Alembert* 118; Pl. 5:107). Only those who either have no attachments or who are totally attached to their communities will find no attraction in the love story.

The audience in the middle ground can be carried away by the love story because they are all too prone to think that their own supposedly natural feelings take precedence over the artificial obligations of society. Through their acquaintance with characters who are good but weak, these readers will finally be brought to confront the fact that the standard of love is not as natural as they thought, and that it conflicts with other standards with an equally good (or bad) claim to naturalness (*Julie*, CW 6:165–71; Pl. 2:202–6). Having learned this, they will be more open to the lesson of the second half of the novel concerning the satisfactions of a retired domestic life. This gradual transition will be more effective than the stark opposition between love and virtue in *The Death of Lucretia*.

Merely describing the nature of the moral transformation that *Julie* is meant to bring about does not explain how this transformation can happen.[33] In both *Emile* and the *Letter to d'Alembert*, Rousseau shows his attentiveness to the subtle ways in which the effects of literature escape the intentions of the author. In his discussion of *Julie* in the *Confessions*, he admits, "I fell into the flaw that I reproached in the Abbé de St. Pierre" with respect to some of his goals (*Confessions*, CW 5:366; Pl. 1:436). He does not, however, imply a failure of the novel as a whole. Perhaps *Julie*'s greatest success in avoiding Saint-Pierre's error lies in Rousseau's depiction of a heroine who engages feelings more than reason.

In spite of the similarities of the situations and lessons of the play and novel, Julie is certainly not Lucretia. Lucretia, unlike Julie, is truly heroic. Rousseau indicates Lucretia's heroic character clearly in a scene in which Brutus reassures her father that her continued love for Sextus poses no threat to her virtue. He says, "Do you know what prodigies of strength and virtue this involuntary love that is subjugated without being acknowledged can produce in her great soul? Learn that passions to conquer are a more powerful goad for heroic souls than cold lessons of wisdom" (*Lucretia*, Pl. 2:1032). Her ability to subjugate her love entirely to virtue using only her own strength gives her a heroic status.

In the novel it is not Julie but the less central character of Edward Bomston who has the greatness or strength of soul characteristic of heroes. Moreover, he is the character most concerned with fulfilling his civic duties. Virtually everyone in the novel including Julie (and Rousseau himself as editor) expresses admiration for Edward's strength or greatness of soul (*Julie*, CW 6:104, 129, 148, 171, 456, 613, 620; Pl. 2:127, 158, 182, 209, 558, 750, 759). As we have seen, Rousseau suggests that heroic strength of soul inspires others to imitate it. Julie herself discusses this effect when she describes her own experience of reading the lives of ancient heroes (*Julie*, CW 6:183–84; Pl. 2:223–24). Such admiration for heroes may be real, but in this novel it has a very small effect. Edward may be one of "those strong souls which attract others and raise them to their own sphere," but none of the other characters is radically changed by a desire to imitate his greatness (see *Julie*, CW 6:613; Pl. 2:750). In fact, his heroic attempts to intervene tend only to aggravate the problems of the lovers. He is quite out of place in the modern world, and his adventures (which are not at all political) are relegated to a sort of appendix to the novel.

Unlike Lucretia and Edward, the protagonists of the novel are lovable rather than admirable. St. Preux is said to have "a soul which was weak, but sound and loving virtue" (*Julie*, CW 6:331; Pl. 2:403). Rousseau shows that Julie is not a modern Lucretia in a number of ways. She has a tender but weak soul, and sometimes she is said to be even weaker than St. Preux (*Julie*, CW 6:264, 281; Pl. 2:322, 343). Even when she becomes a virtuous wife, she attributes her steadfastness to a recognition of her own weakness and consequent reliance on faith in God (*Julie*, CW 6:569; Pl. 2:693). Perhaps the most important difference between the play and the novel can be found in the fact that Julie is based on the Christian model of Heloise rather than the pagan Lucretia. This means both that she is further removed from citizenship and that she can play a part in Rousseau's attempt to modify Christianity while making use of it. Rousseau makes her into something quite new, an unheroic heroine. Julie does share something with heroes because her weakness coexists with a very special quality that substitutes for strength. This combination is captured by Claire's attempt to describe her cousin's influence over herself and others. She says, "This is bound to happen with all souls of a certain temper; they so to speak transform others into themselves; they have a sphere of activity within which nothing can resist them; one cannot know them without wanting to imitate them, and from their sublime elevation they attract unto themselves everyone about them" (*Julie*, CW 6:166; Pl. 2:204). Claire attributes this quality to both Julie and St. Preux, as does Edward, but it is clear that St. Preux manifests it principally in his unique ability to love Julie as she should be loved.[34] Julie's very weakness increases her influence by putting her within the reach of others, and her influence affects everyone, including Edward. Instead of a strong soul, Julie and her lover possess expansive or beautiful ones (*Julie*, CW 6:42, 50, 158, 595; Pl. 2:52, 62, 193, 725). These are heroes of a new type suited for people too corrupt to aspire to heroic strength of soul.

Each of these changes from *The Death of Lucretia*—the absence of wickedness, the shift from republican to domestic life, the focus on the love story before marriage, and the creation of a new sort of heroine—could have been made in a play. In fact, Diderot's *Natural Son* and *Father of the Family* are attempts to solve problems in the French dramatic tradition similar to the ones identified by Rousseau. Rousseau's attack on the theater, however, goes beyond treatment of the subject to the form of drama. He argues that no matter how successful a play is at moving its audience, it will not have any practical effect at improving their morals outside of the context provided by ancient republicanism. As we saw in the preceding chapter, Rousseau insists that vicious tyrants can be as moved by portrayals of suffering virtue as decent people are, but they do not become paragons of virtue as a result. To be sure, novels cannot cause radical transformations of character either, but the theater aggravates the problem by covering the selfishness it encourages with the illusion of sociability. Rather than being a genuinely social activity, theatergoing isolates us in a passive enjoyment of something far removed from our genuine social life as citizens and members of a family. This would be true even if the play dramatized citizenship or family life. The very medium of the drama will undermine its message.

Novels can be as much a distraction from duties as plays are. Nevertheless, Rousseau argues that the difference in form does have moral consequences. In the *Letter to d'Alembert*, he suggests that there is a connection between reading novels and a taste for solitude (*d'Alembert* 82; Pl. 5:75). Unlike plays, novels do not engender an illusion of sociability. Rather than going out into the public for the sake of a purely private pleasure, novel readers remain in private. Even in their privacy, however, these readers need not be as passively self-absorbed as theatergoers are. Reading novels aloud can be a shared pleasure. In the "Second Preface" to *Julie*, Rousseau says, "I like to picture a husband and wife reading this collection together, finding in it a source of renewed courage to bear their common labors, and perhaps new perspectives to make them useful" (*Julie*, CW 6:16; Pl. 2:23). The medium and the message are in accord.

If one wishes to preserve or recapture genuine public-spiritedness, the fact that novels more openly grant primacy to private pleasure than plays do is a poor recommendation. That is why upon opening *Julie* one is greeted by the declaration "Great cities must have theatres, and corrupt peoples Novels" (*Julie*, CW 6:3; Pl. 2:5). The incompatibility of novels and republican citizenship is indicated by the fact that this is one case in which

Rousseau was unwilling to identify himself as "Citizen of Geneva" on the title page of a book. Even within the context of the novel, Rousseau's endorsement of this form of literature should not be overstated. Julie and her family do not read novels (although Emile and Sophie do), and Rousseau does not recommend letting children read or listen to his novel. Even so, *Julie*'s illustration of a domestic life in which one shares simple pleasures with one's family is preferable to the institution of theater, which lures one away from home to display oneself to other members of the audience while enjoying a purely individual pleasure, or to other novels, which make one dissatisfied with domestic life by instilling a longing for adventure.

To strengthen *Julie*'s influence, Rousseau makes a special effort to engage its readers. Numerous scholars have noted that in both prefaces Rousseau coyly refuses to say whether the story is true or not.[35] As these scholars observe, the stratagem of playfully or seriously presenting a novel as a true story was a commonplace in the eighteenth century, but they do not adequately note that Rousseau in fact departed from this practice. His novelty does not come from the implication that his story might be true, but from his refusal to deny that his book is a novel. Rather than attempting to usurp the status of a factual account for his book, Rousseau presents its ambiguous character as a sort of test of the reader rather than of his own veracity. In the first preface, he brushes aside the question of whether the entire correspondence is a fiction by saying, "Worldly people, what matters it to you? It is surely a fiction for you" (*Julie*, CW 6:3; Pl. 2:5). The readers must decide whether the book is fiction or not, but Rousseau implies that they themselves will be judged by their verdict. If they decide (correctly) that it must be fiction, that decision will show that they are too corrupt to believe in the possibilities shown in the novel. The interlocutor in the "Second Preface," who is the novel's first reader, repeatedly indicates his perplexity in the face of this challenge (*Julie*, CW 6:7–8, 21; Pl. 2:12, 29). Similar challenges to the readers are issued frequently in the "editor's" footnotes.[36]

This is not the only time that Rousseau turned negative judgment of his works against the very readers who make them. *Rousseau Judge of Jean-Jacques* is an extended demonstration of the way misreadings of Rousseau and his books reflect on their readers. He also defends *Emile* by saying, "If I have said what must be done, I have said what I ought to have said. It makes very little difference to me if I have written a novel. A fair novel it is indeed, the novel of human nature. If it is to be found only in this writing, is that my fault? This ought to be the history of my species. You who deprave it, it is you who make a novel of my book" (*Emile* 416; Pl. 4:777; translation altered).[37] The same is true for *Julie*, whose readers are constantly challenged to be worthy of Julie's influence. If those who deprave human nature make *Emile* into a novel, those who make *Julie* into a history can redeem human nature.

Such a moral, or moralistic, reading of *Julie* is subject to the challenge made in its most extreme form by Paul de Man, who acknowledges Rousseau's expressions of concern about how readers will be affected by his book, but dismisses them by asserting that "what he actually says about this may be quite silly."[38] In part, de Man's dismissal of Rousseau's moralism is based on his observation that the novel itself undercuts its presumed lessons. The moral lesson of the second half of the novel follows from Julie's recognition that the absolute status she and St. Preux had granted to their feelings was based on an illusion (*Julie*, CW 6:279–301; Pl. 2:340–65). She becomes a virtuous wife by becoming a rigorous critic of the illusions involved in love. Nevertheless, her new moral stance also relies on religious and moral feelings that are ultimately shown to have no more solid a basis than the love they supersede.[39] As Philip Stewart has pointed out, in her final letter written from her deathbed, Julie announces her awareness that her belief that she had overcome her love for St. Preux was only a salutary illusion that allowed her to maintain her virtue.[40]

That the moral lesson of *Julie* is not given a consistent and rational foundation in the novel should not be surprising, however. As we have seen, Rousseau was led toward the novel by the philosophic insight that denied that such a foundation could have any effect on readers. What could be called Rousseau's literary turn away from discourses and toward the novel follows from his premise that people are led by passion rather than reason and his resulting insistence that one must begin by taking people as they are. Accordingly, support for morality must be based on replacing one passion (and its accompanying illusions) with another set of passions (with their accompanying illusions).[41] Rousseau does insist that a full appreciation of the subtlety of his work requires a sophisticated reading that transcends the capacities of his provincial readers (*Confessions*, CW 5:457; Pl. 1:546–47), but this fact need not destroy the effect of the novel on the less sophisticated. In the final analysis, both Julie the character and *Julie* the novel enact precisely what is argued in the theoretical writings: the triumph of passion over reason in most people and the possibility of making this triumph salutary.

In sum, the use of the novel can be seen as the consequence of Rousseau's analysis of the relation between reason and politics, an analysis that underlies his insistence on the importance of heroes. Rousseau is well aware of *both* the limits and the possibilities of the novel. While he regards it as a suitable medium for a teaching that supports the retirement of domestic life and he takes great care to influence how readers will respond to his work, this does not mean that he expects to bring about a total transformation of society. Rather, in a political situation in which there are few means of effective persuasion, he makes use of the scarce resources that are available to foster a partial amelioration.

VIII. Conclusion

Rousseau's picture of the possibilities for citizenship in the modern world is not a rosy one, but drawing a different picture must depend on more than a wishful thinking that refuses to reflect on his understanding of heroic citizenship and the premises on which he bases this understanding. Each of the types of citizenship he describes has its appeal, but each can be viewed accurately only when juxtaposed to the others. Only heroic citizenship can fully satisfy longings for a complete sense of community, but Rousseau's analysis shows us the dangers of heroes even as it magnifies their allure. Moreover, a comparison between heroic citizenship and the antiheroic citizenship of Emile demonstrates how much personal independence must be sacrificed to the former. At the same time, this comparison highlights the limitations imposed on attempts to build community spirit on a base of personal independence. The rareness of either heroic or antiheroic strength of soul tempts us to look for a form of citizenship that can dispense with strength of soul altogether. Rousseau is willing to provide guidance for this attempt, but not without reminding us of the price that it will require.

The images of the heroic citizen, the independent citizen without heroes, and the "beautiful soul" do not exhaust Rousseau's account of the options available. Framing the descriptions of citizenship contained in Rousseau's writings is his own literary activity as a citizen. Rousseau was extremely proud of the fact that his writings earned him the nickname of "Citizen." This literary citizenship will be the theme of the next chapter.

CHAPTER FIVE

"A Hermit Makes a Very Peculiar Citizen": Rousseau and Literary Citizenship

The preceding two chapters have discussed Rousseau's treatment of how citizens are made. Chapter 3 focused on his account of the role the arts can play in making good or bad citizens by helping to form shared identities. Chapter 4 focused on the way Rousseau's books applied this account in concrete ways by giving models of heroes for emulation. This chapter will turn attention back to Rousseau himself as a writer who emphatically insists on his identity as a citizen. As we have seen, Rousseau usually identified himself as "Jean-Jacques Rousseau, Citizen of Geneva," on his title pages. Indeed, he originally identified himself as "A Citizen of Geneva" even before he adopted his policy of always naming himself and before he had recovered legal status as a citizen. His friends gave him the nickname "Citizen" and he was extremely proud of this, which suggests that he saw himself as an exemplary citizen even, or especially, in his role as an author.

That Rousseau's own activity would be consistent with his understanding of good citizenship may not seem surprising. It is peculiar, however, that participating in Genevan politics while living abroad would constitute an exemplary form of citizenship. Nevertheless, this is precisely what will be argued here, that is, that the perfect model of Rousseauian citizenship is a particular form of literary activity that can even take place from a distance. This chapter, then, is concerned with the practice of citizenship rather than with the formation of citizens. It will begin with a general account of this issue in Rousseau's thought and then turn to Rousseau's own practice of what could be called literary citizenship. While critics have frequently looked at Rousseau's account of how citizens are formed, they have tended to misread his account of how they behave and to ignore his account of his own activity as a citizen.

Rousseau's critical distance on Genevan politics indicates that his own form of citizenship is not what has been identified above as heroic citizenship. Nevertheless, this particularly intense form of identification with a community is the necessary starting point for an understanding of any form of citizenship. Heroic citizenship leaves itself open to the objection, discussed briefly in chapter 1, that Rousseau leaves no room for debate and dissent with regard to those matters that make up the everyday substance of political life: principles, laws, and policies. People with identical sentiments of sociability and the same heroes (both of which are cultivated by a government-controlled education) will, it is sometimes argued, be likely to agree spontaneously on all politically relevant matters. A public dissenter will be regarded as simply alien to the community. To respond to this objection, it will be necessary to show concretely, and in greater detail than was done either in chapter 1 or chapter 3, how Rousseauian citizens act in the crucial case of deliberating over matters affecting the whole community.

I. Speechless Citizens? The Problem of Rousseauian Deliberation

In one of the most noteworthy recent attempts to defend a version of republican political theory, Michael J. Sandel distinguishes his own brand of republicanism from those that fall victim to what he calls the two republican "pathologies" of exclusion and coercion. Rousseau's version of republicanism serves as Sandel's prime example of the coercive pathology. "Unable to abide disharmony, Rousseau's republican ideal seeks to collapse the distance between persons so that citizens stand in a kind of speechless transparence, or immediate presence to one another." Citing numerous passages from the *Social Contract* that emphasize the desirability of unanimity and the dangers of dissension, Sandel argues that Rousseau seeks a situation in which "there is no need for political argument." He concludes that "Rousseau's unitary vision" of a healthy society leads to coercive attempts to enforce harmony.[1] In Sandel's view, Rousseauian citizens are speechless citizens, having neither need nor ability to discuss anything with one another.

Such a view of Rousseau's understanding of healthy politics has a long and quite varied pedigree, dating back at least to Benjamin Constant. At its most generous, this criticism argues that Rousseau's insistence on the need to cultivate civic virtue ultimately undermines any commitment he might have to democratic participation.[2] At its least generous, it asserts that

Rousseau's own submissive temperament made him long for a society in which manipulative quasi-totalitarian control is used to make citizens compliant.[3] The claim to be defended here is that while these critics see something real in Rousseau, his concrete treatments of deliberation and activism show that they overstate the difficulty because they miss the major point of his attack on factionalism or disunity.

In essence, these criticisms stem from a tension inherent in Rousseau's doctrine of the general will. On the one hand, by locating ultimate sovereignty in the will of the people, Rousseau emphasizes the importance of universal consent as opposed to wisdom, social standing, wealth, military virtue, et cetera, as the sole source of political authority. On the other hand, by insisting that people do not naturally cooperate with one another and that social interaction tends to exacerbate their selfishness, he claims that genuine consent depends on the government's successful formation of the citizens' character. Rousseau's critics argue that the second of these features of his doctrine erodes his commitment to the first, that is, that citizens who are molded by the government are incapable of giving genuinely free consent.

In sum, the general will requires a government that is unusually active in two ways, both of which run counter to freely given consent. First, in order for the general will to predominate, citizens must think like citizens; that is, they must be willing to think about the good of the community rather than their own interest when they deliberate. Even though it may be true that the benefits that all receive from legislation will tend to reinforce this type of deliberation, something must make them think in terms of the common good in the first place. The cultivation of this disposition requires a government concerned with forming the character of the citizens through the use of education, the arts, heroes, and so on. Moreover, this is likely to take place without the citizens who are its object understanding what is happening to them, and certainly without them consenting to it. This is the formative aspect of Rousseau's republicanism objected to by Sandel and the duplicitous aspect objected to by Lester Crocker.

Second, the legislative power that Rousseau puts in the community as a whole is limited to laws in the sense of general propositions applying to the community as a whole. Any application of these propositions, including many things normally regarded as laws, are to be made by the government. There is no necessity for, and important reasons to exclude, direct citizen involvement in these matters, and Rousseau attacks direct democracy for blurring the distinction between laws and their application to particular matters (*Social Contract*, CW 4:173; Pl. 3:404). Both of these consequences appear to move in the direction of reducing the role of citizens to endorsing (or rejecting) in a simple vote measures proposed by a government that, moreover, has conditioned them to accept its recommendations.

An important element in Rousseau's analysis that at first glance appears to reinforce this tendency to undermining genuine consent is his discussion of factions.[4] Because people do not automatically subordinate their individual interests to the common good, it is quite likely that if they are left to themselves, they will form factions in order to further their interests at the expense of the community as a whole. In doing so, they will have joined a small community—a state within the state—whose general will they will prefer to the larger general will. In a key passage in the *Social Contract*, Rousseau describes what is necessary to avoid factions, saying, "If, when an adequately informed people deliberates, the Citizens were to have no communication among themselves, the general will would always result from the large number of small differences, and the deliberation would always be good." He goes on to say, "In order for the general will to be well expressed, it is therefore important that there be no partial society in the State, and that each Citizen give only his own opinion [*n'opine que d'après lui*]" (*Social Contract*, CW 4:147–48; Pl. 3:372).[5] If citizens must be kept from having any communication among themselves in order to prevent the emergence of factions, participation in the actual making of decisions seems to be drastically limited.

Judgment of the precise nature and extent of this limitation depends on assessment of several phrases in this passage. Each of these phrases has been the subject of considerable commentary. What does Rousseau mean by "adequately informed," by "no communication among themselves," by "deliberation," and by "give only his own opinion"? In addition, the expression "the general will would always result from the large number of small differences" has been notoriously difficult to interpret, in large part because its interpretation depends in crucial ways on what one makes of the other only slightly less puzzling expressions in the passage.

It has been claimed by one of Rousseau's critics that by "informed" he really means "indoctrinated" and by "deliberates" he means only "reflects what he has been told."[6] Others grant that when Rousseau says "informed," he means "given sufficient and accurate information" and that he excludes misleading the citizens. Laying stress on the required lack of communication between citizens, these critics point to Rousseau's hostility to demagoguery. Consequently, they argue that he wishes to exclude any sort of debate over legislation that would invite misleading rhetorical appeals. Accordingly, they argue that by "deliberation" Rousseau means "decision making" and, similarly, that by "giving one's opinion" he means stating yes or no.[7] In effect, they claim that deliberating and giving one's opinions are both synonyms for voting in the sense of casting a ballot. In this view, the requirement that citizens must not communicate among themselves means that they must be essentially passive except when they are voting. At most, they are wrestling inside themselves over whether they will endorse the general will rather than their own particular will.[8]

On the face of it, this is a very plausible interpretation of the passage in the *Social Contract*. Nevertheless, such an interpretation fails to account for what Rousseau actually says. In *Letters Written from the Mountain*, Rousseau warns (with particular reference to critics of the *Social Contract*), "When they do not judge me on what I said, but on what they assert I wanted to say, when they seek in my intentions the evil that is not in my Writings, what can I do? They give the lie to my discourses by my thoughts. When I said white, they assert that I wanted to say black" (*Mountain*, CW 9:141; Pl. 3:696). These critics ignore Rousseau's extreme sensitivity to the ambiguities of language and his frequent recourse to a technical vocabulary at variance with the usages of other writers. Later in the *Letters*, he argues with specific reference to the terms at issue here that it is important to follow his technical political language with great care. He says:

> For example, *To Deliberate*, *To Give an Opinion* [*Opiner*], and *To Vote* are three very different things that the French do not distinguish enough. *To Deliberate* is to weigh the pro and the con; *To Give One's Opinion* is to state one's advice [*avis*] and to give the reasons for it; *To Vote* is one's suffrage, when nothing is left to do but to collect the votes. First the matter is put into deliberation. On the first round one gives one's opinion; one votes on the last round.
> (*Mountain*, CW 9:253; Pl. 3:833)

The stress that Rousseau puts on these distinctions makes it clear that he also made them in the key passage of the *Social Contract*. In sum, he clearly distinguishes deliberating and giving one's opinion both from casting ballots and from each other.

If citizens give their opinions prior to voting, how can Rousseau say that "they have no communication among themselves"? A possible answer to this can be found in the context of the passage that stresses the danger not of demagogic rhetoric, as his critics often suggest, but of faction. The point is not to keep citizens from hearing what a demagogue has to say, but to keep them from expressing and voting for the opinion of a faction rather than their own. Thus, the "communication" to be prevented is the formation of caucuses in which, outside of the public eye, factions coalesce.[9]

Even in light of this evidence, the critics who focus on the role of the government in forming civic virtue and in handling the details of application of laws are not likely to surrender their claim that Rousseau allows for no genuine deliberation. They can still argue that while he does distinguish in principle between giving an opinion and voting, in practice the opinions offered will simply be endorsements of what the government has conditioned the citizens to accept. Focus on the formative role of governments can distract attention from what is, in fact, a constant feature of Rousseau's thought: a radical suspicion of all governments. This suspicion of governments is simply a necessary consequence of the hostility toward factions that everyone agrees plays such an important part of the discussion of voting. The very existence of a government distinguished from the people means that a permanent faction exists in—but in some sense apart from—the rest of the community. The government itself forms a society within the larger society.

As suggested above, Rousseau objects to direct democracy, which might seem to avoid this problem by making the government identical to the people, on the grounds that this form of government will fail to distinguish between the generality of laws and the particularity of their application to individual cases. Democracies tend to invest their minutest decisions with the sanctity that belongs only to laws, and minorities will fall victim to this tendency of the majority, which itself is only a large faction. Other forms of government can mitigate this problem by remaining more clearly aware of the fact that any governmental action is merely an application of the more fundamental law that has its source in the people as a whole. Even so, Rousseau insists that in any society the government will inevitably set itself up against the general will and that it eventually will replace legitimate authority with arbitrary tyranny by usurping the legislative power of the people as a whole (*Social Contract*, CW 4:186–88; Pl. 3:420–23). He describes the unavoidable character of this drift of government into despotism in *Letters Written from the Mountain*. There he argues that time necessarily favors this drift. Each individual attempt on the part of the government to usurp a portion of sovereign power either succeeds or fails. Each success is made permanent by the moral force of precedent. Each failure, on the contrary, is only a temporary failure that will be turned to success in the future (*Mountain*, CW 9:237–55; Pl. 3:813–35).[10] Thus, although he does both, Rousseau encourages a distrust of the government as the source of all political problems even more than he encourages an intrusive government. This distrust of the government is perhaps the fundamental reason why Rousseau insists that there must be real citizen involvement in deliberation over issues of public importance. It should be emphasized that citizens need extreme vigilance merely to retard the drift toward government usurpation of sovereignty. To reverse it is essentially impossible. There is no solution to the inherently self-destructive character of politics.

One additional passage seems to lend support to those who belittle Rousseau's commitment to democratic deliberation. Rousseau begins his chapter on voting in the *Social Contract* by saying that "the way in which general matters are handled can provide a rather precise indication of the current state of the morals and health of the body politic" (*Social Contract*, CW 4:199; Pl. 3:439). He claims that a description of the actual deliberative process of a community is a reliable guide to the health of that community. He explains how to measure this indication by contrasting unanimity (which shows the dominance of the general will) with "debates, dissensions, and tumult" (which show the dominance of private interests). The view that the existence of debate is a sign of ill health supports the reading of Rousseau as favoring coercive control of public opinion, but the broader context suggests a more complicated picture. A few paragraphs earlier he associates "contradictions and debates" with a middle period, one in which the social tie has begun to slacken, but in which ruin is not yet at hand. The third stage occurs when debates are purely masks for private interest. In fact, this stage can lead to a condition in which a new public unanimity can occur because of widespread corruption and the practice of selling votes (*Social Contract*, CW 4:198–99; Pl. 3:438).

In sum, Rousseau identifies three distinct political conditions.[11] In the first, unanimity predominates; in the second, debate; and in the last, selling votes. The presence of unanimity, in itself, could indicate either great health or terminal illness because it can occur in either the first or last stage. The interesting case is the middle one. The condition should not be dismissed because it involves the transition from health to death since Rousseau insists that this transition begins at the very birth of every community. Slackening and decline are the ordinary conditions of even relatively healthy communities and cannot be avoided. Moreover, there is some reason to believe that Rousseau does not regard even the first condition of unanimity as simply desirable at any cost.

Perhaps the sole example of anything that is not an extremely small and simple community that belongs in the first category is Sparta—itself smaller and simpler than most political communities—which Rousseau regularly exalts as the model case of citizen identification with and devotion to the community. As he says in defending the *First Discourse*, "The embarrassment of my adversaries is visible every time Sparta must be mentioned" (*Final Reply*, CW 2:119; Pl. 3:83). His new adversaries today, however, are not embarrassed to cite Rousseau's admiration of Sparta because it can be used as an example of his embrace of coercive formation of citizens. This understanding, or misunderstanding, of Rousseau's position is encouraged by Rousseau himself, who both anticipates the arguments of, and leaves himself vulnerable to, his critics in his treatment of political debate. His desire to show that, contrary to the experience of subjects of absolute monarchies like France, devotion to the community is a real possibility causes him to appeal to historical examples of such devotion, particularly of a Spartan sort. In these cases his rhetoric sometimes overwhelms the complexity of his analysis.

It is, however, not Spartans but Romans whom Rousseau describes as the "model of all free Peoples" (*Second Discourse*, CW 3:4; Pl. 3:113), and it would be a mistake to assimilate these ancient examples with each other. Rousseau's critics frequently fail to notice that, in spite of their many similarities, Sparta and Rome represent rather different alternatives.[12] At one time Rousseau intended to write a parallel treatment of these two successful ancient republics, and the fragments of this parallel support the idea that he views Sparta as the model of patriotism and Rome as the model of freedom. For example, he says, "Ever ready to die for his country, a Spartan loved the fatherland so tenderly that he would have sacrificed freedom itself to save it. But the Romans never imagined that the fatherland could outlive freedom or even glory" (*Political Fragments*, CW 4:63; Pl. 3:543). In sum, the case for Sparta is a case for patriotism that is quite compatible with a high degree of coercion. The case for Rome, the turbulent domestic history of which makes it an unlikely example of total social cohesion, is a case for a sort of patriotism that is intimately linked with freedom.

Rousseau attributes the difference between these two communities to the different way they handled the relation between morals and laws. In Sparta the laws were the source of morals, whereas in Rome the morals were the independent source of the laws. The fact that morals were explicitly legislated in Sparta gave them a particular firmness and constancy. Spartan patriotism—the manifestation of these legislated morals—took the form of total devotion to their ancient laws and resistance to any change in them. The disadvantage of this was that as long as the laws themselves remained unchanged, the Spartans were inattentive to the way the government applied the laws. Spartan heroes are models of self-sacrifice for the sake of the laws, but they are not models of resistance to government abuses.

Roman patriotism, quite differently, took the form of total devotion to morals (in the form of freedom and glory) rather than laws (*Political Fragments*, CW 4:26, 36; Pl. 3:488, 503). These morals served as a standard independent of the laws and their application by the government. As a result, unlike the Spartans, the Romans were devoted to the laws only to the extent that they remained compatible with these morals. They were capable of resisting the government when its application of the laws departed from them. In the *Discourse on Political Economy*, Rousseau argues that the source of the devotion of the Romans to their republic was in its protection of their rights, "but the Romans stood out over all the peoples of the earth for the deference of the government toward private individuals and for its scrupulous attention to respecting the inviolable rights of all members of the state" (*Political Economy*, CW 3:153; Pl. 3:257). In his marginal notes to *De l'esprit* by Helvétius, Rousseau makes a similar remark without limiting it to Rome. Objecting to Helvétius's statement that "everything becomes legitimate and even virtuous for the public welfare [*salut public*]," Rousseau writes that "the public welfare is nothing if all the private individuals are not in safety [*sureté*]" (Pl. 4:1126). The issue, then, is not whether Rousseau is giving a strictly accurate account of Roman history; although it is important that he uses an example taken from history rather than a merely imaginary case. What is important is that he praises Rome for having a standard within itself that can be used to criticize the government. His position represents a middle ground between adopting a standard outside of society (such as natural law) that can always be used against it and allowing no standard other than whatever any government might call a law.

In Sparta the laws were the unquestionable foundation of everything else, whereas in Rome they were seen as instrumental to freedom, morality, and glory. Being instrumental, they are always in principle open to the question of whether they are the best available instruments in the service of these goals. Rousseau certainly does attribute a formative and even duplicitous role to the Roman government, but at the same time insists that the particular way Roman citizens were formed made them vigilant against government intrusions. As we have seen in the preceding chapter, his praises of Roman heroes include both those who sacrificed themselves for the good of their fatherland against foreign enemies and those (like Lucretia or Cato) who stood up against tyranny at home. Rome lacked the unanimity and resistance to change present in Sparta, but it gained resistance to the usurpations of the government.

Thus, while Rousseau has great admiration for the result of the Spartan political experiment of making the laws the source of everything, he does not endorse it in an unqualified way. Because Sparta represents the frictionless extreme of unanimous subordination of the particular to the general will, it is always appealing to Rousseau. Nevertheless, his considered judgment appears to be that this way of making the general will predominate comes at too high a price. This is why he can praise the "excellent regulations" of Sparta and, in the same breath, refer to them as "monstrously perfect" (*First Discourse*, CW 2:18; Pl. 3:24). As was argued in chapter 2, rather than simply dominating, and hence stifling, the political scene, genuine Rousseauian patriotism provides the necessary atmosphere in which a sort of public discussion can take place. Rome, as presented by Rousseau, represents the model of this sort of patriotism.

There is no permanent solution to the political problem. In the long run, every state that does not adopt the Spartan alternative will be ruined, but the long run can be very long indeed. In Sparta the preeminence of the laws slowed decay almost, but not quite, to a stop. In Rome the preeminence of morals was almost as effective and, in addition, allowed recourse to public criticism of attempts by the government to increase its power. In sum, the middle or declining stage—in which Rome and virtually every other community finds itself—is the politically relevant one both for allowing deliberation and for preserving freedom.

It seems certain, then, that Rousseau leaves room for something short of spontaneous unanimity in deliberation, although it must also be said that the critics are right in contending that this deliberation cannot take the form of bargaining and compromise we normally think of in the political process.[13] As Daniel Cullen puts it, "The common interest is expressed rather than manufactured in actions of sovereignty," or as Crocker puts it, the general will is "confirmed" or "discovered."[14] Also, while the fact that the outcome of Rousseauian deliberation is a sort of discovery gives it a similarity to a sort of Aristotelian deliberation in which opposing arguments are weighed, a sequential stating of opinions is quite different from a rational debate. Thus, exactly what Rousseauian deliberation might look or sound like remains to be seen.

Finally, those who wish to argue that there is little room in Rousseau's politics for anything like what we would recognize as a deliberative process can point to the rather scanty evidence of such a process to be found in the text of the *Social Contract*. The reason for this lack, however, is not because Rousseau considers it to be unimportant. On the contrary, although its relative absence does suggest that he does not regard its consideration to be essential in an outline of the "principles of political right," he does say, "I could make many reflections here about the simple right to vote in every act of sovereignty—a right that nothing can take away from the Citizens; and on the right to give an opinion, to make propositions, to analyze, to discuss, which the Government is always very careful to allow only to its members. But this important subject would require a separate treatise, and I cannot say everything in this one" (*Social Contract*, CW 4:199; Pl. 3:438–39).[15] Thus, far from being insignificant, the deliberative process is both important and extremely complex in Rousseau's view. Moreover, this process includes more than the simple right to vote; it also involves the right to express opinions and to analyze existing or proposed legislation.

To be sure, Rousseau's critics have given alternative readings of this passage, arguing that his right to vote is only an empty plebiscite and that he explicitly endorses the efforts of governments to restrict discussion of legislation to officials, rather than warning against this practice as a symptom of the effort of governments to usurp legislative power.[16] They are correct in pointing out that Rousseau does endorse placing restrictions on who can propose new legislation, but that is far from the only issue here. As was argued in chapter 1, Rousseau does not propose restrictions on analyzing existing legislation for its flaws or expressing opinions about proposed new laws. Nevertheless, it remains the case that Rousseau's failure to write the required "separate treatise" on public debate means that some effort is required to reconstruct his position.

From the discussion above, we can isolate three very distinctive features of the sort of deliberative process identified by Rousseau that make it very different from the sort that liberal democratic communities consider normal. First, Rousseau insists that speakers should attempt to identify what the general will is, rather than arguing on behalf of their own interest, or even their own understanding of what is just. When he says that it is important "that each Citizen give only his own opinion," he makes it clear that this opinion is not to be understood as the expression of purely personal preference. By specifying that giving an opinion includes stating the reasons for the statement, Rousseau cultivates distrust of speakers who fail to demonstrate that what they are proposing is contrary to their own interest.[17]

Second, Rousseau is resolutely opposed to interest group politics with its accompanying compromises and trade-offs. Each interest group, including the government itself, is a society within the society having a general will opposed to the general will of the community as a whole. Thus, Rousseau calls for some sort of isolation to ensure the purely personal statement of opinion.

Third, Rousseau discusses the general will as something to be discovered rather than constructed. He says, "The first to propose new [laws] merely states what everyone has already felt, and there is no question of intrigues nor of eloquence to pass into law what each has already resolved to do as soon as he is sure that others will do likewise" (*Social Contract*, CW 4:198; Pl. 3:437). This characteristic of legislative discussion is related to the first one: because the speaker is stating his sense of what the community as a whole thinks rather than his own preference, it is not surprising that others can be expected to recognize his statement as reflecting their own judgment about what the community as a whole thinks, rather than about their own personal preferences.

The three characteristics make up the essence of the sort of political discussion Rousseau endorses. The brevity of his discussions makes it rather difficult to envisage how they would be realized in any practical sense. I would like to suggest that Rousseau gives examples of the sort of political participation that can meet these different requirements in his own activity as a citizen, first, in writing the *Letter to d'Alembert* to influence Genevan debate on the question of whether to establish a theater and, second, in writing *Letters Written from the Mountain* to comment on the Genevan political situation after the censorship of his works. In these works Rousseau acts as a citizen by commenting on proposed legislation and by protesting against government violations of existing laws, and analyzes the fundamental constitution of Geneva, thereby covering the fundamental material that would be dealt with in his "separate treatise" on deliberation. That he does this in the form of published open letters proves to be uniquely fitted to his notion of civic participation.

Rousseau had cause to reflect on the question of the relation between his Genevan citizenship and his residence in France between his decision not to return to his fatherland in 1755 and his publication of the *Letter to d'Alembert* in 1758. When Diderot sent Rousseau a copy of his recently published play *Le Fils naturel* in 1757, Rousseau took great offense upon reading the line "Only the wicked man is alone," which he took as a public rebuke of his decision to leave Paris for a life in the country. Rousseau's view that the line was meant to apply to him is supported by the fact that the speech in which it occurs argues that people of unusual talents have an obligation to use those talents for the good of society, and that they cannot fulfill this obligation if they remove themselves from society. Although Diderot attempted to reassure Rousseau, the very letter in which he makes this reassurance repeats the argument, pointing out the possible harm that could come to others from Rousseau's retirement. Diderot's letter ends, "Farewell Citizen! Nevertheless a hermit makes a very peculiar citizen" (*Confessions*, CW 5:558). Diderot questions Rousseau's title to the nickname "Citizen," upon which he prided himself so much. What we will investigate now is how a hermit can be an exemplary citizen through his writing.

II. Orator versus Actor: The *Letter to d'Alembert*

The *Letter to d'Alembert* is a response to the proposal, made by d'Alembert in volume 7 of the *Encyclopédie*, that Geneva establish a theater. Such an establishment was understood by all to represent a significant departure from the traditional Calvinist laws and therefore amounted to a proposal for the repeal of an old law and the establishment of a new one. Rousseau's attack on this proposal represents the first of his two literary efforts to influence Genevan policy in a particular crisis.

Rousseau's position in writing the *Letter* is a peculiar one. Since the beginning of his literary career, he had always identified himself as Jean-Jacques Rousseau, Citizen of Geneva, in spite of the fact that he had forfeited his citizenship upon his conversion to Catholicism in 1728 and regained it only in 1754. After briefly considering a permanent move to his homeland, he continued to live in France after regaining his citizenship. In the *Confessions* he gives several reasons for his decision not to return to Geneva, two of which are relevant to the *Letter to d'Alembert* (*Confessions*, CW 5:331–33; Pl. 1:395–97). First, he hesitated because of the cold response of the government of Geneva to the publication of the *Second Discourse*, which he had dedicated to his fatherland. Second, he says that he realized that Voltaire's decision to take up residence near Geneva in 1755 would bring about a revolution in Genevan morals that he would be powerless to reverse. Being on the scene would only embroil him in unpleasant and unfruitful controversy. In fact, the controversy over the theater was the direct result of Voltaire's request to d'Alembert to suggest its establishment in his article.

In addition to these negative considerations, Rousseau adds a positive one for keeping his distance from Geneva. By staying in France, he gained a considerable freedom to write without interference. He says, "I would have been much less free at Geneva itself, where, wherever my books might be printed, the magistracy had the right of caviling over their contents." To his he adds that "unless one is a man of intrigues, if one wants to dedicate books to the true good of the fatherland, one must not compose them in its bosom" (*Confessions*, CW 5:341; Pl. 1:406). Thus, both in general and especially in the particular circumstances existing in Geneva after Voltaire moved there, speaking out on public matters runs the risk of contributing to the sort of factional intrigues that can undermine the general will. Strangely, then, the ideal circumstance for preserving one's integrity as a citizen seems to be to live hundreds of miles from one's community and to address one's fellow citizens through an open letter nominally addressed to a foreigner.

In the *Letter* itself Rousseau calls attention to the peculiar character of this way of addressing his fellow citizens a number of times. In his preface he makes it clear that this work is very different in character from his earlier writings. He says, "In the first place, I am not dealing here with vain philosophical chatter but with a practical truth important to a whole people. I do not speak here to the few but to the public, nor do I attempt to make others think but rather to explain my thought clearly. Hence, I had to change my style" (*d'Alembert* 6; Pl. 5:6). This passage—discussed in the preceding chapter in relation to the similar tactic of addressing the general public in *Julie*—sets up a series of distinctions. On the one hand, there are writings like the *First* and *Second Discourses* which (1) are philosophic, (2) are directed to the few readers competent to consider such matters, and (3) attempt to make these readers think for themselves. On the other hand, the *Letter* itself (1) is practical, (2) is directed to the broader public, and (3) explains Rousseau's own thought. The third element in each of these series is the striking one. Together they suggest that he does not necessarily reveal his own thoughts clearly in his theoretical writings, an issue that will be addressed in the next chapter. More significantly in this context, they deny that Rousseau is attempting to influence his readers' thought in the *Letter*. As he says immediately before this statement, "My countrymen have no need of my advice; I know it well." Thus, he is not offering advice; he is merely giving his own opinion.

He similarly plays down the threat posed by deceptive political rhetoric when he distinguishes the orator and preacher from the actor later in the *Letter*. He says:

> The orator and the preacher, it could be said, make use of their persons as does the actor. The difference is, however, very great. When the orator appears in public, it is to speak and not to show himself off; he represents only himself; he fills only his own role, speaks only in his own name, says, or ought to say, only what he thinks; the man and the role being the same, he is in his place; he is in the situation of any citizen who fulfills the functions of his estate. (*d'Alembert* 80–81; Pl. 5:74)

Here, as in the *Social Contract*, the emphasis is on the isolation and independence of the citizen who fills his role by offering his own opinion. The citizen is not a mouthpiece for a faction, which would be like an author writing a speech for an actor.

Rousseau's claim that the orator ought to say only what he thinks requires some clarification. In the *Letter* he regularly calls attention to the fact that he himself does not say everything that is on his mind. For example, at the beginning he informs d'Alembert that he will discuss only the points on which they disagree and will remain silent about those on which they agree (*d'Alembert* 9; Pl. 5:9). In addition to suppressing some of his thoughts, Rousseau also seems to go to some lengths to use the sort of arguments that will affect his fellow citizens. In both cases he is less than perfectly candid.

The *Social Contract* allows us to determine what is meant by saying only what one thinks. As we have seen, when voting the citizen is not to think about what he wants. Instead, he is to think about what the general will is. Although the general will tends to work in the interest of particular citizens, it is frequently opposed to self-interest in the narrow sense. While it is a common feature of democratic politics for speakers to deny that what they are recommending is good for them, Rousseau radicalizes this demand. Accordingly, he declares that he opposes the theater even though he is an avid theatergoer and says, "Love of the public good is the only passion which causes me to speak to the public; I can then forget myself" (*d'Alembert* 132; Pl. 5:120). The best guarantee that one can have that the orator has forgotten self-interest is if he speaks against it.

Because a citizen is attempting to estimate what the general will is, losing a vote means only that he is mistaken—not that he will be deprived of what he wants—and therefore is the cause of no resentment. This is why, in a sense, it does not matter whether he fails to persuade others of his position. Reflecting this in the *Letter*, Rousseau says such things as "After having said what I think, I see no harm in it if my opinion is not accepted," and "If my sentiments are mistaken, at least the error can hurt no one" (*d'Alembert* 11, 16; Pl. 5:11, 15). It would be possible to regard these statements as reflecting an indifference to results, stemming from a sole regard for his own moral purity: having done his duty by speaking, Rousseau washes his hands of the matter, reserving only the right to say "I told you so" when things go badly.[18] That this is not the thrust of these remarks can be seen by considering the argument of the *Letter* as a whole.

Rousseau claims to be astonished that d'Alembert's discussion of the nonexistent theater takes up so much space in his article about Geneva (*d'Alembert* 3; Pl. 5:3), but it is equally astonishing that the reverse is true about his own discussion in the *Letter*. It is remarkable how little of this work is actually devoted to explicit discussion of the issue of whether Geneva should establish a theater. Rousseau does not turn to this issue in precise terms until approximately two-thirds of the way through the *Letter*, after treating such issues as the Genevan clergy, dueling in France, and a number of topics relating to drama in general. It is only after these lengthy preliminaries that he asserts that the establishment of a theater in Geneva will cause a revolution and then says, "Will this revolution be good or bad? It is time to examine this" (*d'Alembert* 98; Pl. 5:90).

A reader might think that the issue has been settled prior to this point in the *Letter*. A significant part of the preliminary matter is devoted to demonstrating that the theater is bad for communities with healthy morals and good for those with unhealthy morals.[19] Implicitly adopting the comical presupposition that vice never sleeps, Rousseau suggests that in Paris the crime rate is reduced by one-twelfth by encouraging theater attendance for two hours a day, but that in a small city the theater takes the place of more salutary occupations (*d'Alembert* 59; Pl. 5:54). Rousseau illustrates this assertion with a lengthy digression in which he speculates on the effects the introduction of a theater might have on farmers who live on a mountain near Neufchâtel. He argues that the simple and pure morals of these mountaineers would be completely undermined by the expense and luxury associated with the theater (*d'Alembert* 60–65; Pl. 5:55–59).

It is natural to assume that what is said about these mountaineers could be applied to the Genevans, who live only fifty or so miles away, but this is exactly what Rousseau does not assume. He concludes this discussion with the remark, "It follows from this that, in order to decide if it is proper or not to establish a theatre in a certain town, we must know in the first place if the morals [manners] are good or bad there, a question concerning which it is perhaps not for me to answer with regard to us" (*d'Alembert* 65; Pl. 5:60). In other words, far from assuming that the Genevans are as moral as the mountaineers, he raises the question of whether they are and pointedly refuses to answer it. A few pages later he says, "One of the inevitable effects of a theatre established in a town as little as ours will be to change our maxims, or if you please, our prejudices and our public opinions, which will necessarily change our morals [manners] for others, better or worse I do not say" (*d'Alembert* 74; Pl. 5:67–68). This reluctance to state an opinion on what one would think is precisely the issue that caused Rousseau to write the *Letter* is remarkable.

When Rousseau does finally turn to his discussion of Geneva thirty pages later, the reasons for this hesitation become clearer. In many ways Geneva resembles Paris more than the mountains outside of Neufchâtel. First, while it is not a large city, its restless commercial activity makes it appear four times as big as it is. Moreover, accompanying this commercial activity is a decline in morals. Rousseau says, "One must not dissemble; the intentions are still upright, but the morals [manners] already noticeably incline toward decadence" (*d'Alembert* 111; Pl. 5:102). He professes ignorance of exactly how close inequality of wealth is to undermining the republic (*d'Alembert* 115; Pl. 5:105).

In sum, Rousseau leaves it very much of an open question how much Geneva resembles the small community of the mountaineers and how much it resembles Paris. The purpose of his discussion of Neufchâtel and Paris is to present the two extremes of a continuum as a preparation for determining where Geneva lies. Although it is clear in which direction his hopes lie, he does not prejudge the matter. In fact, one could say that the issue of the establishment of a theater is an occasion for the Genevans to decide what sort of community they, in fact, are (as opposed to what they might like to be) and that Rousseau's goal is to sketch out the alternatives.

This explains why he can say that it does not really matter whether he is correct in his own judgment (or wish) that Geneva is as morally close to the mountaineers as it is physically. He says that he dares to think that his community is a healthy one, but admits that he could be mistaken (*d'Alembert* 118; Pl. 5:107). If he is mistaken, no harm is done because the Genevans will vote for a theater. In itself, this will not begin the corruption; it will merely increase the corruption that has already proceeded further than Rousseau hopes it has. "When this alternative has ceased to alarm us, the actors can come; they can do us no more harm" (*d'Alembert* 123; Pl. 5:112). It is only a small overstatement to say that the Genevans cannot really make the "wrong" decision about the theater. If they are moved by Rousseau's arguments and reject the theater, they will demonstrate that their morals are good and, therefore, that the theater would be bad for them. If, on the other hand, they are persuaded by d'Alembert and embrace the theater, they will demonstrate that their morals are not good and, therefore, that the theater would be good for them.

Thus, Rousseau is not exactly offering advice to the Genevans about what to do. He is stating his opinion of the current state of the Genevan general will, but he must admit he was mistaken if his side loses. He can regret that his city does not meet the standards he thought it did, but he could not claim that they were wrong to reject his counsel. What he is offering is advice about the meaning of the issue the Genevans are being asked to decide; he is making sure that they are adequately informed about what is at stake in this issue. Without this advice, they might think that this is a minor issue not worth worrying about or—seduced by d'Alembert's claim that the theater and good morals go together—they might unknowingly hasten their decline. What Rousseau argues is that decisions like this one are important because they require that the community define what it believes about itself and therefore what it is. The only "mistake" that can be made is to fail to realize this. That failure in itself would be a sign of a significant corruption in the community.

That Rousseau is merely stating an opinion rather than offering advice does not mean that he is simply making an empty gesture. Sometimes the mere public statement of an opinion about what the community believes can tip the balance of a community unsure about what it does believe. In the *Social Contract* Rousseau attributes such a role to the Roman censorial tribunal, which "far from being the arbiter of the people's opinion, merely declares it." Such a tribunal can determine opinions when they are uncertain (*Social Contract*, CW 4:214–15; Pl. 3:458–59). In the *Letter to d'Alembert* Rousseau proposes the reform of the Court of Honor regulating duels in France in precisely this spirit (*d'Alembert* 67–75; Pl. 5:61–69). Of course, these are examples of governmental institutions meant to direct public opinion, but Rousseau insists that private individuals have a role in this process that is quite independent of and immune to governmental control. For example, he argues that the female gossips of Geneva, who are in no way agents of the government, "almost perform the function of censors in our city" by making public judgments about scandalous behavior (*d'Alembert* 106; Pl. 5:97). Similarly, his own *Letter* is an example of attempting to determine uncertain opinions made by a citizen outside of the government.

In sum, living in the country outside of Paris, Rousseau is isolated from the political factions that exist in Geneva. As a result, he gives his own opinion rather than, like an actor, reciting the lines that are given to him by the faction to which he belongs. Because the opinion he offers is contrary to his interest as an avid theatergoer, he can claim that when he speaks he forgets about himself and considers only the general will. He gives his estimate of the current state of the general will in Geneva in the hope of settling an unfixed opinion, but is prepared to accept a result opposed to the one he proposes as a more accurate expression of the general will. If he turns out to be wrong, it is because he has failed to discover the general will. Rousseau's literary activity as a writer of a letter is a model of civic participation as he understands it.

III. The Citizen Renounces Citizenship: *Letters Written from the Mountain*

Rousseau's second intervention into Genevan politics took place with the publication of *Letters Written from the Mountain* in 1764, six years after the *Letter to d'Alembert*. Once again he chose to intervene through public letters written from abroad, this time to an anonymous (or hypothetical) Genevan correspondent who is intelligent but has not decided whether to join those citizens who are protesting the government's condemnation of Rousseau's works. The subject of these *Letters* is also quite different from that of the *Letter to d'Alembert*. Rather than commenting on a proposed change in legislation, Rousseau is concerned with a subject that is at the same time narrower and broader. These *Letters* are a response to the public situation after the condemnation of *Emile* and the *Social Contract*. In the first place, they concern an issue that is related directly to Rousseau's own personal interest. Moreover, they concern the application of the law rather than a change in legislation.

In the second place, these *Letters* also concern something more fundamental than the mere application of the law. Rousseau argues that the violation of legal procedures in his case is the symptom of a deep constitutional crisis in Geneva in which the members of the governing Small Council were attempting to usurp power. Thus, these *Letters* concern something other than ordinary legislative deliberation of the sort illustrated by the *Letter to d'Alembert*. They concern the sorts of recourse available to citizens who perceive both incidental and fundamental injustices in the government's administration of the laws.

As we saw in the discussion of the *Letter to d'Alembert* and the *Social Contract*, Rousseau insists that deliberation requires that citizens forget about themselves or their own particular interests. This is clearly not possible in the case in which one is the object of criminal proceedings. In fact, as was pointed out in chapter 1, Rousseau goes to some trouble to combat the argument that he has suffered no personal injury by having his books condemned and burned. While the Genevan government argues that an author is not injured by a punishment inflicted on his book, Rousseau claims that this could be true only in the case of anonymous authors (*Mountain*, CW 9:218–19; Pl. 3:791–93). From the beginning, he says, "I feel that it is impossible for me to forget myself in a quarrel in which I am the subject" (*Mountain*, CW 9:134; Pl. 3:687).

After spending six of the nine *Letters* analyzing the prosecution of his books, Rousseau turns to the general political situation in Geneva, apologizing for the length of time spent on discussing his books and saying, "In speaking about myself I was thinking about you; and your question depends so much on mine, that the one is already resolved only with the other, there is nothing left for me but to draw the conclusion" (*Mountain*, CW 9:237; Pl. 3:813). Rousseau could claim with some plausibility that the agitation over his prosecution has led to a general constitutional crisis and that in this instance his private interest in proper legal procedure is identical to the common good. Nevertheless, his arguments that concern for private interest necessarily blinds one to the general will would make such a claim highly suspect. What can a Rousseauian citizen do to lay suspicions to rest in a case in which the personal and the political are so intermingled?

Living away from Geneva is not enough to keep Rousseau from involvement in intrigues in this case. Accordingly, he takes the extreme step of renouncing his citizenship so that he cannot be suspected of manipulating the current crisis for his own gain. The partisans of his cause are no longer partisans for him because he is no longer a party to the legal proceedings at issue. He says, "Far from the ostracism that exiles me forever from my country being the result of my faults, I have never fulfilled my duty as a Citizen better than at the moment I cease to be one, and I would have deserved the title of one by the act that made me renounce it" (*Mountain*, CW 9:226; Pl. 3:801). Although he still maintains a stake in his reputation, which is sullied by the attacks on his books, by renouncing his citizenship, Rousseau disposes of self-interest as an issue as much as possible. Like one of his legislators, he gains a sort of moral authority based on disinterestedness by removing himself from politics altogether. Rousseauian political activism, then, requires that one remain open to the possibility of complete withdrawal from the community as part of the fulfillment of one's civic duty.

Just as he follows the path set in the *Letter to d'Alembert* of establishing himself as an outsider, Rousseau also follows the same path by emphasizing that this is a book written for ordinary citizens. Here again he emphasizes that his previous books have not been directed to a popular audience (*Mountain*, CW 9:211; Pl. 3:783). Rousseau admits that if he were writing only to his anonymous correspondent, he might conduct his argument on a general and abstract level using technical vocabulary, but "the subject of these Letters interests an entire people, composed in its greatest number of men who have more sense and judgment than reading and study" (*Mountain*, CW 9:284; Pl. 3:871). Rather than attempting to seduce these readers with big words, as his political opponents do, Rousseau promises them "the truth in all its simplicity." The only change between this statement and the *Letter to d'Alembert* is that in this context Rousseau is more concerned about the deceptive rhetoric of his opponents and less concerned with the philosophic style of d'Alembert. This approach is very reminiscent of the beginning of Plato's *Apology* in which Socrates insists upon his own lack of sophistication as a rhetorician, but Socrates, unlike Rousseau, does not feel that it is necessary to do away with the charge that he is speaking in his own interest.

In the substance of his argument, Rousseau also follows the path he set for his response to d'Alembert. Turning away from his treatment of his own position, he poses the questions that presumably interest his Genevan reader, "You ask what the present state of your Republic is, and what its Citizens ought to do? It is easier to respond to the first question than to the other" (*Mountain*, CW 9:237; Pl. 3:813). One might think that the second question is the crucial one, but once again Rousseau spends most of his time on the first. Having devoted two-thirds of the *Letters* to the particularities of his own case, he then devotes virtually all of the rest of the work to describing the present state of Geneva. Five paragraphs from the end, he finally turns to the question of what is to be done, "Here I am, Sir, at the conclusion of these Letters. After having shown you the condition in which you are, I will not undertake to trace out for you the road that you must follow in order to leave it. If there is one, being on the very spot, you and your Fellow Citizens must see it better than I can; when one knows where one is and were one ought to go, one can direct oneself without effort." Shortly thereafter he repeats, "I propose nothing" (*Mountain*, CW 9:305, 306; Pl. 3:895, 896).

Certainly a part of Rousseau's reticence here is due to the tension between his long-felt abhorrence to civil unrest in his native city and his desire to receive justice.[20] Nevertheless, his procedure is identical to the one he follows in the *Letter to d'Alembert*. The issue for Genevans is not exactly what to do, but what sort of community they see themselves as belonging to. If, on the one hand, they rally to the support of those who have petitioned the government for redress, they show that they form a community that will protect itself against government usurpation of sovereignty. If, on the other hand, they belittle the danger posed by what could be regarded as an isolated case, they show that they are already too far down the road of decline. Whichever decision they make will be the right one because it shows what they are.

What then is the present state of Geneva? In fact, Genevan public opinion is divided on this question. "Some People of very good sense tell you: we are the most free of all people, and other People of very good sense tell you: we are living under the harshest slavery." Rousseau's hypothetical correspondent is the perfect example of someone whose opinion is not yet fixed and whom Rousseau (acting like a censor) is trying to tip in a particular direction. Rousseau's own answer to the question is that both sides are right. He says, "Nothing is more free than your legitimate state; nothing is more servile than your actual state" (*Mountain*, CW 9:237; Pl. 3:813). In principle and by its laws, Geneva is free, but in fact and by its government's abuse of the laws, it is not free. Rousseau's judgment or hope is that the present servility has not progressed so far as to prevent a return to the legitimate state. The bulk of this part of the letter is an attempt to inform the Genevans adequately about the issue by reconstructing the constitutional principles underlying the Genevan government and opposing them to the practices of the existing government.[21] Which of these more accurately reflects the present Geneva is for the citizens as a whole to decide.

In both the *Letter to d'Alembert* and *Letters Written from the Mountain*, Rousseau stops short at the first round and only gives his opinion. In neither case does he move on to the last round and cast his ballot. In *Letters Written from the Mountain*, in fact, he has renounced this privilege along with his citizenship. The extent to which in both works he makes himself into a radical outsider who, nevertheless, identifies with the community makes Rousseau seem more like a legislator who offers his advice and then leaves. This raises the question of whether Rousseau's model of civic activism can be adopted by more ordinary citizens who lack his literary gifts and, more importantly, live in their community and plan on staying there.

Letters Written from the Mountain answers this question in the affirmative. Rousseau's argument is that the real constitutional crisis faced by Geneva is not caused by the suppression of his works as much as it is by the government's treatment of those who have rallied to his support. These supporters have presented a *representation*, or remonstrance, to the government, accusing it of violating legal procedures in Rousseau's case. The government has, in turn, denied their right to have this remonstrance presented to the General Council, or sovereign legislative body. In effect, these remonstrators are letter writers like Rousseau. They have written an open letter to the government, publicly protesting its behavior and demanding that the people as a whole judge it through the General Council. As Rousseau is writing an open letter to defend the remonstrators, they have written an open letter defending him.

Rousseau argues that the right to make such remonstrances against the government and have them presented to the sovereign is an absolutely fundamental right. He says that in any state in which the sovereignty is ultimately in the hands of the people, "the Legislator always exists, although it does not always show itself." Moreover, "its members are scattered, but they are not dead" (*Mountain*, CW 9:263; Pl. 3:845). Since (as we saw above) the inevitable decline of any society begins with the usurpation of legislative functions by the government, any effort to retard this decline depends on a mechanism to call the government's attempts to the attention of the sovereign. Making remonstrances against the government is this mechanism. It is the way that the invisible sovereign can be summoned forth to show itself.

Rousseau concedes that in one of its forms such actions are dangerous and can be thwarted by the government, that is, when citizens attempt to propose new laws. In such cases he argues that the government may veto the remonstrance. Nevertheless, even when the government does refuse to submit proposed laws to the sovereign, the citizen making the proposal has at least succeeded in making his opposition to the existing law known to the public, which can read his remonstrance. As argued in chapter 2, Rousseau is quite insistent that public criticism of existing laws cannot legitimately be forbidden. In cases of complaining against the government's transgressions against existing laws, moreover, Rousseau insists that these complaints require the attention of the assembled sovereign rather than simply members of the government (*Mountain*, CW 9:264–65; Pl. 3:846–48). In making remonstrances, citizens are acting as members of the sovereign, but they are not voting, which can be done only in the sovereign body. Instead, they are "stating their opinion [*opiner*] about matters that ought to be brought there" (*Mountain*, CW 9:264; Pl. 3:845). Because this is not a vote, the number of remonstrators is irrelevant to the seriousness of their case. In fact, counting the signatures on a remonstrance would encourage a faction to present itself as the sovereign. The remonstrance of a single citizen, in principle, means as much as one signed by a majority.

In sum, the model of civic activism held up in the *Letter to d'Alembert* and *Letters Written from the Mountain* applies to all citizens, not merely to an occasional great figure comparable to the legislator. In these works Rousseau gives models of civic activism that include deliberation about proposed legislation, oversight of the administration of existing laws, and reflection on the constitution as a whole. These examples demonstrate that the critics who insist that Rousseau's principles lead to a fundamentally passive citizenry are incorrect. Their criticisms do, however, have the advantage of calling attention to the peculiarities of Rousseauian activism, among which are (1) the pressure to show oneself as disinterested even to the point of renouncing citizenship, (2) the need to speak in popular language, (3) suspicion of speakers who speak in defense of their own interest, (4) a tendency to turn every debate into a discussion of the fundamental character of the community, and, finally, (5) the literary character of the open letter or petition in which one gives one's own opinion rather than aligning oneself with a faction. Each of these features may be very problematic and may, in practice, perhaps lead to some of the tendencies that Rousseau's critics deplore, but they can also lead in unexpected other directions.

Rousseauian citizenship can be understood as a peculiar variant of the favorite Enlightenment community: the republic of letters. The Enlightenment republic of letters is a cosmopolitan community that at its best engages in rational debate in an attempt to come to a consensus and at its worse (as shown in the critique outlined in chapter 1) uses satire and calumny to mobilize a faction of intellectuals. Rousseau's republic of letters is made up of citizens of a small homogeneous republic who live independently of one another, even to the point of residing hundreds of miles away from their fellows. Rousseau's critics are right to point to a significant formative role for legislators and governments in Rousseau's politics. His citizens may regularly withdraw from their isolation to meet in speechless transparency during festivals that reinforce their civic identity. In political debate, however, they write countless open letters and circulate petitions, not to find the truth or hammer out a compromise, but to tip the balance of unsettled opinion about what sort of community they live in. Rousseau's citizens may rush to the assembly, but they will make sure to stop at the bookseller to pick up their copy of the latest open letters on the way, after having mailed their own letter to the editor in plenty of time for publication.

IV. Conclusion

In concluding the *First Discourse*, Rousseau refers to wise men who behave as good citizens and suggests that they be given "the only recompense worthy of them: that of contributing by their influence to the happiness of the People to whom they will have taught wisdom." A few pages earlier, he suggests that the motive for such wise men might well be glory (*First Discourse*, CW 2:22, 19; Pl. 3:30, 26). We have seen in Rousseau's discussion of heroes that he regards this motive as a possible but unstable basis for virtue. The same could be said for compassion as the basis of patriotism, because compassion is usually not strong enough to counter self-interest.

Rousseau presents himself as a good citizen even in the act of renouncing his citizenship, but the basis of his citizenship is not clear. At the very least it must be acknowledged that by refusing to identify himself as a citizen on the title page of some of his books, Rousseau did not consider himself to be nothing but a citizen. The concluding chapter will turn to the consideration of Rousseau as not a citizen, but a philosopher who is also an author.

CHAPTER SIX

PHILOSOPHIC GOOD AND BAD FAITH

In the last several chapters, emphasis was placed on Rousseau's view of the public responsibility of authors, on authorship as citizenship. It must be acknowledged, however, that Rousseau also wrote for a more specialized readership, "those who know how to understand" ("Bordes," CW 2:185; Pl. 3:106).[1] In *Letters Written from the Mountain*, he even claimed that his books were always the sort "that are not written for the people" (*Mountain*, CW 9:211; Pl. 3:783). Coming from the author of the best-selling novel of the eighteenth century, this is a very strong claim; its absolute character must be understood in relation to the context of self-defense. Even so, it does indicate an important part of Rousseau's literary project. The purpose of the present chapter is to address, first, Rousseau's critique of the literary projects of other philosophers and, second, his account of how to write for other philosophers without forgetting the public. This does not represent a complete departure from the argument developed to this point. In Rousseau's view, any writing for publication is necessarily an act of (good or bad) citizenship, whereas philosophic investigation of the truth is necessarily indifferent to the effect of that investigation on others. Even in his most philosophic works, Rousseau never set aside his responsibility.

We have seen that Rousseau identifies *Julie* and the *Letter to d'Alembert* as the works in which he is most exclusively concerned with a popular audience. One could suggest that the *Second Discourse* and *Reveries of the Solitary Walker* stand at the opposite pole. In beginning the first of these, Rousseau says, "I shall imagine myself in the Lyceum of Athens, repeating the Lessons of my Masters, with Plato and Xenocrates for judges" (*Second Discourse*, CW 3:19; Pl. 3:133). This would be an announcement that the *Second Discourse* was a purely philosophic work if Rousseau did not immediately add, "and the human Race for an audience." What Rousseau would say to Plato and Xenocrates in front of the human race is by no means identical to what he would say "in secret, in the decent and frank expansiveness of philosophic intercourse" (*d'Alembert* 11; Pl. 5:10).[2] Analogously, Rousseau begins the *Reveries* by insisting that this book is being written for himself alone, but his frequent addresses to its readers indicate that he was well aware that he was writing to himself with "the human Race for an audience." The same point is made at the beginning of the *Confessions*, where Rousseau announces, "Let the trumpet of the last judgment sound when it will; I shall come with this book in my hands to present myself before the Sovereign Judge." Even before such a judge, Rousseau will demand, "Eternal Being, assemble around me the countless host of my fellows; let them listen to my confessions" (*Confessions*, CW 5:5; Pl. 1:5).

At the conclusion of this chapter, I will discuss an occasion in which Rousseau claimed to be addressing himself to a philosopher in a private letter. There was at least one other occasion in which he addressed the issue of the publication of a book of philosophy written for philosophers. Not long after the publication of *Julie*, while the manuscripts of *Emile* and the *Social Contract* were in their final stages of preparation, Rousseau received one of the more remarkable of the many letters sent to him by aspiring authors. His correspondent, the Benedictine Dom Deschamps, announced that he had completed a manuscript containing nothing less than "that metaphysical Truth so sought after until now" by all philosophers. He asked Rousseau's advice about publishing his *True System or the Key to the Metaphysical and Moral Puzzle* (Leigh 8:306). Rousseau responded that even if Dom Deschamps's claim to have discovered the truth were accurate—a claim that would also be made by all mistaken philosophers—this would be no reason to publish. He proceeds, "I will add that it is not Enough to consider the good that a book contains in itself, but one also ought to weigh the evil to which it can give rise, it must be considered that it will find fewer readers who are well disposed than who have bad hearts and ill-formed heads. Before publishing one must compare the good and the bad it can do and the uses with the abuses; which of these two effects prevails over the other decides whether it is good or bad to publish" (Leigh 9:29). As Rousseau expected, his correspondent was not dissuaded and he continued to write for assistance, not only to Rousseau, but also to Helvétius, d'Alembert, and Diderot, and eventually to less distinguished thinkers. Doubtless, Rousseau's advice was in part inspired by his judgment of his correspondent's intellectual capacity and the quality of his manuscript; nonetheless, it is quite consistent with his own practice.

A full treatment of Rousseau's understanding of philosophy is beyond the scope of this book, which is intended to show the preconditions for such a treatment. Completeness would require full-scale studies of at least the *Second Discourse*, *Emile*, the *Confessions*, and the *Reveries*. A partial treatment of this theme is unavoidable here, however. Although Rousseau published no systematic metaphysical treatise, no *True System*, his actions in writing the way he did and his arguments explaining and justifying these actions reveal how deep and comprehensive his thought was. Even the glimpse into the ultimate basis of his thought unraveled in the present study indicates that he did not bury this thought in impenetrable privacy. The issues addressed in this chapter, then, will include Rousseau's understanding of the defects of previous attempts to deal with the private character of philosophy in relations with the public and his presentation of his own understanding of this issue to other philosophers. The book will then conclude by addressing the peculiarity of Rousseau's understanding of himself as a thinker who both is and isn't a philosopher.

I. Rousseau and the Background of the Esoteric Doctrine

As we have seen, Rousseau insisted that his good faith made him virtually unique as a writer. He regularly insists that other writers were guided by their private interest rather than concern for truth. As a result, they wrote not to express the truth, but to further the agenda set by their private interest. While Rousseau attributes this tendency to writers in general, he insists that philosophers in particular are prone to it. In fact, precisely in the work in which he most insists on his own good faith, he says, "I have never prided myself on philosophic good faith; for I have never been acquainted with any such thing" (*Beaumont*, CW 9:71; Pl. 4:991).

Rousseau addressed himself very explicitly to the tension between the private doctrines of philosophers and the bad faith to be found in their public expressions, in reference to what he called the internal or esoteric doctrine (*doctrine intérieur*). He discusses this phenomenon in four different contexts, ranging from the beginning of his literary career to the end of his life, in the *Observations*, the *Confessions*, the *Dialogues*, and the *Reveries*. Taken together these discussions show the complexity and consistency of Rousseau's understanding of the core significance of the doctrine. A look at these discussions can both clarify the phenomenon at issue and show what is distinctive in his understanding of it.

Because the rather startling account of the history and nature of philosophy that Rousseau constructs around his discussions of the esoteric doctrine might seem to be odd, or even perverse, to some readers today, some preliminaries are necessary to set the stage for an account of these discussions.[3] First, it should be said that Rousseau would presume that many of his contemporaries would not regard his discussion as odd. Although some intellectuals would have objected to his negative evaluation of the esoteric doctrine, they were far from denying its existence. In fact, in many ways it formed the centerpiece of their own understanding of the history of philosophy. Discussions of the esoteric doctrine were abundantly available to Rousseau.[4] A brief look at the seventeenth- and eighteenth-century background of the esoteric doctrine as it was accessible to Rousseau can help us see what is distinctive in his account.

Some immediate antecedents of Rousseau's view are quite easy to identify. Victor Gourevitch has provided useful suggestions about sources well known to Rousseau, including Diderot, Barbeyrac, Locke, and the article in Bayle's *Dictionary* on Spinoza.[5] To these one should add Warburton (to whom Rousseau refers in the *Social Contract*), whose *Divine Legation of Moses Demonstrated* contains a lengthy discussion of the "double doctrine," claiming that it was held by all moral philosophers in antiquity.[6] One could also add the French freethinkers, or so-called *libertins érudits*, who regularly distinguished themselves as *déniaisés* from the vulgar and who, in the description of Joan DeJean, "transmit their message of intellectual and narrative freedom in a devious manner that serves to camouflage the message."[7] DeJean indicates that she believes that Rousseau was unfamiliar with these writers,[8] but, in fact, he makes a rather elaborate reference to one of the preeminent libertine texts, Cyrano's *Histoire comique*, in *Le Persiffleur*, which was written before the *First Discourse* (Pl. 1:1111). Rousseau also knew a later version of the libertine arguments from Nicolas Fréret's *Lettre de Thrasybule à Leucippe*, which he read in manuscript years before its publication in 1768.[9] This work, which presents itself as a translation of a translation of a Greek manuscript, contains a systematic argument against religion. Its supposed writer counsels his addressee "to regard all religion as a tyrannical opinion, invented to dominate minds, and to which wise men must conform in the exterior."[10] According to Rousseau's friend Duclos, Fréret wished to restrict access to this manuscript to "friends *interioris admissionis*."[11] Duclos, who apparently supplied Rousseau with the manuscript, evidently regarded him as such a friend.

Beyond the information provided by these sources, which are meant to be illustrative rather than comprehensive, one can link specific sources to the details of Rousseau's accounts. For example, Rousseau fairly regularly connects Pythagoras with the origins of philosophy and usually makes a rather positive judgment about him, but he also presents him as the originator of the esoteric doctrine. The classic presentation of Pythagoras in relation to the esoteric doctrine can be found in Pierre Bayle's *Dictionnaire historique et critique*. In his article on Pythagoras, Bayle makes the distinction between initiates and the profane among Pythagoras's students. This account was repeated in many sources available to Rousseau and his contemporary readers.

Rousseau also refers to the existence of the esoteric doctrine in China. Reports arriving from China after the establishment of Jesuit missions there at the end of the sixteenth century brought about a serious reevaluation of European self-consciousness.[12] Detailed reports became available about this unquestionably highly civilized, apparently well-governed, non-Christian country, which, moreover, had a recorded history stretching back further than that of any Christian country. What was to be made of this rival? The dispute over the relation between the morality of Chinese society and its religious traditions, in particular, gave birth to some peculiar divisions and alliances, and it is in the disputes over this issue that the esoteric doctrine makes its appearance. The earliest accounts of China, those sent back by the missionary Matteo Ricci, featured both the good morals of the Chinese and the purity of their intellectual tradition. This remained the predominant Jesuit view and was endorsed by figures such as Leibniz and Voltaire, who seized the opportunity to promote a universal rational natural religion and toleration.[13] Ricci's views were opposed by his successor in the Jesuit mission, Nicholas Longobardi, who argued that the ancient Chinese sages were materialists and that their modern followers were closet atheists who concealed their atheism behind outward conformity to traditional religious practices. Their atheism is the essential component of their esoteric doctrine. This view of these thinkers was adopted by writers such as Malebranche, who opposed the Chinese tradition as a variant of modern Spinozism, and Bayle, who defended this tradition on precisely the same ground. Bayle used the supposed atheism of the Chinese literati as an example to illustrate his notorious thesis that a society based on atheism could thrive. In sum, assertions about the esoteric doctrine were used both to vilify the Chinese literati as closet atheists and to praise them for precisely the same thing.

Rousseau was well acquainted with significant parts of this literature. He took an interest in the question posed by China when he was in his twenties, during the period in which he made his greatest effort to educate himself. In the *Confessions* he gives an account of his daily routine of studies during this period. As a part of his studies, Rousseau used the *Abrégé chronologique de l'histoire universelle sacrée et profane* by the Jesuit Denis Pétau, a work that discusses China at some length, and began to write his own "Universal Chronology or General History of the Times Since the Creation of the World to the Present" (Pl. 5:487–92). Bayle, Leibniz, and Malebranche were among the authors he studied carefully in the 1730s, and China is also discussed by Locke, whom he also studied during this period. Toward the end of the 1740s, he also immersed himself in historical literature, including works about China while he worked for the Dupin family. Also while working for the Dupins, Rousseau was involved with writing a refutation of Montesquieu's *Spirit of the Laws*, which contains numerous discussions of China. In the *Second Discourse*, he refers favorably to the Jesuit accounts of China (*Second Discourse*, CW 3:85; Pl. 3:213). In short, Rousseau was very familiar with literature about China, including discussions of the esoteric doctrine, written by missionaries, travelers, and philosophers. Significantly, he refers to China as an example of a combination of the extremes of both atheism and fanaticism (*Confessions*, CW 5:474; Pl. 1:567).

Rousseau singles out one additional source of information about the esoteric doctrine that deserves special attention. In book 9 of the *Confessions*, he refers to "the esoteric doctrine about which Diderot talked to me so much, but which he never explained to me" (*Confessions*, CW 5:393; Pl. 1:468). The complexity of Diderot's view deserves more study, and only a sketch of the issues involved can be given here. Some scholars have argued that Diderot was both opposed to and constitutionally incapable of systematic dissimulation. They argue that his very openness about the existence of the esoteric doctrine indicates that he did not accept the concealment it implies. Peter France, for example, cautions against exaggerating the possibility "that Diderot cultivated disorder and ambiguity as protective devices in an age of repressive censorship."[14] Nevertheless, France himself immediately cites a statement from Diderot that says as directly as possible that this is precisely what he does. Others have been less hesitant to attribute a form of the esoteric doctrine to Diderot. Following Eugène Meyer, J. Robert Loy argues that Diderot held two different moral positions: one for the people based on traditional notions of virtue and another for the wise based on radical materialism.[15] Certainly, Diderot frequently insists that terms such as "virtue" and "vice" are essentially meaningless and should be used only as a concession to prevailing opinions. Such language is part of public statements concealing a private doctrine. In the letter to Landois of June 29, 1756, for example, he distinguishes between the way preachers speak about morality and the way philosophers do. The former talk about virtue and free will, while the latter talk about beneficence coming from physical temperament.[16] Victor Gourevitch has identified this as an example of the esoteric doctrine and points out that it is one of the modern philosophic doctrines Rousseau attacks in the *First Discourse*.[17]

Diderot would have been familiar with the doctrine through his study of the major English deists from the turn of the century, among whom the esoteric, or double, doctrine was a common (and fairly openly acknowledged) position.[18] For example, Toland, whose materialism influenced Diderot, wrote a work specifically on the subject, "Clidophorus: or Of the *Exoteric and Esoteric Philosophy*," and referred to it in other works. Among the English thinkers who discussed the systematic dissimulation of opinions, or "defensive raillery," was Shaftesbury, whose *Essay concerning Virtue and Merit* was translated by Diderot near the beginning of his friendship with Rousseau. In his "Discours préliminaire" to his translation, Diderot refers to the virtuous pagan philosophers whose professions of piety might be "either from the heart or only in appearance."[19] In the same context, he makes a similar profession himself, saying that the goal of the work is to demonstrate that there is no virtue without belief in God, which is very different from what Shaftesbury's work (and Diderot's translation) actually argues.

Diderot's expertise on the doctrine is shown most clearly through its numerous appearances in the *Encyclopédie*, a work that announced its own practice of yielding to "national prejudices" in conspicuous articles only to undermine them in more obscure articles referred to in cross-references. As it happens, Rousseau's first reference to the doctrine occurs only a few months after the publication of volume 1, and his second reference concerns the period shortly before the publication of volume 7 in 1757. The doctrine is referred to frequently in these volumes, the intervening ones, and, indeed, subsequent ones. In volume 1 explicit references occur in the articles "Ame," "Aristotelisme," and "Asiatiques" (the first two written by the abbé Yvon and the last by Diderot). Among the additional articles from the first seven volumes with explicit reference to the esoteric, double, or interior doctrine are the following: "Celtes," "Egyptiens," "Eléatiques," "Encyclopédie," and "Grecs," all but the first of which were written by Diderot and the other by the abbé Yvon. After the resumption of publication in 1765, the doctrine is mentioned in "Japonais," "Indiens," "Ioniques," "Juifs," "Platonisme," "Pythagorisme," "Samanéen," and "Xenxus."[20] As these lists show, avid readers of the *Encyclopédie* would be well acquainted with the idea that the doctrine had been held in many different places since early antiquity. Given this abundance of material, what should most surprise a reader of Rousseau's references to the doctrine is his claim not to know much about it.

Given the multiple authorship of the *Encyclopédie*, it is not surprising that there are variations in the treatment of the doctrine, even though the articles are largely drawn from Brucker's *Historia critica philosophiae* or from Warburton. The most extensive and, possibly, the most typical discussion is also the most thematic one. Formey's article "Exotérique and Esoterique" from volume 6 begins, "The ancient philosophers had a double doctrine; one external, public, or *exoteric*; the other internal, secret, or *esoteric*." Formey is at pains to deny that this doctrine could have arisen out of low motives such as "pettiness of mind." Following Warburton, he repeatedly claims that philosophers made use of this double doctrine only for the public good, although he concedes that it later might have degenerated. Furthermore, he finds it in Egypt, Persia, India, and ancient Gaul. He associates it with both Greek philosophic sects and with political and religious leaders.

Clearly, the *Encyclopédie* presents the doctrine as ubiquitous. Its accounts are mostly descriptive or rather positive. At best, they claim that dissimulation arose from the public-spiritedness of philosophers who wanted to support salutary beliefs or, at worst, that it was a necessity imposed by intolerance. Significantly, the only unambiguously negative discussion of the doctrine in the *Encyclopédie* occurs in the article "Celtes" by the abbé Yvon, where the object of the attack is its use by religious leaders rather than philosophers. In other articles the abbé praises the philosophic, as opposed to religious, use of the doctrine. There is an obvious tension in such treatment of the doctrine: praise of the doctrine gives publicity to something it admits should be kept private. For example, in the article "Aristotelisme" the abbé Yvon calls Aristotle indiscreet for acknowledging the existence of an interior doctrine—a doctrine that he discusses himself—and, even more, for openly and dogmatically rejecting the immortality of the soul. Yvon makes the same claim in virtually identical language in "Ame." In both cases he is simply paraphrasing Warburton.

Although he sometimes follows the view outlined by Formey, Diderot himself inclines toward publicity. One of his clearest statements occurs in "Grecs." Diderot says, "If a discovery is essential to the good of society, to deprive society of it is to be a bad citizen; if it is of pure curiosity, it is worth neither the trouble of making nor that of being hid. Useful or not, to keep it secret is to understand poorly the interest of one's reputation." Diderot chides the adherents of the esoteric doctrine for being insufficiently interested in fame. Moreover, he implicitly denies the possibility that the doctrines kept secret might be worse than useless to society. In the article "Encyclopédie," Diderot stresses the goal of complete clarity. He laments that this goal has not been met by past thinkers and will not be met in the

Encyclopédie because of such factors as intolerance and "the failing of the double doctrine." In "Aius-Locutius" he proposes that censors protect the public by censoring only works written in the vernacular and leave complete freedom to works written in scholarly languages. This would not do away with the esoteric doctrine, but it would allow it to come out-of-doors.

In sum, Diderot's position appears to be an example of what Paul Bagley has called conditional esotericism: out of a concern for safety, he concealed certain opinions but ultimately aimed at the abolition of the necessity for dissimulation.[21] The presuppositions of such an understanding are stated at the conclusion of the article "Pyrrhonienne ou Sceptique Philosophie," in remarks removed by the publisher because of their boldness. Diderot says, "A truth, whatever it may be, even if harmful for the present, will necessarily become useful in the future. A lie, whatever it may be, even if advantageous at present, will necessarily become harmful in time." This position justifies the conclusion that "when certain truths may not be stated openly, this can only be due to poor legislation."[22]

In short, discussions of the esoteric doctrine were abundantly available to Rousseau. What is distinctive in his treatment is his denial of both Diderot's presupposition (that the truth is necessarily useful for society in the long run) and his conclusion (that one should attempt to insinuate truths that shock conventional views). What makes the esoteric doctrine so objectionable to Rousseau?

II. Rousseau and the Esoteric Doctrine

Rousseau's earliest mention of the doctrine is also his most extensive discussion of it. It occurs in the *Observations by Jean-Jacques Rousseau of Geneva on the Reply Made to His Discourse*, the work discussed in chapter 1 in which he openly asserts his authorial identity. Objecting to Rousseau's claim in the *First Discourse* that philosophy undermines religion, Stanislaus had argued that "books of moral philosophy" were in fact powerful supports for Christianity (*Observations*, CW 2:43; Pl. 3:43). Rousseau responds by asserting, first, that philosophy was both alien and hostile to early Christianity; second, that subsequent Christians turned to it only out of self-defense, "to learn the doctrine against which one had to defend oneself" (*Observations*, CW 2:46; Pl. 3:47); and, finally, that this defensive introduction of philosophy into Christian apologetics eventually corrupted the original doctrine.

In a note to this attack on philosophy, Rousseau provides a catalog of "the pernicious maxims and impious dogmas of the various sects." This catalog covers theological issues such as the denial of providence, the existence of God, and the immortality of the soul, and moral issues such as defenses of theft and adultery or the debunking of friendship and patriotism. Rousseau concedes that the philosophic sects of antiquity did not all agree with one another about any of these dogmas; in fact, he insists that they disagreed not only on these but also on virtually all other substantive questions.[23] Beyond claiming that each fell into "some dangerous error," he identifies the one thing they did share as the esoteric doctrine. His long comment on the doctrine is worth quoting in full:

> And what shall we say about the distinction between the two doctrines so eagerly received by all the Philosophers, and by which they professed in secret sentiments contrary to those they taught publicly? Pythagoras was the first to make use of the esoteric doctrine. He did not reveal it to his disciples until after lengthy tests and with the greatest mystery. He gave them lessons in Atheism in secret and solemnly offered Hecatombs to Jupiter. The Philosophers were so comfortable with this method that it spread rapidly in Greece and from there in Rome, as may be seen in the works of Cicero, who along with his friends laughed at the immortal Gods to whom he so eloquently bore witness on the Rostrum. The esoteric doctrine was not carried from Europe to China, but it was born there too with Philosophy. And to it the Chinese owe the large number of Atheists or Philosophers they have among them. The History of this deadly doctrine, written by an informed and sincere man, would be a terrible blow to ancient and modern Philosophy. But Philosophy will always defy reason, truth, and even time, because it has its source in human pride, stronger than all those things. (*Observations*, CW 2:45–46; Pl. 3:46)

This passage has several noteworthy features. First, Rousseau identifies the esoteric doctrine as a distinctively philosophic doctrine. In fact, he presents it as the only distinctive philosophic doctrine: the only other characteristics shared by all philosophers are the possession of one or more of a variety of errors and disagreement with one another. Second, he insists that far from being a historically contingent fact connected with the dissemination of Greek philosophy, the doctrine arises wherever philosophy appears. Finally, he accounts for the persistence of the doctrine by the fact that philosophy has its origin in pride, as opposed to concern for reason or truth. How does philosophic pride lead to the concealment characteristic of the esoteric doctrine?

The esoteric doctrine can be seen as the logical consequence of its root in the following way. Their distinctive pride causes philosophers to seek to distinguish themselves from others. It makes them wish to flatter themselves for their exclusive possession of the truth and consequently to overestimate the extent to which they do possess it. They disdain the opinions of nonphilosophers and disagree with all other philosophers, in both cases without any particular regard for truth (*Narcissus*, CW 2:191; Pl. 2:966). These philosophers will buttress their self-esteem by cultivating a circle of initiates who endorse their doctrines, which must remain private both to avoid the consequences of outraging public opinion and to maintain exclusivity.

The particular vulnerability of philosophers to pride is a regular theme in Rousseau's works. In the *First Discourse* he places the origin of the study of both nature and of morality not in wonder (as Aristotle did) but in pride and similar vices (*First Discourse*, CW 2:12; Pl. 3:17). Rousseau ultimately argues that this philosophic pride gives birth to a certain misanthropy in the following way. He says that "by dint of reflecting on humanity, by dint of observing men, the philosopher learns to appreciate them according to their worth, and it is difficult to have very much affection for what one holds in contempt" (*Narcissus*, CW 2:192; Pl. 2:967). The judgment about others is not simply wrong. As Rousseau says, "The people show themselves such as they are, and they are not lovable" (*Emile* 225; Pl. 4:509). The problem lies in the contempt that accompanies this judgment. The philosopher's "contempt for others turns to the profit of his pride: his amour-propre increases in the same proportion as his indifference to the rest of the universe" (*Narcissus*, CW 2:192; Pl. 2:967). Finally, in the *Second Discourse* Rousseau attributes the lack of compassion in philosophers to their combination of amour-propre and reason (*Second Discourse*, CW 3:37; Pl. 3:156). In each of these cases, pride is the inseparable companion of philosophy.

In sum, pride causes philosophers to overestimate the power of their own reason and to press their inquiries beyond their ability. In doing so, they reach dogmatic conclusions that gratify their vanity even though these conclusions would fail to satisfy a genuinely impartial reason. This, in turn, causes them to congratulate themselves on their superiority to other humans and to seek confirmation of this superiority from a small group of followers. Philosophic pride thus causes both dogmatism and sectarianism. Both of these support the esoteric doctrine, which manifests itself in deception of the public for the purpose of furthering the private selfishness of philosophers.

Thus, what might seem to be merely a formal similarity among philosophers—their possession of unconventional secret doctrines that they share with a few trusted disciples—entails a more substantive agreement. Philosophers conceive their own interest not only independently, but in defiance of conventionally held standards of morality. They may vary in their precise understanding of what their own interest is, but they agree in defining it in distinction from the opinions of the majority of people. In practice, this leads to a policy of selfishness combined with a defensive masquerade of virtue.

This element of vice masquerading as virtue is stressed in Rousseau's second discussion of the esoteric doctrine. In the *Confessions* he discusses the moral principles of his former friend Grimm, saying that they can be reduced to a single article; "namely that the sole duty of man is to follow the inclinations of his heart in everything" (*Confessions*, CW 5:393; Pl. 1:468).[24] Rousseau goes on to identify this as "the esoteric doctrine about which Diderot talked to me so much, but which he never explained to me." Throughout the *Confessions* Grimm is shown manipulating public opinion to acquire a reputation as a man of unsurpassed sensitivity and honor. His concern with reputation ranges from conspicuously pretending to be seriously ill as a result of being rejected in love to spending hours each day in the application of cosmetics.[25] Grimm's principle implies that any concern expressed for morality would be merely exoteric, a part of his effort to present a respectable public image to put himself in a better position to satisfy his own inclinations. It could be said, then, that the esoteric doctrine is connected with a systematic and reflective effort to dupe public opinion for one's own advantage. Victor Gourevitch has aptly described it as "systematic hypocrisy reduced to principle."[26] Intellectuals like Grimm do in a rigorous way what high society people do less reflectively.

One might think that precisely the interior character of the doctrine would make it a relatively harmless, though distasteful phenomenon. While a Grimm might use it to further his ambition, philosophers tend to be less enterprising. In fact, the secret character of the doctrine itself would tend to make it vulnerable to extinction. In antiquity, even when versions of the doctrine were written down and circulated within a sect, these writings frequently became lost. As Rousseau says, "The impious writings of Leucippus and Diagoras died with them" (*First Discourse*, CW 2:20; Pl. 3:27). Rousseau, however, calls the esoteric doctrine "deadly." The problem is that over the long run, leaks are inevitable. Some sectarian followers of philosophy are bound to be indiscreet. Moreover, as Clifford Orwin has pointed out, the ancient sects engaged in a public relations campaign to elevate the status of philosophy.[27] This campaign had two unfortunate results. First, even when it employed a more respectable exoteric doctrine, it also attracted more and more adherents for the interior doctrine. Many of these yielded to the temptation to flaunt their unorthodoxy in relatively daring public displays.[28] A few prideful, unorthodox thinkers might be harmless, but their pride ultimately leads to swarms of adherents who necessarily have a pernicious effect on society. Second, as argued in chapter 3, even fairly innocuous philosophic discourse can damage the persuasive character of political speech.

Rousseau's last two discussions of the esoteric doctrine are concerned with precisely this consequence, which, he argues, has become much more dangerous in modernity. One of these discussions occurs in the *Dialogues* and the other in the *Reveries*. With their focus on writing and publication, they add a new element to Rousseau's description. The passage from the *Reveries* applies what Rousseau had earlier said about the doctrine in the *Observations* and *Confessions* to contemporary writers. He divides the morality of his opponents into a "rootless and fruitless morality which they pompously display in books or in some striking scene on the stage without any of it ever penetrating the heart or the reason" and "this other secret and cruel morality, the esoteric doctrine of all their initiates, for which the other only serves as a mask, which is the only one they follow in their conduct. This purely offensive morality is of no use for defense and is good only for aggression" (*Reveries*, CW 8:26; Pl. 1:1022). The reference to hypocritically moralistic plays written by philosophers is certainly directed against Diderot and possibly Voltaire. Rousseau deprives those who follow the esoteric doctrine of the justifications of public-spiritedness and self-defense. The morality expounded in their exterior doctrine is empty in spite of its high-sounding rhetoric, and the morality taught in private is used only for the aggressive pursuit of selfish goals.

The passage in the *Dialogues* suggests an even more aggressive distinctively modern version of esotericism. Rousseau insists that bold statements occasionally found in his own books are much less dangerous than the superficially innocuous contents of other contemporary books. He says, "Our philosophers have what they call their esoteric doctrine, but they teach it to the public only while concealing themselves, and to their friends only in secret. By always taking everything literally, one would perhaps actually find less to reproach in more dangerous books than in those we are talking about here" (*Dialogues*, CW 1:28; Pl. 1:695; translation altered). This discussion repeats the charge of duplicity against the adherents of the esoteric doctrine, but it also adds something curious. While Rousseau's other discussions claim that the esoteric doctrine (here said to be taught in secret to friends) is accompanied by an exterior doctrine that pompously (but uselessly) proclaims its adherence to conventional morality, this one asserts that the public is also taught the *interior* doctrine in books in which it is hard to find anything to reproach. How can a pernicious morality be taught in books in which it is hard to find anything offensive? Also, how can a doctrine that is taught to the public be considered an esoteric doctrine?

Rousseau seems to claim that the adherents of the esoteric doctrine write two sorts of books, one that they publish using their own names and another that they publish anonymously. In the first sort, they do not directly present any shocking doctrines; rather, they pay an empty lip service to conventional teachings. In the second, they appear to do the same thing, but in fact undermine the positions they praise by giving feeble defenses for them (what John Toland called "the bounceing [sic] compliment") or alternatively by what David Hume called the "secret insinuation" of unorthodox opinions).[29] This suggestion is confirmed by what Rousseau says later in the *Dialogues*, referring sarcastically to the "brilliant Authors of this Century" who preach "the love of virtues and the hatred of vice," but who also teach "that there is neither vice nor virtue in the heart of man, since there is neither freedom in his will nor morality in his actions" (*Dialogues*, CW 1:140; Pl. 1:841–42). Once again, Diderot is the foremost of these authors.

The attempt to insinuate into the public doctrines normally reserved for the initiated represents an innovation in the esoteric doctrine. This form of modern esotericism is very different in its consequences from the practice Rousseau describes in his earlier discussions. In the ancient version, the adherents had only a relatively unintentional effect on society as a whole. In the new version, they aim at its radical transformation and are aided by the invention of the printing press.[30] The usual name for this phenomenon is enlightenment, not esotericism, but Rousseau suggests that rather than enlightening, the new adherents of the doctrine are inculcating a new prejudice. They are more interested in imposing their own reason on the public than in making the public reasonable; they are guided by a "proselytizing fury" (*d'Alembert* 11; Pl. 5:11). Their pride aims not merely at distinguishing their own opinions from those of the vulgar, but also ruling the vulgar. Thus, in its modern form, the esoteric doctrine characterizes a group of intellectuals who are attempting to satisfy their own vanity by making themselves into a privileged elite (or insiders) who control public opinion (*Dialogues*, CW 1:178, 238; Pl. 1:889, 967). Rousseau develops this picture of modern intellectuals in great detail at the end of the *Dialogues*. There he attributes to them the complex strategy of teaching doctrines most likely to gain supporters while simultaneously working secretly to undermine traditional morality. Their goal is to make themselves into absolute authorities by being the "supreme interpreters" of what is natural (*Dialogues*, CW 1:238–39; Pl. 1:967).

From the four passages in which he discusses the esoteric doctrine, one can deduce a coherent account of Rousseau's view of it. First, he presents it as the distinctive characteristic of philosophers and other intellectuals deriving from their pride. It bears many resemblances to the hypocrisy pervading modern societies but differs from this hypocrisy by being a reflective doctrine. Second, rather than being a defense of salutary public opinions or an educational device introducing students to the truth after lengthy preparation (both of which are forms of deception endorsed by Rousseau), the esoteric doctrine is essentially a manifestation of the prideful desire for distinction. Finally, in antiquity it was essentially a defensive doctrine, but in modernity it has gone on the offensive: it is part of a covert attempt to control public opinion.

It might seem strange that Rousseau would attack the esoteric doctrine so vehemently when he, himself, argues that philosophic argumentation should be kept out of the public arena. Nevertheless, his own insistence on the essentially, not merely prudentially, private character of philosophy is very different from the position he attacks. In the final analysis, Rousseau objects to the esoteric doctrine as held by his predecessors and contemporaries because of its source in pride and the goal it serves of manipulating public opinion for selfish purposes. He especially rejects the provisional esotericism defended by Diderot. Its selfish, prideful origin makes it seek public effects. Strangely enough then, Rousseau's view of the esoteric doctrine is that in its traditional form, the doctrine has not been interior enough.

Different sources and different goals, it would seem, could justify a different sort of private, or esoteric, philosophic doctrine. In practice it might be difficult to distinguish between the illegitimate and a more legitimate version, just as it is difficult to distinguish between self-serving lies and more justifiable ones. The practical difficulty of distinguishing between the two does not imply that the distinction between the two sorts of separation of private doctrine and public profession is meaningless.

Rousseau's defense of his own literary practices implies that he regards himself as exempt from the vices that characterize other writers. His account of the esoteric doctrine, its origin in pride, and its pernicious consequences raises the question of whether there might be a cure for these consequences by means of a cure for its source, philosophic pride. Such a cure would free philosophers from both their contempt for nonphilosophers and their dogmatism. Usually Rousseau is unwilling to stimulate the hope for a purged philosophy because of his views of the deep-rootedness of the problem.[31] Nevertheless, on one occasion he explored this possibility in the form of an allegorical story that he chose not to publish, but that he did entrust to his literary executor.[32]

III. Rousseau's Philosophic Dream

In his so-called "Fiction, ou Morceau allégorique sur la révélation," a work that has drawn very little attention from scholars in the English-speaking world, Rousseau describes a philosopher who has been cured of his pride and gives an account of how he might act toward the public.[33] Much of the importance of this work stems from the fact that it treats a range of topics of persisting importance for Rousseau. In it, he directly addresses the nature of philosophy, gives his judgment of Jesus and Socrates, and—significantly for our purpose—presents his view of the obstacles faced by philosophers who wish to have an influence on the public. There is, however, some dispute over how these topics fit together in the "Fiction," or what its major focus is. The title given to it by its first editor, "Fiction, or Allegorical Fragment on Revelation," designates both a subject and a literary form, as well as the incompleteness of the work. This title also indicates the editor's judgment about the central topic of the "Fiction," namely, religious revelation. This judgment was accepted and amplified upon in the first treatments of the work. In one of the first reviews, Sainte-Beuve says that it "shows us Rousseau in all the fervor of his religious enthusiasm" and that it demonstrates that Rousseau should be included among those people who are "Christians by instinct, feeling and desire."[34] Fifty years later Saint-Beuve's evaluation, which had been shared by numerous contemporary critics, was called into question by Pierre-Maurice Masson, who argued that the work's early interpreters had been led astray by the misleading title and by faulty assumptions about the completeness of the work.[35] Masson argues that the "Fiction" is characterized primarily by its opposition to any sort of philosophic or religious dogmatism. Most importantly, he very reasonably insists that a proper judgment of this work and its significance must depend on evaluation of its contents, rather than on presuppositions about Rousseau's thought on any subject. The argument here is an elaboration of Masson's suggestions.

A. The First Philosopher

From the beginning of the "Fiction," the focus is on philosophy, not revelation. It recounts the story of "the first man who attempted to philosophize" ("Fiction," Pl. 4:1044). There is some ambiguity as to whether Rousseau is concerned here with a historical question concerning the origins of philosophy or with issues that perennially concern anyone who attempts to philosophize. He does not identify this first philosopher, although at one point in the manuscript he originally identifies him as Pythagoras only to cross out this identification. He usually refers to him only as "the Philosopher."

Prior to any confrontation with public opinion, Rousseau's first philosopher retreats from the bustle of the city to the countryside and solitude for his meditations. This sort of retreat differs markedly from the activity of thinkers like Diderot or Socrates who thrive in the city. In his rural retreat, the philosopher is surrounded by objects that give him a pleasant sense of the orderliness of nature. His curiosity about this order is stirred particularly by the sight of the complex motions of the heavens. Rather than being comforted, however, he is troubled about the source of this order. His perplexity centers on two general issues. The first of these concerns the source of the order of the physical universe, and the second concerns his own ability to perceive this order or to construct it in his thought. His meditations dwell on the first of these issues.

The philosopher is unsure about whether physical order is the result of a purely "fortuitous arrangement" or the consequence of some ordering principle ("Fiction," Pl. 4:1046). In effect, he is torn between materialist explanations of the world and teleological accounts. He spends much more time considering the first option than the second. In particular, he ponders the difficulties facing materialists: the apparent spontaneity of motion in animals, the nature of sensation, and his own experience of thinking and free will. Although he sees no satisfactory materialist account of these issues, he concedes that such an account is not outside the realm of possibility.[36] He professes stronger reservations concerning what he regards as the indispensable assumption of materialism, that is, the claim that motion is intrinsic to matter and that this motion can ceaselessly generate new combinations. The philosopher's most profound meditations are unable either to resolve or to solidify his reservations, and the spectacle of the order of nature becomes only a source of uneasiness for him.

The fact that Rousseau's philosopher refers to the Epicurean doctrine of the "swerve," which is needed to make moving atoms collide, shows that he is considering a very old issue. Rousseau was well aware that the relation between the orderliness of the heavens and natural teleology had a long history. In one of the fragments to *Emile*, he cites Aristotle as arguing against the materialist position on the key issue of whether matter can be conceived of as having motion intrinsic to it (Pl. 4:876). In short, Rousseau regards this issue as coeval with philosophy and as unsolvable, or at least unsolved.

The rest of the formulation Rousseau gives to the philosopher's perplexity is very reminiscent of the discussion of the same issue in Diderot's *Pensées philosophiques* (published in 1746)[37] and also his philosophical allegory, *La Promenade du sceptique* (written the next year).[38] Diderot uses the newly fashionable study of probability to argue that the orderliness of the universe does not refute atheism. In fact, he claims that atheism is favored by this orderliness because in the infinity of time an orderly universe must necessarily arise out of randomness. While the first philosopher concedes the force of Diderot's argument, he also insists that it falls far short of a demonstration, given that it assumes without proving that motion is intrinsic to matter and, therefore, that God is unnecessary to begin motion.

The fact that the first philosopher spends so much time thinking about the objections to the materialist doctrine (and particularly about the indecisive character of these objections) and none thinking about the objections to the alternative is striking. It is as if the materialist view is attractive to his reason but repugnant to his heart. His admission of uncertainty leads him to the brink of abandoning his reasoning about these unsolvable questions. He sees that rather than being a reasonable pursuit of knowledge, further investigation will only be in the service of his sense of pride. Unlike the philosophers Rousseau criticizes, his first philosopher gives up his prideful desire to settle every question.

It is only when he has recognized and overcome the temptation of philosophic pride—his conviction that his reason alone can settle the issues he has been debating—that the first philosopher has the experience that led the original editor to call this the "Fragment on Revelation": "All at once a ray of light happened to strike his mind and to unveil to him those sublime truths which it does not belong to man to know by himself and which human reason serves to confirm without serving to discover them. A new universe offered itself so to speak to his contemplation" ("Fiction," Pl. 4:1047). As a result of this new insight, or revelation, the first philosopher is able to conceive of the world as the work of a divine being. He now can see the "invisible chain that links all beings," a doctrine closely associated with optimism as formulated by Leibniz and Pope. Optimism is only one of the possible alternatives to materialism, and the version presented in the "Fiction" has a strong theological cast. Rousseau was well aware of other alternatives. For example, in the citation of Aristotle's opposition to the supposition of eternal motion referred to above, Rousseau says that this philosopher rejected the materialist view, even though he "did not appear to have thought too well of the Divinity" (Pl. 4:876).

In effect, the first philosopher turns away from materialism and toward optimism. He does so, however, not as a turn from a faulty philosophic doctrine to another that is demonstrably true. The rather tentative, or imprecise, character of the "revelation" given to the first philosopher is indicated by the way it is described in the "Fiction" itself. Although it is said that the "sublime truths" seen by the philosopher are compatible with human reason, he makes no attempt to provide a completely rational account of his new understanding. There are still "perplexing sophisms" that he is unable to resolve. The basis of his commitment to his new view is not its revealed character; rather, he relies on his "interior sentiment" to decide between two alternative rational, but imperfectly proven, accounts of the world, one of which is consoling and the other of which is not. His conclusion is not what reason would decide by itself; it could be called an article of faith of natural religion.[39]

The philosopher's excursion into philosophic meditation has taught him the futility of attempting to resolve his remaining doubts. His reason has become aware of its own limits, and his philosophic pride is replaced by a humility that leaves him open to consolation. The effect of this change of feeling in the philosopher is that he is inspired by a new philanthropy, the opposite of the misanthropy all too typical of philosophers. While, to begin with, he is seen only outside of society and there is no indication that he philosophizes for any reason other than to satisfy his own curiosity, under the influence of his new enthusiasm, he suddenly acquires a desire to share his consoling discovery. He believes that what he has discovered can be put into the service of virtue. Philosophy becomes philanthropic only after it becomes aware of its own limits.

The opposition between the old philosophic pride and the new philosophic philanthropy can be understood in the following way. It was argued above that Rousseau claims that pride is both the root and the product of philosophy. Their pride makes philosophers look for the wickedness and misery of humanity, and when (as is all too easy to do) they find these things, their pride is inflated. Because of this relation between pride and observation, it is impossible to say that these philosophers are the best observers of human nature. As Rousseau says in *Emile*, "It is not philosophers who know men best. They see them only through the prejudices of philosophy" (*Emile* 243; Pl. 4:535). Observers not motivated by pride in the first place will not draw a conclusion that increases pride. The observation of human wickedness and misery, unaccompanied by prideful prejudice, can lead, for example, to a doctrine of natural goodness corrupted by society, such as the one Rousseau himself teaches. Rousseau (and his student Emile) draws the conclusion that men are pitiable rather than contemptible. Thus, philosophy purged of pride leads to philanthropy.

B. The Fate of the Wise

The first philosopher now longs to share his discovery with the world, but his meditations have lasted into the night, and while waiting for the dawn, he falls into a deep sleep and begins to dream. In his dream the philosopher finds himself in an immense temple, with a dome supported by seven statues, each of which has the shape of one of the seven deadly sins.[40] These statues accurately portray the hideousness of the vices they represent; but—by a trick of perspective—they appear beautiful when seen from inside the temple. In the center of the temple is an altar upon which there is an eighth statue that is veiled. This statue is worshiped in a variety of ways by its devotees, each of whom imagines it in terms of his own dominant passion. Sadistic perversity reigns everywhere. The forms of worship either prohibit natural acts or require an unnatural cruelty.

The ministers of the temple, marked by "a modest and contemplative air" that thinly conceals their "pride and cruelty," make sure that those entering the temple are blindfolded until they reach the point of perspective at which the seven statues will take on their deceptively beautiful appearance ("Fiction," Pl. 4:1048). Unlike the people who commit atrocious acts because they are under the spell of illusion, the ministers are well aware of the deformity of their idols but serve them out of self-interest. They profit from the fanaticism they help to inculcate.

In the "Fiction" the prephilosophic world is one of fanaticism and prejudice. It is characterized by the same qualities Rousseau elsewhere identifies as the distinctive marks of corrupt religion: "iniquity, falsehood, hypocrisy, and tyranny" ("Franquières," CW 8:266; Pl. 4:1142). In such an atmosphere, the philosophic gesture of stripping away the veil, of undermining respect for irrationally held opinions, cannot appear in the sinister light it usually takes on in Rousseau's treatments of philosophy. In this instance, up to a point, Rousseau makes common cause with his erstwhile friends who were committed to enlightenment. In the philanthropic first philosopher's dream, the issue is less justifying philosophy than it is the tactical question of how philosophy can combat religious prejudices.

One of the striking features of the "Fiction" is that prior to his dream, the philosopher is quite unaware of the precise nature and extent of the prejudices from which his fellows must be liberated. To be sure, he knows that they are in need of enlightenment, and he hopes to make them happy and virtuous by filling this need. Nevertheless, his own enlightenment took place entirely outside of a social context, and he, himself, was liberated from doubt rather than from prejudice. Rousseau seems to understand meditation and reasoning as a source of and cure for the former, but not the latter. In this first part of the dream, the philosopher learns that the public is in even greater need of his discovery than he had thought: his discovery is an alternative to the fanaticism he observes here as well as being an alternative to materialism. In fact, one could say that the most significant revelation experienced by the philosopher comes not from his sudden illumination about the order of the universe, but from what he learns from the dream about the obstacles that fanaticism opposes to the spread of the truth.

The theme of public enlightenment in Rousseau's image is introduced by a mysterious voice that says to the philosopher, "You have just contemplated the blindness of peoples, it remains for you to see what the destiny of the wise is in this place" (Pl. 4:1051). The Pléiade editors suggest that the invisible source of this voice may be connected with the illumination the philosopher has already experienced.[41] It should be considered, however, that the illumination took place before the dream and was not accompanied by any voices. The uncertain source of the voice (and Rousseau's several hesitations in the manuscript about how to characterize it) betrays the unfinished character of the "Fiction." The function of the voice in the work as we have it is to introduce the theme of the remainder of the dream.

The destiny of the wise is revealed by three characters who successively enter the temple, each of whom confronts the corrupt religion with a different tactic. Rousseau offers no account of how each of them acquires his wisdom; each has it already upon his arrival at the temple. Like the first philosopher, none of them appears to learn the truth from his encounter with the false opinions of society. Significantly, Rousseau gives no hint of any disagreement among the three concerning the truth about nature. They either agree, or their disagreements are unimportant. What is important is their shared philanthropy.

Two of the three wise men are easy to identify. The details of the second intruder's experiences clearly correspond to the death of Socrates as portrayed in Plato's *Crito* and *Phaedo*, and the third is identified as the "son of man," a clear reference to Jesus.[42] It has proven to be more difficult to attach a name to the first wise man. His only clearly distinguishing mark is that he is dressed like the first philosopher. Since it is in this part of the "Fiction" that Rousseau originally identified the first philosopher as Pythagoras, some scholars have identified the first wise man as a Greek, specifically Xenophanes.[43] Others assume that the intruder is dressed like Rousseau himself and accordingly identify him as a contemporary, for example, Diderot.[44] I would suggest that this man whose face is not visible is the first philosopher himself as he would be if he awoke at this point and tried to communicate his newfound wisdom.[45]

This first wise man's behavior is already marked by a degree of caution because he has seen the deceptive character of the temple and the power of its clergy. Instead, "discreetly touching the blindfold of those who were led [to the altar] he returned the use of sight to them without causing any apparent displacement" ("Fiction," Pl. 4:1051). His strategy, then, is gradual and discreet enlightenment rather than a direct public challenge of religious authority. This strategy certainly can be compared in some ways with that of the *Encyclopédie*, the "Preliminary Discourse" of which does, indeed, contain an important reference to "removing the blindfolds from the eyes of their contemporaries."[46] Masson supports the link to Diderot with a reference to the *La Promenade du sceptique*, in which Diderot uses an image of an army in blindfolds to portray Christians and discusses the possibility of removing the blindfolds. Against Masson, it should be pointed out that in the *Promenade* and elsewhere, Diderot shows himself to be very conscious of the fate in store for anyone who attempts to remove the blindfolds of prejudice. Consequently, it seems likely that both Diderot and Rousseau share the same reservations about the approach taken by the first wise man. In any event, it is certain that this wise man represents a general strategy as much as any particular individual. This strategy would be the one that would immediately occur to someone in the position of the philosopher.

The object of the enlightenment given by this wise man is the exposure of the hideous character of the seven statues and of the atrocities incited by the clergy. He pays no attention to the central statue and teaches nothing about the truth concerning nature or divinity. The enlightenment he offers is largely negative in character. It is successful in that those whose blindfolds have been displaced refuse to worship the statues, but their lack of discretion in attempting to convince others to behave the same way is the cause of this strategy's failure. The ministers trace this sedition to its source and "immolate" the wise man on the spot to great popular acclaim.

This first strategy of enlightenment fails for two main reasons. First, its gradual nature leaves it vulnerable to persecution by the ever-vigilant ministers, who will destroy any threat to their power before it becomes strong enough to challenge them effectively. Second, because it depends on avoiding detection, this strategy places too heavy a weight on the newly enlightened. The wise man's own behavior is quite discreet, but those who have been enlightened by him, that is, those who have not been wise enough to enlighten themselves, are incapable of the discretion necessary for the success of this conspiracy. With this example Rousseau seems to be issuing a warning against a struggle for allegiance against the forces of prejudice.

The second intruder, or Socrates, avoids these causes of failure through a combination of greater caution and greater boldness. His caution consists in an apparent devotion to the cult of the temple: he avoids the blindfold by claiming to be a blind man in search of a cure from the divinity. In other words, he dissimulates about his own enlightenment: he claims to know less than he does. In fact, his claim to blindness is quite analogous to the Socratic claim of ignorance. It is the ironic claim to know nothing, but to be free of the illusory claims to knowledge characteristic of the populace.

This deception allows the second intruder to draw near enough to the altar so that he can leap onto it and strip the veil off the central statue. Rather than contenting himself with exposing the vices of the clergy to a few, with one stroke this wise man gets to the heart of the matter by exposing the very nature of fanaticism to the many. The central statue is now revealed to be a combined image of ecstasy and rage. Its eyes gaze tenderly toward heaven, but it stifles humanity underfoot and holds an inflamed heart in one hand and a dagger in the other. This image, which the worshipers had previously fashioned after their own passions, is now revealed to be one of fanatical intolerance, both passionate and dangerous. To complete his action, the wise man gives a speech indicating the self-destructive character of this form of religious devotion. This revelation of the destructive character of the religion of the temple does not have its desired effect. The spectators are incapable of seeing the statue for what it is even after its veil has been stripped off. What the philosopher sees as cruelty, the crowd sees as "celestial enthusiasm" ("Fiction," Pl. 4:1052). Accordingly, the wise man is seized, tried, and put to death in the manner of Socrates' execution.

The first philosopher finds something unfathomable in the behavior of this second wise man after he is sentenced to death. In an apparent allusion to Socrates' final words, "Crito, we owe a cock to Asclepius," Rousseau observes that "the last speech of the old man who made a very distinct homage to that very statue which he had unveiled cast into the Philosopher's mind a doubt and a perplexity from which he was never able to extricate himself very well" ("Fiction," Pl. 4:1053). How can it happen that the man who willingly goes to his death for opposing fanaticism, as Rousseau's Socrates does, openly professes a devotion to one of the objects of the cult he opposed?[47] The philosopher imagines two possibilities. First, the statement could be understood allegorically rather than literally: for example, by saying that he owes a sacrifice to the god of healing, Socrates may be indicating that he regards life as a sickness from which he is about to be released and that he indicates no particular devotion by his remark. Second, Socrates may merely be making an act of submission to the laws that command a particular mode of worship: "For if all manners of serving the divinity are indifferent to it, it is obedience to the laws that must be preserved." The first alternative is uncertain and depends on an unverifiable interpretation. The second leaves an apparent contradiction between this public submission and Socrates' earlier defiance of the publicly ordained worship of the temple. The story of Socrates here seems to show the intractability of the problem of combining the enlightenment gesture of stripping away the veil with a proper submission to public authority.[48]

The second interpretation that the philosopher finds for Socrates' final words, in fact, makes Socrates into an adherent of something like Rousseau's own position. As argued in chapter 2, Rousseau strictly insists on dividing religion into three elements: external worship, dogmas that serve as the basis of morality, and purely speculative dogmas having no connection to morality. He insists that the last of these is merely a matter of individual belief. The other two are within the legitimate scope of legal regulation. Thus, the paradox in the second wise man's behavior could be resolved if he, like Rousseau, made these distinctions. This would allow him to oppose fanaticism—which attempts to force not only actions, but belief in purely speculative dogmas—on civic grounds while continuing to observe the religious practices of the community that are not inextricably bound to fanaticism.

The similarity between Rousseau's own position and the philosopher's second interpretation of the Socrates of the dream suggests either that Rousseau shares the contradiction that he finds in Socrates or that he has reservations about Socrates' action in stripping off the veil. The difficulty is this: it appears possible to maintain the distinction between the essentials of religious belief and the inessential public religious worship only when the latter does not require the immoral actions found in the temple. When the public religion does make such demands, in other words, when it uses speculative dogma to justify immoral actions, some sort of opposition to that religion seems necessary.

In the end the problem is less with Rousseau's Socrates' bold opposition to some aspects of religious fanaticism than with his failure to oppose it successfully. The failure of the Socratic strategy of unveiling was its underestimation of the people's attachment to their passions, its belief that the mere exposure of worship as fanaticism would cure that fanaticism. As Rousseau says elsewhere, "The Philosopher can give the Universe some salutary instructions, but his lessons will never correct either the nobles who scorn them or the People which does not hear them at all. Men are not governed in that way by abstract views" (*Hero*, CW 4:2; Pl. 2:1263). The characterization in the "Fiction" of Socrates, the proponent of the noble lie, as the champion of public enlightenment who fails because he overestimated the capacity of the many to understand the truth can strike one as odd. In fact, in the *First Discourse* Rousseau presents Socrates as his own predecessor in arguing against the public dissemination of learning (*First Discourse*, CW 2:9–10; Pl. 3:13). Nevertheless, the fact that Socrates was put to death for his philosophizing is evidence that can be cited to show that his behavior was excessively bold and involved a miscalculation. Be this as it may, the failure of this approach to overcome fanaticism leaves the question of whether there is an alternative to the sort of enlightenment symbolized by the Socratic gesture of stripping off the veil.

The third intruder in the dream, the "son of man," presents such an alternative. The first wise man offered an exposure of the effects of fanaticism; the second revealed the nature of fanaticism itself. The third wise man offers something to the passions that fuel fanaticism to supplement the purely negative criticism given by his two predecessors. He seizes the statue, throws it to the ground, and takes its place on the pedestal: he offers the populace not philosophy, but a new object of worship in his example. He teaches not with rational demonstrations, but with fables and parables that have an inspiring effect on even the least intelligent of his audience. His effect is precisely to transform the passions and feelings that supported fanaticism. It can be said that, like Julie, the legislator, heroes in general, and other figures in Rousseau's works, he gives his audience new souls, or changes them into different people.[49]

It is important to note, as most commentators do, that there is nothing supernatural about the "son of man" aside from a mysterious voice that announces his appearance. He performs no miracles, and Rousseau does not make even a hint of a reference to the resurrection. Like Rousseau's legislator, it is his great, but thoroughly human soul that is the strongest source of the conviction he inspires. Furthermore, he does not appear to redeem men from their sins. Rather, he says, "I come to atone for and cure your errors" ("Fiction," Pl. 4:1053).[50] His mission is no different from the one undertaken by the two other wise men. The only difference is the means he employs, and even these means are not supernatural. In short, the Jesus of the dream is a particular sort of wise man, and his superiority to his predecessors in the dream is based on the superiority of his tactics rather than his divinity. The "son of man" is also described as having less affectation than the second wise man. In other words, he is even more thoroughly cured of philosophic pride.

The tactics used by the "son of man" are less a rejection than the completion of the strategy used by the second wise man. It would have been quite possible for him to overturn the central statue even if it had not been unveiled, but his replacement of this statue with himself is aided by the fact that he can be compared with the unveiled image of fanatical intolerance. In short, the "philosophic" strategy of the second wise man was not useless, but it needed completion by the "religious" strategy of the third wise man. These two tactics complement each other in a way that neither of them complements the strategy of the first wise man, which makes no contribution to the other two. It is very striking that none of the strategies involves saying anything to the people about the issues that had perplexed the first philosopher before his dream or about his resolution of these issues.

At the point that the "Fiction" breaks off, the "son of man" is in triumph. His "revolution" has completely won over the people, although they waver temporarily when he refuses to destroy his enemies. Although the "Fiction" does not provide an ultimate judgment about the "son of man," nothing in it is incompatible with what Rousseau says elsewhere. In other places he presents Jesus as a failed political legislator and as the founder of a transpolitical revolution in the universe ("Letter to Franquières," CW 8:269; Pl. 4:1146). He presents his new revolution negatively as one of the leading causes of the impossibility of sound politics in the modern world (see *Social Contract*, CW 4:216–24; Pl. 3:460–69) and positively as one of the few remaining barriers to the harshest despotism ever seen, a despotism founded on the dogmatic antireligious spirit of modern philosophy.

The "Fiction" leaves its readers with a very strong impression of Rousseau's view of the superiority of Jesus to the alternatives presented in this work. Perhaps this impression should be tempered a bit by the acknowledgment that the fragment breaks off with no reference to Jesus' death, which would match the violence of the death of the first intruder in the temple.[51] Furthermore, we do not know how the dream would have concluded or how the first philosopher might behave when he wakes up. Does he worship Jesus or imitate him? Does he seek and perhaps find an even better strategy for enlightening the public, or does he abandon such hopes to return to his private reveries? Each of these alternatives can be found in Rousseau's works or in interpretations given to these works.

IV. The Language of the Wise

The "Fiction" is about philosophy in that it is a story about the wise in their effort to teach the people. It is not directly a story about philosophers in communication with other philosophers. As we have seen, none of the three wise men in the temple has anything to say to the people about the issues connected with the revelation that occurs to the first philosopher prior to his dream. Certainly none of them has anything to say about the contending views that preceded this revelation. The story itself, however, does not seem to be intended for a popular audience. It does not urge such an audience to be more receptive to the lessons of the wise; rather, it urges the wise, first, to abandon philosophic pride and, second, to learn how to speak to a popular audience. Thus, it seems plausible to suggest that in this work, Rousseau is writing directly to a philosophic audience about its relations with nonphilosophers.

It might seem strange to suggest that Rousseau would address a philosophic audience through allegory rather than through argument. Even within the "Fiction," the use of such language is characteristic of the "son of man," who speaks to the people through fables. We have also seen that legislators use this sort of language when speaking to people. Nevertheless, Rousseau does not simply identify figurative speech with a popular audience and rational argumentation with a philosophic audience. We have already seen that rational argument has its place in addressing the people in debate about laws and policies. When recommending "persuasion" to legislators, Rousseau does indicate that the wise have "their own language" (*Social Contract*, CW 4:156; Pl. 3:285), but he does not explain what this language is like.

In his "Preface to a Second Letter to Bordes" (which he chose not to complete or to publish), Rousseau explains his own method of developing his ideas "for few Readers" in the *First Discourse* and responses to critics ("Bordes," CW 2:184; Pl. 3:106). With regard to these works, he says, "I have often taken great pains to try to put into a Sentence, a line, a word tossed off as if by chance the result of a long sequence of reflections. Often, most of my Readers must have found my discourses badly connected and almost entirely rambling, for lack of perceiving the trunk of which I showed them only the branches. But that was enough for those who know how to understand, and I have never wanted to speak to the others" ("Bordes," CW 2:184–85; Pl. 3:106). In the *Letter to d'Alembert*, one of the works in which Rousseau says he spoke "not to the few but to the public" (*d'Alembert* 6; Pl. 5:6), he gives—as if by accident—a glimpse of the language he would adopt when speaking to a philosopher without the public as an audience.

Numerous times in the work, Rousseau alludes to the fact that he is simultaneously addressing d'Alembert and the public, with the latter as his primary audience. It is as if he has inverted the *Second Discourse* and is addressing the human race with a philosopher as his audience. For example, he refers to an issue "which it would be superfluous to resolve for you and which it is not here the place to resolve for the multitude" (*d'Alembert* 67; Pl. 5:62). Later Rousseau pretends to have a series of lapses in which he first confuses d'Alembert with the multitude and then confuses the multitude with d'Alembert. This takes place in the discussion of the private men's clubs of Geneva, known as circles, places where frank and private conversation can take place. Rousseau begins a sentence, "If you ask me next what is so bad about abolishing the *circles*," but then breaks off and exclaims, "No Sir, that question will not come from a philosopher." After this apology, he explains, "I must nevertheless answer; for this once, although I address myself to you, I write for the people." Then, ostensibly addressing the people, he begins his answer, "I say, in the first place, that, if the odor of tobacco is a bad thing, it is a very good one to remain master of one's property and to be sure of sleeping at home." Once again he interrupts himself, this time to say, "But I am already forgetting that I do not write for d'Alemberts. I must express myself in another way" (*d'Alembert* 100; Pl. 5:91). Having put the result of a long sequence of reflections into a sentence tossed off as if by chance, he then explains the sequence in twenty-two paragraphs complete with numerous footnotes.

The difference between Rousseau's statement to d'Alembert and his explanation for a popular audience is not only in the compactness of the former. Rousseau also addresses d'Alembert with a series of images rather than a rigorous argument: he invites him to weigh the bad odor of tobacco in the men's clubs against security of household and marriage. In the *Confessions* he gives an example of a similar mode of communication when discussing his friend Marshal George Keith, whom he identifies as "a wise man." In this context he tells the story of Keith recommending a young man to the service of Frederick the Great simply by having him deliver a small bag of peas to the king. Rousseau comments, "These elevated geniuses have a language between them that vulgar minds will never understand" (*Confessions*, CW 5:500; Pl. 1:598). Thus, it would appear that the language of the wise consists in symbolic speech in which complex thoughts are expressed with extraordinary compression. It resembles the persuasive language used by legislators (described in chapter 3) in that it is expressed in concrete images; it differs in that it is meant to convince rather than persuade.[52]

Rousseau's "Fiction" is a lesson for philosophers without exactly being an inducement to philosophy. It teaches about the dangers of philosophic pride and the proper practice of philanthropy. In doing so, it points to, without settling, a variety of perennial issues for philosophers about the nature of the world and the mind's ability to grasp this nature. In the final analysis, Rousseau's philosophic "Fiction" practices what it preaches about the undesirability of letting these issues intrude on the public arena. Like the third wise man, Rousseau teaches through apologues and fables. He presents the need for the use of allegories in the form of an allegory.

V. Rousseau and the First Philosopher

So many of the details of the "Fiction" correspond to Rousseau's self-presentation that it is hard not to identify the philosopher in question as Rousseau himself, in spite of his usual unwillingness to call himself a philosopher. In particular, Rousseau's description of this philosopher's meditations and dilemmas closely resembles his discussion in the second half of book 8 and first half of book 9 of the *Confessions* of his own position around the time he wrote his *First* and *Second Discourses*. Later Rousseau returned many times to Diderot's argument that the order of the world could be understood as the product of chance. His one reservation is precisely the one raised by the first philosopher: the difficulty of assuming that motion is intrinsic to matter ("Letter to Voltaire," CW 3:117–18; Pl. 4:1071; see also "Franquières," CW 8:264; Pl. 4:1139). In sum, while Rousseau is presenting the origins of nonprideful philosophy in general, he is very much concerned with his own experience of philosophy.

The philosopher's initial isolation from the hubbub of public opinion is a typical Rousseauian device. He very commonly insists on the need for some more or less total rupture from the way of life represented by cities, even though he is well aware of how easy it is to "transport the life of the city into the country" both physically and psychologically ("Lettres morales," Pl. 4:1116). Rousseau himself arrived at the argument of the *Second Discourse* in the depths of the forest of Saint-Germain, and most of the great works he wrote from 1756–62 were conceived during his walks in the forest of Montmorency (*Confessions*, CW 5:326, 339; Pl. 1:388, 403–4).

When offering guidance to a young man who had written to him about a condition of perplexity into which he had fallen as a result of studying philosophy, Rousseau declares that the state of doubt in which the philosopher finds himself is completely alien to him ("Franquières," CW 8:259–60; Pl. 4:1134). More commonly, however, he says that this is precisely the condition into which his own studies had put him (See *Reveries*, CW 8:21; Pl. 1:1016; *Emile* 267; Pl. 4:567; and "Lettres morales," Pl. 4:1087–91). In the first two of these passages, he presents doubt as the beginning point of philosophy, but in the third he also insists that—on metaphysical as opposed to moral questions—it is also the terminus. In addition to asserting that doubt is the beginning of philosophy, he consistently claims that uncertainty about certain ultimate metaphysical questions must be the ultimate outcome of philosophic pursuits. Although he frequently attacks skeptics and Pyrrhonists, he does so mainly to object to the moral consequences they draw from their skepticism, not to the skepticism itself.[53]

The parallel between the first philosopher's "revelation" and Rousseau's account of his own "illumination" is unmistakable.[54] In the *Confessions* he describes his sudden insight into the basis of his system by saying, "I saw another universe and I became another man" (*Confessions*, CW 5:294; Pl. 1:351). What distinguishes Rousseau's description of himself from the account of the first philosopher is the quasi-religious language of the latter. However Rousseau may have intended to end the "Fiction," it is clear that its movement reflects his presentation of the movement of his own thought and writing. As we have seen, Rousseau frequently says that, like the first philosopher, his first impulse after making his discovery of "another universe" was to use it to cure men of errors, but he also comes to the conclusion that the way to do this is by providing a new image for people to look up to and imitate. In effect, he adopts a variant of the tactic of the third wise man.

Whether or not Rousseau should be seen as the "first man who attempted to philosophize," the lesson of the "Fiction" remains the same: Philosophic pride must be rejected. His insistence in the *Observations* that pride is more powerful than either reason or truth means that pride will always be a temptation for philosophers, particularly since to abandon pride also entails remaining in doubt about fundamental issues. Therefore, a newly founded philosophy would have to be particularly attentive to the dangers posed by those who are attracted to philosophy for the wrong reason. Consequently, it would have to be less concerned with its own propagation than traditional philosophy has been. In general, Rousseau is much more concerned with warning about the dangers of pride than he is with encouraging anyone to philosophize.

It is also true that Rousseau is quite willing to let potential philosophers shift for themselves. In *Emile* he even suggests that education that would lead such promising young people to philosophy is impossible. "Only ordinary men need to be raised; their education ought to serve as an example on for that of their kind. The others raise themselves in spite of what one does" (*Emile* 52; Pl. 4:266). In the *First Discourse* he asserts, "Those whom nature destined to be her disciples needed no teachers" (*First Discourse*, CW 2:21; Pl. 3:29). To overstate only slightly, philosophic education is unnecessary, impossible, and dangerous.

Because he did not complete or publish the "Fiction," the evidence it provides about addressing a philosophic audience might seem inconclusive, or even to suggest that Rousseau ultimately rejected such a project. Nevertheless, this evidence is very compatible with a work in which Rousseau clearly did address a philosophic audience directly, his famous "Letter to Voltaire" of August 1756 on optimism (or providence). Like the "Fiction," this work consists of an insistence of the inconclusiveness of the arguments between materialism and a sort of teleology, a demand to abandon dogmatic pride, the sketch of a consoling alternative to materialism, and a call for a popular, and even poetic, defense of this position. Unlike the "Fiction," the *Letter* does not express Rousseau's lesson allegorically, but spells it out quite clearly.

Unlike the *Letter to d'Alembert* or the *Letter to Beaumont*, the "Letter to Voltaire" was originally simply a private letter sent to Voltaire. It was first published in 1760 without Rousseau's permission. Certainly Rousseau knew from the beginning that it might be published someday because Voltaire had published an earlier exchange of letters between them. Still, unlike the letters intended for immediate publication, the "Letter to Voltaire" proceeds as if its primary addressee were Voltaire rather than the more general audience that might eventually read it. Thus, in this work Rousseau comes as close as possible to writing directly to a philosophic audience, although he does so without forgetting other potential readers.

He begins the letter by identifying himself as "a friend of truth who speaks to a Philosopher" ("Letter to Voltaire," CW 3:108; Pl. 4:1059).[55] The substance of the "Letter" is a discussion of Voltaire's attack on Pope's optimism in his *Poem on the Lisbon Disaster*. Rousseau gives a detailed account of the inadequacies of a number of Voltaire's arguments. In doing so, he does not claim to have demonstrated the truth of optimism. While optimism presents itself as an argument for divine providence, in Rousseau's view, it assumes the existence of God rather than proving it ("Letter to Voltaire," CW 3:115; Pl. 4:1068). He argues only that the case against optimism and, more generally, against theism is based only on "possibilities" while the case on the other side is based on "probabilities" ("Letter to Voltaire," CW 3:117; Pl. 4:1070). In the face of the resulting uncertainty over two alternatives that "are equally convincing," he declares his support for the one that "persuades" him by being more consoling ("Letter to Voltaire," CW 3:118; Pl. 4:1071). As indicated by his appeal to persuasion rather than demonstration, Rousseau admits that his preference could reasonably be labeled a mere prejudice. Just as was the case in the "Fiction," an impasse of reason leads to a commitment to a consoling position. It should be noted that Rousseau's most candid statement of the strength of the argument for materialism and his claim that the position he is defending could be called a prejudice come in a part of the letter that was not sent to Voltaire, and that was published only after his death. This is almost a genuinely private statement.

Rousseau insists to Voltaire that the lack of certainty possessed by the latter's position should make him less dogmatic in asserting it. This uncertainty should lead him to reject the "inhumanity in troubling peaceful souls, and in afflicting men to no purpose, when what one wishes to teach them is neither certain nor useful." He blames Voltaire for using his poetic gifts to popularize distressing teachings.[56] He concludes the *Letter* by urging Voltaire to turn away from the "subtleties of Metaphysics" and to use his talent to write "a civic profession of faith" that will teach a tolerant moral code ("Letter to Voltaire," CW 3:120–21; Pl. 4:1074–75).

In sum, Rousseau recapitulates the indecisive reasoning of his own first philosopher about the order of the world, explains the unphilosophic grounds of his philosopher's consoling conclusion of the argument, and urges Voltaire to communicate his new moral law to the people. Rousseau indicates in the *Confessions* that Voltaire declined the invitation to join in this project and responded by using his poetic gifts to attack optimism even more vigorously in *Candide* (*Confessions*, CW 5:361; Pl. 1:430). Voltaire's failure to be persuaded or convinced by Rousseau's plea, however, does not detract from the force of his arguments or presentation.

As he was to do again a few years later in the *Letter to d'Alembert*, Rousseau attempts in the "Letter to Voltaire" to give a philosopher a lesson in his public responsibility as an author. In both cases the lesson might seem to be a practical or moral, as opposed to philosophic, one, were it not for the fact that in both works Rousseau's practical lesson is supported by rational arguments against his addressee's views. Rousseau tries to show d'Alembert that philosophy cannot settle theological issues in the political arena, and he tries to show Voltaire that he has not succeeded in giving his rejection of optimism a rational foundation. It is a philosophic demonstration of the problems in Voltaire's arguments that prepares the way to the moral lesson. In both these works and the "Fiction," Rousseau shows that he sees the possibility of philosophy cured of its prideful and dogmatic tendency. These works also show how far he is willing to go in appealing directly to philosophers on their own terms.

VI. Conclusion

This completes the account of Rousseau's authorship. The essential consequences of this account can be summarized as follows. In his demands upon citizen authors, Rousseau drives a wedge between self-interest and the demands of citizenship that leads to renouncing citizenship while practicing it. In his demands upon philosopher authors, he practices philosophy while constantly denouncing it. The different parts of his conception have had profound influence on different successors, but it is doubtful that anyone else could combine them. It is no wonder that Rousseau paid a heavy personal price attempting to live up to his own understanding of what it means to consecrate one's life to the truth.

POSTSCRIPT

Philosophers and the Friend of the Truth

The major argument of this book could be viewed as an attempt to follow Rousseau's development of his criticism of d'Alembert (and others) for failing to see that philosophy and authorship are in large part incompatible activities. Rousseau's insistence that authorship is an essentially public and political activity leads to his demand that authors take public responsibility for their works by naming themselves. This same insistence leads him to take on the guise of "Citizen of Geneva" for almost all of his major works. These works help to promote good citizenship, or to replace it when it is impossible. Moreover, Rousseau's authorship is, itself, a model of what he understood good citizenship to be.

In the last chapter, attention was turned back to the other side of Rousseau's distinction, to the philosophers, particularly insofar as they attempt to be authors. In the course of this discussion, two ambiguities remain slightly beneath the surface. First, on the one hand, Rousseau is presented as a critic of an entire tradition of philosophy, but, on the other hand, he is presented (through his presentation of the "first philosopher") as a genuine philosopher. Second, Rousseau argues that philosophy intrinsically belongs in private, but he engages in public communication with philosophers in his books. While a complete treatment of the issues raised by these ambiguities can hardly take place in a postscript, it is possible to make these issues emerge more clearly. The main issue here is Rousseau's view of philosophy and of his participation in it.

The obvious necessary beginning point for a consideration of this issue is to observe that Rousseau regularly (but not always) attacked philosophy. Moreover, he steadfastly refused to call himself a philosopher and objected when others referred to him as one. These features were consistent from the beginning of his career as an author until the end. To a critic of the *First Discourse* who attacked him for his reproaches against philosophy and asserted that we should use even the philosophers' errors to correct ourselves, Rousseau responded, "Yes, let's correct ourselves and philosophize no more" (*Final Reply*, CW 2:127; Pl. 3:94). A decade later, in *Emile* he declared, "Be aware that if all the kings and philosophers were taken away, their absence would hardly be noticeable and that things would not be any the worse" (*Emile* 226; Pl. 4:510). When the archbishop of Paris accused him of being "a man full of the language of Philosophy without being a genuine Philosopher" (CW 9:3), Rousseau responded, "Oh, I agree! I have never aspired to that title, to which I acknowledge I have no right; and I am surely not renouncing it through modesty" (*Beaumont*, CW 9:81; Pl. 4:1004). Even when private correspondents referred to him as a philosopher, he typically answered, "I do not know why philosophers are made, nor do I care to know it" (Leigh, 5:178).

To be sure, one can find some passages in which Rousseau praises philosophy and says that it is good for people like "Socrates and Minds of his stamp" (*Second Discourse*, CW 3:38; Pl. 3:156). Leonard Sorenson has assembled this evidence to argue that in the final analysis, Rousseau concluded that "philosophy constituted man's natural purpose." Qualifying this claim slightly, Sorenson argues that philosophy is "the only purely natural good *now* available to man" (emphasis added).[1] Nevertheless, even if one granted this, one would have to concede that there are few things that separate Rousseau more sharply from Socrates than the ways the two of them characteristically spoke about philosophy.

Heinrich Meier has argued that this difference between Rousseau and Socrates is a consequence of the very different situations in which they found themselves rather than a genuine disagreement.[2] Plato's representation of Socrates, and hence of philosophy, is part of an attempt to make philosophy publicly respectable in the face of the threat to its existence exemplified in the trial of Socrates. Rousseau faced a situation in which philosophy had become too respectable and was in danger of becoming nothing more than a partisan opinion held unreflectively. Rousseau laments the fact that the word "philosophy" had become fashionable (*Confessions*, CW 5:68; Pl. 1:81) and, as discussed in the preceding chapter, was resolute in his attack on its partisan character. In Meier's view, both Plato's Socrates and Rousseau are equally supporters of genuine philosophy, and each would have behaved the same way in similar circumstances.

One could build on Meier's suggestion by saying that Rousseau rejected the word "philosophy" but not the thing. In the "Letter to Voltaire," Rousseau identified himself as a "friend of the truth who speaks to a

Philosopher" ("Letter to Voltaire," CW 3:108; Pl. 4:1059). In later writings Rousseau continued to refer to himself as a friend of the truth, even in works in which he denied that he was a philosopher (*Emile* 110, 260; Pl. 4:348, 558; *Beaumont*, CW 9:48, 51, 53; Pl. 4:962, 965, 968; *Mountain*, CW 9:228; Pl. 3:803). Rousseau was not at all averse to inventing new terms if he thought they could be useful; he could well have thought that the usurpation of the old "philosopher" by people like Diderot made a new term necessary. Rousseau's adoption of the term "friend of the truth" is part of an effort to recover the original meaning of philosophy as a distinct way of life devoted to inquiry. It is not surprising that Rousseau explicitly links it with his motto, *vitam impendere vero*.

Certainly Rousseau's contemporaries adopted a nontraditional view of philosophy, and Rousseau frequently compares these new philosophers unfavorably with their predecessors. Nevertheless, as we have seen, his criticisms of philosophy extend to the predecessors as well. His antiphilosophic rhetoric has had the effect of discrediting both the word and the thing among many intelligent readers. Consequently, Meier's thesis that Rousseau provides a "poetic presentation" of his own activity—which, if properly understood, constitutes a defense of philosophy—requires further support to become convincing.

If this intriguing explanation of Rousseau is indecisive, it remains the case that even in his attacks on philosophy, Rousseau uses the tools of philosophic argumentation. This has been noted as one of the great paradoxes of his work from the beginning. Early on, Voltaire, for example, chided Rousseau for his attack on learned activities such as philosophy by saying, "You are like Achilles who gets carried away against glory, and like Father Malebranche whose brilliant imagination wrote against the imagination" (CW 3:103). Rousseau acknowledges the truth of a similar claim made by the king of Poland and compares himself to the church fathers who scorned "worldly sciences," which "they nonetheless used to combat the Pagan Philosophers" (*Observations*, CW 2:40; Pl. 3:39). His goal is to undo the bad effects of philosophy without adding to its seductiveness. In at least these circumstances, philosophy is useful, and even necessary. That philosophy is a cure for ills is a very traditional view. What is untraditional in Rousseau's position is that it is also the cause of these very ills.

This side of Rousseau's presentation has been explored in a number of works by Jean Starobinski. Starobinski's view is summarized in his statement "And we must not forget that Rousseau came to consider his philosophical *oeuvre* as an ill into which he let himself be swept away, but the consequences of which he must suffer for the remainder of his life, but while attempting to set them right through new writings."[3] This remark is deliberately ambiguous about whether Rousseau regarded his philosophical writings as connected with an illness for which he sought a cure, or with an evil committed for which he sought atonement. Starobinski's position agrees with the qualified version of Sorenson's position described above in that both see philosophy as good in present circumstances. Starobinski's view is the opposite of Sorenson's in that it does not see philosophy as a natural good, except in the sense that an otherwise poisonous remedy can be considered as a natural good.

Starobinski has provided a rich account of the numerous ways Rousseau presents the advantages and disadvantages involved in looking for a remedy in the evil itself.[4] The use of philosophy is never without such risks. To extend this medical analogy, one could say that in this interpretation, philosophy can prevent the social ills caused by philosophy if it can inoculate readers against the temptation to philosophize; but for anyone for whom the inoculation is too late, it must serve as an antidote. Such an individual was among those who wrote to Rousseau for guidance in the 1760s. Although it is unlikely that Rousseau regarded his pseudonymous correspondent "Henriette" as a philosopher, it is clear that he regarded her as a very intelligent woman and, as Starobinski has noted,[5] his advice to her fits his own case as well. Rejecting the possibility that this unhappy woman could be made happy by returning to a simple life, Rousseau says, "It is no longer a question of reducing you to knitting and crocheting."[6] The reason for this is that "once it is in effervescence the mind always remains there, and anyone who has thought will continue to think his whole life." Thinking can make one keenly aware of the ills caused by thinking, but far from curing them, awareness only increases them because "all our efforts to leave them only entangle us in them more" (Leigh 20:19).

Although this illness is "great and without a remedy," it is possible to seek a "palliation." Rousseau insists that the greatest part of Henriette's misery is caused by her vanity. Like most so-called philosophers, she is obsessed with demonstrating her superiority to those around her. She must learn to renounce the hope for admirers of her wisdom. At this point Rousseau ceases to talk about a mere palliative and says, "Henceforth study is for you the lance of Achilles which should cure the wound it has made."[7] Philosophy can effect a cure by changing its aim. Rousseau says, "You want to distract yourself by means of philosophy. I would like it to detach you from everything and restore you to yourself" (Leigh 20:21). Such a reorientation will be painful because it involves renouncing the one desire that has dominated Henriette's life, but this is the only solution to her problem.

It should be noted that Rousseau's advice to Henriette is complicated by the fact that it involves an appeal to the very vanity that must be overcome as well as to her desire for happiness. She will undertake her treatment only to show that she is worthy of Rousseau's good opinion. This appeal to her vanity indicates his skepticism about her ability to undergo a genuine cure. Nevertheless, the letter does suggest that philosophy can bring about a complete cure for the ills it causes not merely for society, but for philosophers themselves. It begins to appear that philosophy may indeed offer the best way of life for anyone outside of the pure state of nature described in the *Second Discourse*. It should quickly be added, however, that philosophy is not quite presented as intrinsically good. It is a means rather than an end in itself. It is not understanding as such, but being restored to oneself that is the goal. Philosophy gives us back to ourselves and therefore would be quite unnecessary for those who have not lost themselves in the first place. In the letter to Henriette, it would appear that philosophy has a positive, although still instrumental use. Returning to oneself, the ultimate goal, is connected with the strength of soul that, as was argued in chapter 4, is the substratum for the experience of the sentiment or feeling of one's own existence, which is the true basis for happiness according to Rousseau.[8]

In the "Letter to Voltaire," the sentiment of existence plays a crucial role in the argument. Against Voltaire's claim that few people would wish to experience their lives over again because life contains more burdens than pleasures, Rousseau argues that if this were so, the human race would die out from despair. He then says that so many philosophers have agreed with Voltaire on this point because philosophers "in comparing what is good and bad always forget the sweet feeling of existence, independent of any other sensation." In fact, Rousseau concedes that the existence of literary people and the rich is miserable, but he contrasts their lives to those of "an honest bourgeois," "a good artisan," or "a peasant" who lives in a free country. Appealing to an example that also had been featured prominently in the *Letter to d'Alembert*, he concludes, "I dare to state that perhaps there is in the upper Valais not a single Mountaineer discontented with his almost automatic life, and who would not willingly accept, even in place of Paradise, the bargain of being reborn unceasingly in order to vegetate thus in perpetuity" ("Letter to Voltaire," CW 3:111; Pl. 4:1063). Such lives are impossible for people who have begun to think, but the goal of philosophy, as it is presented in the letter to Henriette, is to make possible for such people a life that is comparable to this existence. Philosophy, then, is a necessary means for happiness for some, but not in principle for all. Even though Rousseau discovered the importance of the sentiment of existence only through philosophic investigation, this sentiment in itself is quite separable from philosophy.

Given that philosophy certainly causes ills, it might appear difficult to understand how philosophical awareness could make any contribution to a cure for misery. Oblivion would seem to be far more useful. Indeed, in the *Reveries* Rousseau presents a remarkable account of the delightful sensation of being reborn after being knocked senseless in a collision (*Reveries*, CW 8:11–12; Pl. 1:1005), and his analysis provides a very suggestive account for understanding those who escape misery through various forms of self-induced stupefaction. Nonetheless, it remains the case that "anyone who has thought will continue to think his whole life." For those who think, thinking becomes a part of their feeling of existence. The brief account that follows will attempt to show how philosophy, or something like it, can be more than merely a dangerous medicine.

The discussion of chapter 3 raised, but did not answer, the question of whether artistic activity can contribute to a life of independence. There it was argued that in its purer forms, the natural life—either in the pure state of nature or the more civilized life of the young Emile—is an essentially inartistic life. We can now add that these forms of natural life are essentially unphilosophic as well. Naturally, the beautiful is reduced to the good, the good is reduced to the pleasant, and the pleasant is reduced to what pleases the senses. Good taste is literally identical to what tastes good, and knowledge is restricted to knowledge of pleasure and pain. Although this sort of life is possible in the sense that it is the truest expression of human nature, it is certainly not possible for humans in societies as we know them. We cannot go back to living in the forest with the bears, and even Emile cannot maintain his natural independence perfectly for long after he reaches the age of fifteen and discovers other humans.

Are there any other options for living a life of independence, or do the links that Rousseau establishes among departure from nature, social dependence, and the arts mean that, for us, a life of independence is only an illusory dream? Traditionally, the life of independence could be identified with the philosophic life, which is understood in distinction from both an artistic life and a life of political engagement. The classic statement of this position, of course, is the cave metaphor in Plato's *Republic* in which the appeal of the philosophic life is presented largely in terms of independence or liberation from the chains that bind other humans, and those chains are understood as being forged in large part by the arts, or poetry. There is very strong evidence that Rousseau's criticisms of the arts owe much to the Platonic account,[9] but his alliance with Plato stops with this critique precisely because he does not accept the view that philosophy in its highest sense ultimately has a more natural foundation than the arts do.

This is not to say that Rousseau does not understand philosophy at all in terms of independence or liberation. In fact, while speaking as a citizen, he frequently takes philosophers to task for destroying social bonds. This same process could be presented in a more positive light by saying that philosophy liberates from social bonds. Rousseau does identify a natural source of the desire to know that can be distinguished from the unnatural pride-based one and that also contributes to independence. The natural form of curiosity is based on the "innate desire for well-being" (*Emile* 167; Pl. 4:429), which leads to the desire to know everything connected to one's interest. Rousseau urges us to imagine "a philosopher relegated to a desert island." In an obvious reference to Newton, he says that this philosopher will lose all interest in things such as the system of the world, the laws of attraction, and differential calculus. Instead, he will explore every part of his island. This is not to say that this particular form of the desire to know cannot be extended indefinitely. After all, "the island of humankind is the earth and the most striking object to our eyes is the sun," and we may need to learn differential calculus, the laws of attraction, and more to understand how to use these things; but natural desire to know will always be based on the more or less clear connection between knowledge and our interests. Furthermore, these interests are defined in a material way rather than in terms of some presumed interest we may have in satisfying an erotic longing to know.

This leads to the question of how Rousseau understands his own philosophic activity. A large part of the image of himself that Rousseau has left us is a picture of a solitary man who pursues activities that he loves, indifferent to both the opinions of others and to considerations of interest. Some of these activities seem remarkably unphilosophic in that they consist of dreamlike reveries. Others, however, such as the study of music or botany, look remarkably like philosophy in its traditional sense. In his argument for the primacy of philosophy for Rousseau, Sorenson makes a sharp distinction between reveries and philosophy, but it is not so clear that Rousseau, himself, makes this distinction in his accounts of his own activity.[10] In fact, a close look at these accounts indicate that Rousseau regards the pleasure involved in both reverie and philosophy as deriving from feeling the pleasant activity of one's imagination. In other words, feeling the activity of one's soul.

The best known of Rousseau's accounts of the satisfying character of nonutilitarian knowing occurs in his descriptions of botany in the *Reveries* and *Confessions*. Botany, as he describes it, is a contemplative pursuit that differs from both pride-based and interest-based philosophy. He pursues it by himself without concern for other people's opinions. Most important, he insists that botany should not be pursued as a useful study. The "Introduction" to his botanical dictionary opens with the remark "The first misfortune of Botany is to have been regarded since its birth as a part of Medicine" (CW 8:93; Pl. 4:1201). This utilitarian approach has deformed botany by restricting it to a narrow field and by blinding those who study it to the genuine beauty of plants. These beauties are found by means of the contemplation of the structure or "organization" of plants. Furthermore, these beauties can be appreciated only as a result of prolonged study. One must be a knower in order to appreciate them (*Confessions*, CW 5:537; Pl. 1:641–42).

What causes the satisfaction Rousseau feels in contemplating the structure of plants? Does he recognize a beauty intrinsic to them and, in addition, one that points beyond plants to the beauty of the cosmos? Is the beauty of the structure of plants something like the forms or ideas of classical philosophy? The answer to these questions is somewhat complicated. In the first place, when he writes about botany to others, he makes fairly conventional teleological claims, but when he writes about his own study, Rousseau makes only fairly perfunctory efforts to link botany to ultimate concern about being. We can experience the structures of plants as beautiful without any reference to their connection with anything beyond themselves.[11] Even more importantly, he does not argue that the pleasure of botanizing increases in direct proportion to the knowledge that is gained. He describes his own intense pleasure by saying:

> To wander nonchalantly in the woods and in the country, here and there to take up mechanically, sometimes a flower, sometimes a branch; to graze on my fodder almost at random, to observe the same things thousands of times, and always with the same interest because I always forget them, was enough for me to pass eternity without being bored for a moment. I was, and my lack of memory ought to have always kept me at that fortunate point of knowing little enough about it so that everything was new to me and enough so that I was able to feel everything. (*Confessions*, CW 5:537; Pl. 1:642)

The pleasure of botanizing requires a degree of knowledge but consists more in the novelty of ever-renewed discovery of particular beauties than in the contemplation of eternal principles. Forgetting is at least as important an element in Rousseau's account as understanding is. In traditional accounts, one does not find a bad memory this high on the list of qualities necessary for philosophic contemplation.

Contemplation as Rousseau liked to practice it resembles more an aesthetic activity than a philosophic one, a pleasant stimulation of the imagination, a walk through an art gallery admiring the beauty of one painting, but moving on to another before an inevitable boredom can set in. A large part of the reason for this need for novelty comes from the fact that in Rousseau's account the structure or organization of beautiful objects is more the occasion for the experience of beauty than it is the locus of beauty. As was argued in chapter 3, the artistic experience is one of identifying with feelings, and the person having the experience can identify only with feelings he is capable of recognizing or in some manner already has. A work of art, or a natural object experienced as beautiful, is only the medium for the stimulation of these feelings. As Rousseau says at least twice in quite different contexts, "Except for the single Being existing by itself, there is nothing beautiful except that which is not" (*Emile* 447; Pl. 4:821; and *Julie*, CW 6:569; Pl. 2:693). Because he insists that we have no access to this single Being existing by itself, this is the same as to say that there is nothing beautiful except our experience of beauty, an experience that is a form of the feeling of our own existence. Because of this, it would be a mistake to conclude from Rousseau's praise of botany that love of the beautiful is necessarily connected with an appreciation of the orderliness of nature. The disorder of tempests and the wildness of waterfalls can reflect the feelings of the soul as beautifully as the structure of plants can.

Throughout Rousseau's works there are numerous accounts of his experience of satisfaction with this new type of nonphilosophic contemplation. He gave his most comprehensive account in an attempt he made to explain that, contrary to what most of his acquaintances thought about him, he led a life of happiness rather than misery. His description of a happy day has three stages. First, having left his home early to avoid pestering visitors, he observes the beauty of plants. Second, he imagines a society of friends and lovers to share his pleasure. An identification with even imaginary fellows is necessary to complete the pleasure. He shows how much even this pleasure comes from the act of imagining rather than real company by saying, "If all my dreams had been turned into realities they would not have been enough for me; I would have imagined, dreamed, desired again. I found an inexplicable void in myself that nothing could fill." Naturally enough this inexplicable void drives him to consider the traditional concerns of philosophy. His mind moves "to all the beings of nature, to the universal system of things, to the incomprehensible being who embraces everything." But when faced with these ultimate concerns, he says, "I did not think, I did not reason, I did not philosophize." Instead, he abandons himself to confusion and lets his imagination roam. He sums up this experience with a final antiphilosophic remark, "I believe that if I had unveiled all the mysteries of nature, I would have felt myself to be in a less delightful situation than that stupefying ecstasy to which my mind abandoned itself without reserve" ("Letters to Malesherbes," CW 5:579; Pl. 1:1140). Ultimate clarity is less delightful than stupefying ecstasy is, although clarity is necessary to sustain this ecstasy.

In what sense is this particular sort of independent life an artistic one in the precise sense of imitation or identification with human emotion? In the following way: Rousseau's peculiar form of confronting being is to see his own restless longing reflected in the universe itself. In contemplating the universe, he identifies with his own feelings. The universe becomes a metaphor for himself. Thus, Rousseau describes a life of self-sufficiency as the highest human happiness, but this is a life of aesthetic contemplation, imaginative creation, and stupefying ecstasy; it is a poetic rather than a philosophic life, or, rather, it is a life in which the distinction between poetic creativity and philosophy is impossible to make.

I tentatively conclude that philosophy is the base of Rousseau's happiness in three ways. First, philosophy is an essential (but not the only) part of the cure of the ills caused by thinking, ills such as vanity and unreasonable fears and hopes. Second, philosophic understanding provides the necessary precondition for other activities such as writing novels like *Julie*, or reverie. Finally, philosophic contemplation of a sort forms a part (but not the only part) of the reveries in which Rousseau experiences the feeling of his own existence. In the final analysis, after sifting through much evidence and many qualifications, it is hard to avoid the conclusion that for Rousseau, philosophy—only when understood as the attempt to return to oneself and experience both the feeling of existence and the feeling of the power of one's own imagination and aesthetic sensibility—is the best life available to anyone who has begun to think. It may well be valuable because it contributes to the heroic activity of a legislator or the imaginative activity of a poet or composer. Philosophic understanding in the more traditional attempt to understand the truth about the whole is important only to the extent that it can provide the solid basis for fulfilling but nonphilosophic experiences.

In one and the same work, the *Dialogues*, Rousseau said both, "I am neither a philosopher nor austere," and "I doubt that any philosopher ever meditated more profoundly, more usefully perhaps, and wrote more in so little time" (*Dialogues*, CW 1:137, 1010). This book has attempted to show that he engaged in sustained philosophic reflection on the highest level in considering the significance of his activity as an author. Nevertheless, even while consecrating his life to the truth, Rousseau found himself compelled to explain philosophic activity in terms of something (the sentiment of existence) that he regarded as more fundamental and that he claimed philosophers always forgot about. It may be that his deepest understanding made it impossible to describe even his philosophic activity in any other way.[12] However that may be, he is certainly true enough to his claim that authorship is public and philosophy private not to present himself as a philosopher in his published or unpublished writings.

The intention behind this postscript is not to dispose of the question of Rousseau and philosophy, but only to set it on its proper footing. To have gone even this far is, perhaps, excessive in a book that took title pages as its point of departure.

NOTES

Introduction

1. On the close relation between *Emile* and *The Republic*, see Ellis, *Rousseau's Socratic Aemilian Myths*.

2. Diderot's precise role in advising Rousseau about the position he took in the *Discourse* is much debated. A sober summary of the evidence is presented in Cranston, *Jean-Jacques*, 227–29.

3. The most complete edition of the attacks on Rousseau's *Discourse* is the three-volume *Die Polemik um den Ersten Discours von Rousseau in Frankreich und Deutschland*, ed. Tente. Translations of the attacks to which Rousseau responded can be found in CW 2, along with Rousseau's responses.

4. D'Alembert, *Preliminary Discourse to the Encyclopedia of Diderot*, trans. Schwab, 103.

5. Translated as *Jean-Jacques Rousseau: Transparency and Obstruction*, trans. Goldhammer.

6. Translated as *Of Grammatology*, trans. Spivak.

7. An older work that focuses on Rousseau's intention in the *First Discourse* is Strauss's "On the Intention of Rousseau," originally published in *Social Research* 14 (1947); republished in *Hobbes and Rousseau*, ed. Cranston and Peters, 254–90.

8. See, in particular, Johns, *The Nature of the Book*. Johns focuses on the situation in England. The notes to chapter 1 indicate some of the relevant scholarship about France.

9. Translated by Thomas Burger with Frederick Lawrence.

10. Goodman, *The Republic of Letters*, 53–89. Goodman's introduction presents a very useful account of recent issues in Enlightenment historiography. The most useful recent attempt to integrate Rousseau into the Enlightenment is Hulliung, *The Autocritique of Enlightenment*.

12. Kelly, *Rousseau's Exemplary Life*.

Chapter One

1. The details of this sequence of events can be found in Gouhier's excellent study of the relations between Rousseau and Voltaire, *Rousseau et Voltaire*, 195–234. While acknowledging that the difference of opinion over anonymity played a role in Voltaire's behavior, Gouhier does not give it the same importance I do here.

2. For the details of this, see ibid., 289–304.

3. See Gourevitch, "Rousseau on Lying," 97. I am indebted to the excellent discussion in this essay.

4. Also among these early writings was Diderot's first major publication, the *Essai sur le mérite et la vertu*, a translation of Shaftesbury. Not only was this work published anonymously and with a fake Amsterdam imprint, but Shaftesbury was identified only as S.

5. For an account of the endless uncertainties involved in the publication of books in England in the century before Rousseau wrote, see Johns, *The Nature of the Book*. Sources of uncertainty analogous to the ones identified by Johns still existed in France in the eighteenth century.

6. For more complete accounts of censorship in France in the eighteenth century, see Hanley, "The Policing of Thought," 265–95; and Roche, "Censorship and the Publishing Industry."

7. For accounts of Malesherbes's career as director of publishing, see Birn, "Malesherbes and the Call for a Free Press."

8. Foucault, "What Is an Author?" 126.

9. For accounts of these events, see Cranston, *The Noble Savage*, 344–50; and Patterson, *Censorship and Interpretation*, 239–40.

10. See, for example, the letters to Helvétius in May and September 1763 during the period described above. *Les Oeuvres de Voltaire*, ed. Besterman, 110:199, 228, 404. On this point see Pappas, *Voltaire and Diderot*, 37.

11. Havens, *Voltaire's Marginalia on the Pages of Rousseau*, 138–39; see also 136. Voltaire also refers to Spinoza's use of Latin and his skill in writing as useful for lowering the risks of persecution.

12. The account that follows is drawn mainly from *Les Oeuvres complètes de Voltaire*, 110:199–200, 227–28, and, especially, 403–5. It is meant only to show the elements in Voltaire's strategy that shed light on Rousseau's opposed strategy. A book-length study would be necessary to provide a full explication of Voltaire's understanding of the social role of an author. For a useful beginning point for discussion, see Koselleck, *Critique and Crisis*, 60, 113–17.

13. Quoted in Furbank, *Diderot*, 167.

14. There is one exception to this, the small pamphlet *The Vision of Peter of the Mountain, Called the Seer* (CW 9:309–14; Pl. 2:1232–38), which Rousseau insisted on publishing anonymously in 1765. This pamphlet also violates Rousseau's rule of not writing personal attacks on individuals.

15. Foucault, "What Is an Author?" 124. With this and other references to the characterization of authorship by Foucault, I do not intend to indicate that Rousseau originated any of the practices or understandings of authorship identified. Rather, I wish to show the particular use he made and understanding he had of these prac-

tices. A discussion of Foucault's account that attempts to make his chronology more precise is given by Chartier, *The Order of Books*, 25–59.

16. The story of Voltaire's beating at the hands of the servants of Rohan and his subsequent exile is well-known. For a short account, see Besterman, *Voltaire*, 106–9. On Voltaire's change of name, see ibid., 70–71.

17. Stendhal, *Racine and Shakespeare*, trans. Daniels, 71n.

18. Some of the complexity involved in anonymous publication is shown by Rousseau's account of his strategy in writing his response to Stanislaus. He says that he was aware that Stanislaus had been assisted in writing the "Reply" by a Jesuit and that he was able to separate the parts written by the two authors. Having done so, he could treat Stanislaus with respect while being more bold in attacking his coauthor.

19. Palissot de Montenoy, *Oeuvres complètes*, 1:217.

20. For a complete account of Rousseau's response to the censors of *Julie*, see McEachern, "*La Nouvelle Héloïse* et la censure," 83–89.

21. For a discussion of this, see Roosevelt, *Reading Rousseau in the Nuclear Age*, 247.

22. *Diskurs über die Ungleichheit/Discours sur l'inégalité*, ed. Meier. The relevant passages can be found in CW 3:97–101. Meier also provides a useful account of the atmosphere of censorship at the time of the publication of the *Second Discourse* (lxxviii–lxxxv).

23. On Rousseau's disagreements with the Savoyard Vicar, see Emberley, "Rousseau versus the Savoyard Vicar"; Macy, "'God Helps Those Who Help Themselves'"; Masters, *The Political Philosophy of Rousseau*, 54–55; and Nichols, "Rousseau's Novel Education in *Emile*," 545–50.

24. For a summary of the events surrounding the censorship of these works, see Vanpée, "Rousseau's *Emile ou de l'éducation*," 159–61.

25. On d'Alembert's own caution see Pappas, *Voltaire and Diderot*, 67.

26. D'Alembert, *Oeuvres complètes*, 5:464.

27. Diderot, *Oeuvres complètes*, ed. Assézat and Tourneux, 13:27. See Furbank, *Diderot*, 420–22.

28. The classic interpretation of Rousseau in this light is that of Starobinski, *Jean-Jacques Rousseau*.

29. For a good sketch of the literary strategies of Rousseau, Diderot, and d'Alembert in particular, see Saisselin, *The Literary Enterprise in Eighteenth-Century France*.

30. See, for example, *Correspondance Jean-Jacques Rousseau, Chrétien-Guillaume de Lamoignon de Malesherbes*, ed. Negroni, 347–48.

31. Jackson, "Text and Context of Rousseau's Relations with Diderot."

32. The term translated as "honorable" here is *honnête*, which also means "honest" or "decent." For an alternative translation of this passage, see Gourevitch, "Rousseau on Lying," 97.

33. Shackleton, *Montesquieu*, 85–89.

34. For a discussion of this, see Namer, *Rousseau Sociologue de la connaissance*, 72.

35. This claim is raised on behalf of d'Holbach, who constantly used anonymity and false attribution, by Topazio, *D'Holbach's Moral Philosophy*, 9.

36. Foucault, "What Is an Author?" 123.

37. For a brief account of the intensity of readers' reactions to Rousseau and their identification with him, see Darnton, "Readers Respond to Rousseau."

38. For an elaboration of this issue in the *Dialogues*, see Christopher Kelly and Roger D. Masters, "Introduction," *Dialogues*, CW 1:xviii–xxi.

Chapter Two

1. For Rousseau as a defender of censorship, see Bloom, "Introduction," *Politics and the Arts*. For the view that Rousseau is an enemy of liberty, see Crocker, "Rousseau et la voi du totalitarisme" and "Rousseau's *soi-disant* Liberty"; and Talmon, *The Origins of Totalitarian Democracy*.

2. For examples of this consensus, see Strauss, "On the Intention of Rousseau" and *Natural Right and History*; Masters, *The Political Philosophy of Rousseau*; Gourevitch, "Rousseau on the Arts and Sciences"; Goldschmidt, *Anthropologie et politique*; Bloom, "Introduction"; and Coleman, *Rousseau's Political Imagination*.

3. See *First Discourse*, CW 2:203–4 n. 7.

4. See, for example, Buchanon, *Marx and Justice*; Galston, "Defending Liberalism"; and Habermas, *Communication and the Evolution of Society*, trans. McCarthy.

5. See, for example, MacIntyre, *After Virtue*; Williams, *Ethics and the Limits of Philosophy*; and Winthrop, "Aristotle and Theories of Justice."

6. For an exception, see Ackerman, *Social Justice in the Liberal State*, 99, 323, 341.

7. Rawls, *A Theory of Justice*, 11.

8. Habermas, *Communication and the Evolution of Society*, 185.

9. On the opposition between Calvinism and Socinianism with particular reference to the issue of dissimulation and persecution, see Zagorin, *Ways of Lying*, 63–82, 94–97. This book provides an extremely useful account of the complex attitudes toward dissimulation in an era of religious persecution.

10. D'Alembert, *Oeuvres complètes*, 5:457; emphasis in original. He goes on to indicate that Rousseau's later defense of dancing is more shocking to orthodoxy than his own defense of the theater. See also his "Avertissement sur la justification de l'article *Genève* de l'Encyclopédie," in ibid., 5:423. For a broader discussion of this section of the *Letter to d'Alembert*, see Coleman, *Rousseau's Political Imagination*, 19–31.

11. I am grateful to Joel Schwartz for his observations on this point.

12. Boss, "Rousseau's Civil Religion and the Meaning of Belief," 181.

13. Tocqueville, *Democracy in America*, trans. Lawrence and ed. Mayer, 292.

14. On this point, see Baker, "Eternal Vigilance," 161; and Strauss, *Natural Right and History*, 289.

15. This conclusion is defended by Cullen, *Freedom in Rousseau's Political Philosophy*.

16. See, for example, Walzer, *Interpretation and Social Criticism*, 33–66.

17. For an excellent treatment of the *Letter* in relation to Rousseau's theoretical works on the understanding of women, see Schwartz, *The Sexual Politics of Jean-Jacques Rousseau*.

18. For an account of Rousseau's practical intention in the *Social Contract*, see Melzer, *The Natural Goodness of Man*, 271–73.

19. Marshall, "Art d'écrire et pratique politique de Jean-Jacques Rousseau," 337. On this point, see Strauss, *Natural Right and History*, 287.

20. See, for example, the claim made by Vaughan in *Political Writings of Jean-Jacques Rousseau*, ed. Vaughan, 2:184–85.

21. See Miller, *Rousseau*, 87–104.

22. See Melzer, *The Natural Goodness of Man*, 261–66.

23. This characterization occurs in a discussion of d'Alembert's proposal of the establishment of a theater in Geneva. Rousseau thought, correctly, that d'Alembert had made the proposal in order to gratify Voltaire, who had settled in the neighborhood of Geneva. See Gouhier, *Rousseau et Voltaire*, 119.

24. See Keohane, "'The Masterpiece of Policy in Our Century.'"

25. On the tendency of Enlightenment social criticism to lapse into hypocrisy when it claims to adopt a disinterested standpoint, see Koselleck, *Critique and Crisis*, 113–14.

26. See Strauss, "On the Intention of Rousseau"; and Gourevitch, "Rousseau on Lying."

27. On Rousseau's attack on philosophic pride, see chapter 6.

28. Among the examples of this tactic are the responses to the critics of the *First Discourse* and, in particular, Rousseau's "Letter to Voltaire." This letter consists largely of a refutation of Voltaire's attack on optimism. While it defends Pope and Leibniz against Voltaire's attack, it does not really demonstrate that Rousseau agreed with the optimists: in effect it is anti-anti-optimism rather than pro-optimism. See Kelly and Masters, "Human Nature, Liberty and Progress."

29. My discussion here and below relies on Strauss, "On the Intention of Rousseau."

30. What I have called responsibility as an author could be considered as one version of a more general understanding of integrity in political action. For an excellent account of Rousseau's effort to combine effectiveness with principle in political action, see Grant, *Hypocrisy and Integrity*.

Chapter Three

1. The most complete collection of these responses can be found in the three-volume collection *Die Polemik um den ersten Discours von Rousseau in Frankreich und Deutschland*, ed. Tente. The responses to which Rousseau published answers can be found in CW 2.

2. See d'Alembert, "Discours preliminaire," 1:161–62.

3. In the *Confessions* Rousseau says, "*The Village Soothsayer* put me completely in fashion, and soon there might not have been a man in Paris more sought after than I was" (*Confessions*, CW 5:309; Pl. 1:369). For an account of its composition and success, see CW 5:309–21; Pl. 1:369–82.

4. Voltaire, *Lettre au docteur Pansophe*, 850–51.

5. To avoid the problem posed by exact imitation of ugly things, d'Alembert appeals to the notion of *la belle nature*, which was a commonplace of French treatment of the beautiful in the seventeenth and eighteenth centuries. See Hobson, *The Object of Art*, 159.

6. See d'Alembert, "Discours préliminaire," 1:103.

7. For an identical statement of the hierarchy as dominant in accounts of music around 1700, see Haeringer, "L'Esthétique de l'opéra en France au temps de Jean-Philippe Rameau," 279:11.

8. Hobson uses Rousseau's letter as evidence of the novelty of the position stated by d'Alembert. See Hobson, *The Object of Art*, 283.

9. Consider also this remark from the article "Harmonie": "By reason, since *Harmony* does not furnish any principle of imitation by which Music, forming images or expressing feelings, may be elevated to the Dramatic or imitative genre, which is the most noble part of the Art and the only energetic one, all that regards merely the physics of Sounds being quite limited in the pleasure they give us and having but very little power over the human heart" (*Dictionary*, CW 7:413; Pl. 5:851).

10. For an extensive account of the political importance of Rousseau's treatment of language and music, see Gourevitch, "The Political Argument of Rousseau's *Essay on the Origin of Languages*."

11. For the defenses of politeness, see in particular the *Refutation by Gautier* (CW 2:70–71) and the *Discourse on the Advantages of the Sciences and the Arts*, by Bordes (CW 2:100–1).

12. Although Rousseau usually insists that he would prefer open to concealed wickedness, he occasionally concedes that "in a country in which it is no longer a question of honest people nor of good morals, it would be better to live with rogues than with brigands" ("Preface" to *Narcissus*, CW 2:196; Pl. 2:971).

13. See Grant, *Hypocrisy and Integrity*, 57–101.

14. On the debate over the theater leading up to Rousseau, see Barras, *The Stage Controversy in France from Corneille to Rousseau*.

15. Rousseau does argue, however, that this is true only in the best cases. Frequently people will identify with brilliant success rather than goodness, particularly when they are seeing a comedy. See *d'Alembert* 34–35; Pl. 5:32; and *Emile* 115–16; Pl. 4:356.

16. Rousseau is not alone in promoting an understanding of all of the fine arts as somehow theatrical. See the excellent study of Diderot's art criticism by Fried, *Absorption and Theatricality*. This is one of numerous cases in which Rousseau and Diderot made a very similar diagnosis of a problem and attempted to solve it in extremely different ways and in different fields: Diderot by attempting to invent a new form of theater and Rousseau by abandoning it altogether. The intensely personal nature of their falling-out at the end of the 1750s has obscured the extent to which these philosophic differences of opinion fueled their disputes.

17. See *Confessions*, CW 5:7–8; Pl. 1:8.

18. For negative views of Rousseau's description of the legislator, see Ellenberg, *Rousseau's Political Philosophy*, 27; and Shklar, *Men and Citizens*, 155.

19. Masters, *The Political Philosophy of Rousseau*, 354. Tracy Strong captures the strangeness of the legislator's status by saying, "We must recognize the possibility that there has been, is, might be such a being, but also that no one of us could ever claim to anyone else to be such a being. Nor could anyone make a legislative claim to us." Strong, *Jean-Jacques Rousseau*, 161. No one can claim to be a legislator because that would imply a claim to authority over others denied by natural equality.

20. After noting the very different character of the legislator's various functions, Hilail Gilden suggests that there must be two different legislators who work at different times. See Gilden, Rousseau's "Social Contract," 72–75.

21. Timothy O'Hagan has described these conditions as an "affective field in which the moral agents are situated and make their choice" (*Rousseau*, 14).

22. See, for example, Hall, *Rousseau*, 110–25; and Lemos, *Rousseau's Political Philosophy*, 131–215.

23. For an elaboration of this point, see Kelly and Masters, "Rousseau's *Social Contract*, the Common Good, and the Guilty."

24. In all instances below, the word translated as "persuasion" (or "persuade") is *persuasion* (or *persuader*). Similarly, the word translated as "convince" is *convaincre*.

25. Shklar, *Men and Citizens*, 157–58.

26. Shklar, "Rousseau's Images of Authority," 346. Upon further reflection, Shklar apparently reconsidered this claim; see *Men and Citizens*, 161.

27. For an account of the peculiarities of the dividing point between the state of nature and society, see Derrida, *Of Grammatology*, 255–69. For a cogent, if extremely succinct, critique of Derrida, see Gourevitch, "Rousseau's Pure State of Nature," 35 n. 19.

28. See Gourevitch, "Rousseau's Pure State of Nature," 53–54.

29. For accounts of Moses as the most important example of a legislator, see Baczko, "Moïse legislateur . . . ," 111–30; and Harvey, "Exemplarity and the Origins of Legislation," 211–54.

30. See Plato, *Republic* 398d, 400d.

31. On Monteverdi's use of Platonic authority for his claim that one should "make the words the mistress of the harmony and not the servant," see Tomlinson, *Monteverdi and the End of the Renaissance*, 25. On the subordination of music to lyrics in Lully, see Kintzler, *Jean-Philippe Rameau*. See also Neubauer, *The Emancipation of Music from Language*, 22–23.

32. On this point, see Kintzler, *Jean-Philippe Rameau*, 99–132; and John Scott's introduction to CW 7:xiv–xxvi.

33. For an account of this debate that lucidly explains the contrasting positions of Lully, Rameau, and Rousseau, see Kintzler, *Jean-Philippe Rameau*.

34. For an account of the natural basis of these cultural variations, see Scott, "Rousseau and the Melodious Language of Freedom."

35. For an account of how Louis XIV made conscious use of spectacles for purposes similar to the ones Rousseau attacks, see Isherwood, *Music in the Service of the King*. In their eagerness to attack the application during the French Revolution of Rousseau's endorsement of spectacles, critics do not always notice his reservations about the use of spectacles.

36. Shelley, "A Defense of Poetry," 7:112.

37. On Rousseau's importance for the myth-making and culture-forming projects of the English Romantic poets, see Cantor, *Creature and Creator*.

38. For a sound assessment of Rousseau's view of the political circumstances in which he found himself and its effect on his practical intention, see Melzer, *The Natural Goodness of Man*, 253–82.

39. For further discussion of this passage in relation to Rousseau's understanding of Jesus, see Kelly, *Rousseau's Exemplary Life*, 57–64.

Chapter Four

1. On the centrality of avoiding personal dependence for Rousseau, see Melzer, *The Natural Goodness of Man*, 70–85.
2. For an analysis of these figures, see Shklar, "Rousseau's Images of Authority."
3. Cameron, "The Hero in Rousseau's Political Thought," 416.
4. Ibid., 408.
5. On the most likely source for Rousseau's citation of Bacon, see *Hero*, CW 4:231 n. 23.
6. See Cameron, "The Hero in Rousseau's Political Thought," 401.
7. For a discussion of physical virtue in Rousseau, see Goldschmidt, *Anthropologie et politique*, 318–19.
8. See Melzer, *The Natural Goodness of Man*, 29–49.
9. See also *Reveries*, CW 8:55; Pl. 1:1058. Rousseau's most detailed account of the transition of weakness into vice occurs in *Dialogues*, CW 1:9–10; Pl. 1:669.
10. On the things necessary to turn strength of soul into moral virtue, see *d'Alembert* 96; Pl. 5:88–89; "Franquières," CW 8:267–68; Pl. 4:1143–44; and *Julie*, CW 6:593; Pl. 2:722–23. See also Burgelin, *La Philosophie de l'existence de J.-J. Rousseau*, 447–55.
11. For a more detailed discussion of this passage, see Kelly, *Rousseau's Exemplary Life*, 22–23, 79–82. It should be pointed out that Rousseau's own alienation has two difficulties beyond the fact of alienation itself. First, by reading both novels and Plutarch, he has two contradictory sets of heroes. Second, both sets of heroes (particularly the ones in novels) have no relation to the circumstances in which he finds himself.
12. For a discussion of the details of Rousseau's use of "emulation" in *Considerations on the Government of Poland*, see Kelly, *Rousseau's Exemplary Life*, 25–26.
13. For an elaboration of this point and citations of relevant texts, see CW 2:204–5.
14. See, for example, Talmon, *The Origins of Totalitarian Democracy*, and Crocker, "Rousseau et la voi du totalitarisme."
15. See Kelly, *Rousseau's Exemplary Life*, 99.
16. See ibid., 21.
17. For some intriguing suggestions concerning Rousseau's "oscillation" between admiration of such harshness and his ultimate rejection of it, see Manent, *La Cité de l'homme*, 45, 268.
18. Compare *Julie*, CW 6:540; Pl. 2:657.
19. I have attempted to give such a treatment in *Rousseau's Exemplary Life*. See also "Introduction," *Confessions*, CW 5:xvii–xxxiv. The present study of Rousseau's literary practice and image of what it means to be a writer should also add to this picture.
20. See also "Lettres Morales," Pl. 4:1082. Elsewhere Rousseau suggests that he had always known the futility of this goal. See Leigh 10:226 (discussed in chapter 1).

21. Dena Goodman has argued that the effect of the *Second Discourse* is "to make of the actively critical reader a passive spectator" (*Criticism in Action*, 107). The argument here is that the reason the *Discourses* do not elicit social action is that they are diagnoses of the problem that only implicitly indicate solutions and that they are aimed at a very select audience.

22. That Rousseau was, however reluctantly, willing to take on the function of spiritual adviser to numerous of the people who wrote to him has been illustrated by Jean Starobinski; see *Blessings in Disguise*, 134–37.

23. Rousseau makes a similar claim in the "Preface to a Second Letter to Bordes," written in 1753 ("Bordes," CW 2:185; Pl. 3:107), but he did not finish this work and left the preface unpublished.

24. For an excellent discussion of the issues involved in this sort of deception, see Gourevitch, "Rousseau on Lying."

25. See editors' introduction to Pl. 2:lxxxvi. A recent treatment of the similarity between the works can be found in Matthes, *The Rape of Lucretia and the Founding of Republics*.

26. The story can be found at Livy I, 57–59; and Ovid, *Fasti* II, 685–852.

27. Matthes argues that women in general and Lucretia in particular have the qualities that Rousseau found necessary for a legislator (*The Rape of Lucretia*, 119–25). I argue below that Julie is the legislator of only a nonpolitical sort of founding.

28. Augustine, *City of God*, 1:17–20.

29. This statement is put into the mouth of a character identified only as "R," who is the editor of *Julie*. Because the identification with Rousseau is made implicitly at several points in the dialogue, I will treat the two as the same.

30. On this "cancellation," see Bennington, *Sententiousness and the Novel*, 137–41.

31. On this point, see Jackson, *Rousseau's Occasional Autobiographies*, 138–41. Jackson emphasizes the personal aspect of this description of madness for Rousseau, but the problem has a long history. See, for example, Hobbes, *Leviathan*, ed. Oakeshott, 24, 52; Descartes, *Discourse on Method*, trans. Cress, 4; and Condillac, *Essai sur l'origine des connaissances humaines*, 146. The last of these is of interest because Rousseau was friendly with Condillac and was instrumental in the publication of the *Essai*.

32. For an account of Rousseau's attempt to transform society from below, as it were, see Morgenstern, "Emile et la révolution dans la vie quotidienne."

33. For an account of how the novel accomplishes the transformation from personal feelings to social obligations, see Ray, *Story and History*, 240–69.

34. On this point, see ibid., 256. For a more negative interpretation of this characteristic as a disturbing manifestation of "Julie's obsessive need to control," see DeJean, *Literary Fortifications*, 171.

35. The most complete treatment of the "Second Preface" is the one given by Jackson. For other notable examinations, see de Man, *Allegories of Reading*; and Robinson, "Literature versus Theory." With regard to this preface, de Man claims that "rarely has a preface been less able to shed light on the meaning of a text it introduces" (205), but his own reading of that preface and especially Jackson's shed considerable light on *Julie*.

36. On Rousseau's efforts to weed out the wrong sort of reader, see Stewart, *Half-Told Tales*, 138, 168; and Ray, *Story and History*, 262.

37. For a discussion of this passage, see Bloom's introduction (*Emile* 3).
38. De Man, *Allegories of Reading*, 209.
39. See de Man, *Allegories of Reading*, 217–19.
40. Stewart, *Half-Told Tales*, 209–10. A similar view is at the heart of Ray's interpretation in *Story and History*. See also Starobinski, *Jean-Jacques Rousseau*, 132–34.
41. On this point, see Gourevitch, "Rousseau on Lying," 102.

Chapter Five

1. Sandel, *Democracy's Discontent*, 320.
2. The most thorough examples of such criticism are Cullen, *Freedom in Rousseau's Political Philosophy*, and Trachtenberg, *Making Citizens*.
3. The most persistent of such criticisms comes from Lester G. Crocker in a number of works over the past forty years. Most significant is *Rousseau's "Social Contract,"* and the most recent is "Rousseau's *soi-disant* liberty."
4. See the discussions in Cullen, *Freedom in Rousseau's Political Philosophy*, 151–52; and especially Trachtenberg, *Making Citizens*, 42–50.
5. For a useful survey of interpretations of Rousseau's voting procedure as outlined in this passage, see Parry, "Thinking One's Own Thoughts."
6. Crocker, *Rousseau's "Social Contract,"* 70–71; see also 80, 89.
7. See Cullen, *Freedom in Rousseau's Political Philosophy*, 150; and Manin, "On Legitimacy and Political Deliberation."
8. See Cullen, *Freedom in Rousseau's Political Philosophy*, 159–60.
9. See Trachtenberg, *Making Citizens*, 228–29.
10. For good discussions of Rousseau's view of the government as both a constant threat to liberty and as necessarily engaging in concealed ruling, see Melzer, *The Natural Goodness of Man*, 217–20, 241–44.
11. For a discussion of these stages, see Gilden, *Rousseau's "Social Contract,"* 150–52.
12. See, for example, Crocker, *Rousseau's "Social Contract,"* 49; and Shklar, *Men and Citizens*. Citing Bertrand de Jouvenal, Cullen argues that Sparta falls short of being Rousseau's model (*Freedom in Rousseau's Political Philosophy*, 137), but he does not systematically distinguish Sparta from Rome. See also Miller, *Rousseau*, 29.
13. Trachtenberg argues that the general will can be conceived of as the result of hypothetical bargaining but points out that this is not the form that deliberation takes (*Making Citizens*, 15–23). Thus, unlike Rawls, for example, Rousseau's account of justice involves both a hypothetical bargain and an actual consent.
14. Cullen, *Freedom in Rousseau's Political Philosophy*, 120; Crocker, *Rousseau's "Social Contract,"* 70.
15. For a useful discussion of this passage, see Gilden, *Rousseau's "Social Contract,"* 159.
16. On this point, see Cullen, *Freedom in Rousseau's Political Philosophy*, 215–16 n. 153. The precise limits of this will be discussed below.
17. On a form of this mistrust as characteristic of democracy, see Orwin, "Democracy and Distrust."

18. For an excellent discussion of the relation between the goal of individual moral purity and political prudence in Rousseau, see Grant, *Hypocrisy and Integrity*, 70–71.

19. On this issue, see the discussion in Bloom's introduction to *d'Alembert*, xxii–xxv.

20. *Confessions*, CW 5:181, 509–11. For a slightly different view of Rousseau's position on Geneva, see Miller, *Rousseau*, 87–122.

21. On the character of this reconstruction, see Miller, *Rousseau*, 96–102.

Chapter Six

1. For numerous other passages in which Rousseau refers to the relatively few readers he is addressing, see Strauss, "On the Intention of Rousseau."

2. A number of scholars have identified the *Second Discourse* as Rousseau's most philosophic work. See, for example, Strauss, "On the Intention of Rousseau," and Sorenson, "Natural Inequality."

3. To begin, it should be said that the esoteric doctrine should not be simply identified with the related phenomenon of esoteric writing explored by Leo Strauss. See, for example, *Persecution and the Art of Writing*. Strauss has argued that numerous philosophers—Rousseau among them—have written in a way that allows them to communicate with two different audiences simultaneously, one made up of ordinary careless readers and another made up of careful readers who can read between the lines. The esoteric doctrine as Rousseau discusses it—the existence of a secret teaching—can be understood as the precondition of such writing; nevertheless, one can certainly have an esoteric doctrine without having any desire to communicate it through writing. Indeed, as we shall see, Rousseau's argument is that the desire to communicate the esoteric doctrine through generally accessible writings (as opposed to purely private communication to initiates) is a relatively late development.

4. For useful discussion of the "twofold philosophy," "double doctrine," "interior doctrine," or esotericism in eighteenth-century France, see Manuel, *The Eighteenth Century Confronts the Gods*, 65–69, 225–26; and Payne, *The Philosophes and the People*, 65–70. For philosophic and religious uses of the doctrine in the immediately preceding centuries, see Zagorin, *Ways of Lying*.

5. See *The Discourses and Other Early Political Writings*, ed. Gourevitch, 335.

6. Warburton, *The Divine Legation of Moses Demonstrated*, 1:309–472. For Rousseau's reference to Warburton, see *Social Contract*, CW 4:157.

7. DeJean, *Libertine Strategies*, xii. See also Spink, *French Free-Thought from Gassendi to Voltaire*, 9; and, in connection with Rousseau, 309; and Pintard, *Le Libertinage érudit dans la première moitié du XVIIe siècle*, 86, 176.

8. DeJean, *Libertine Strategies*, 197.

9. See Pinot, *La Chine et la formation de l'esprit philosophique*, 344; and Smith, "Helvétius, Rousseau, Franklin and Two New Manuscripts of Fréret's *Lettre de Thrasybule à Leucippe*."

10. Fréret, *Lettre de Thrasybule à Leucippe*, 10.

11. Cited in Lanson, "Questions diverses," 300–1.

12. For summaries of this debate, see Shackleton, "Asia as Seen by the French

Enlightenment"; Guy, *The French Image of China Before and After Voltaire*; and Mungello, *Curious Land*.

13. Leibniz's writings specifically devoted to China are conveniently collected in *Writings on China*.

14. France, *Rhetoric and Truth in France*, 198 n. 10.

15. Loy, *Diderot's Determined Fatalist*, 163.

16. Diderot, *Correspondance*, 1:213–14.

17. See Gourevitch, *The Discourses and Other Early Political Writings*, 331. This point was made earlier by Fabre, "Deux frères ennemis."

18. For useful accounts, see Bagley, "On the Practice of Esotericism"; Berman, "Deism, Immortality, and the Art of Theological Lying"; and Sullivan, *John Toland and the Deist Controversy*, 173.

19. Diderot, *Oeuvres complètes*, 1:12.

20. Of these, "Indiens," "Platonisme," and "Pythagorisme" were also by Diderot.

21. See Bagley, "On the Practice of Esotericism," 245–47. This seems to be Loy's position on Diderot (*Diderot's Determined Fatalist*, 181). See also Topazio, *D'Holbach's Moral Philosophy*, 104. A generation later Condorcet gave an account of the "secret doctrine" that is a systematic version of one of the strands to be found in the *Encyclopédie*: first, the doctrine was used by priests to establish their power over the people, then it was used by philosophers to protect themselves from the power of the priests, finally it has come into the open.

22. *Encyclopedia: Selections*, 293–94, 293.

23. Rousseau repeats this point in the *Second Discourse*, saying that the ancient philosophers "seem to have tried their best to contradict each other on the most fundamental questions" (*Second Discourse*, CW 3:13; Pl. 3:124).

24. A letter from Rousseau to Tronchin from February 1757 about Mme. d'Epinay shows that Rousseau is not simply inventing this characterization of Grimm's morality for the purposes of the *Confessions* (Leigh 4:162).

25. For a contrast between Grimm and Rousseau, see the editors' introduction to the *Confessions*, CW 5:xxi–xxvi.

26. Gourevitch, "Rousseau on Lying," 98.

27. Orwin, "Rousseau's Socratism," 181.

28. For an interesting account of one episode involving the adherents of the traditional version of the doctrine and their more radical opponents, see Anderson, *The Treatise of the Three Impostors*.

29. On these terms and others, see Berman, "Deism, Immortality, and the Art of Theological Lying."

30. For a development of this point, see Orwin, "Rousseau's Socratism."

31. On this point, see Strauss, "On the Intention of Rousseau."

32. For a translation and more complete account of the "Fiction," see Kelly, "Rousseau's Philosophic Dream."

33. Two factors that may have contributed to the neglect of this work are the fact that its title does not give a very accurate account of its contents and the degree of un-

certainty about when Rousseau wrote the work. Rousseau originally entrusted the manuscript to his friend and literary executor, Paul Moultou, along with many other papers that he wanted to preserve. He left no indication of how he intended to use this fragment, although he took some care to preserve it, unlike other fragmentary works that he took some care to destroy. There is no evidence concerning how Rousseau planned to finish the story that he tells in it or whether it was meant to fit into a larger work as the "Profession of Faith of the Savoyard Vicar" fits into *Emile*, or the "Prosopopeia of Fabricius" fits into the *First Discourse*. The manuscript has no title but was given one by Moultou's descendant Streckheisen-Moultou upon its first publication in 1861 in an edition of previously unpublished works and correspondence by Rousseau.

34. C.-A. Sainte-Beuve, *Causeries du Lundi*, July 22, 1864. The translation is my own. Sainte-Beuve does qualify his claim by adding that in comparison with his contemporary philosophes, "Rousseau was *relatively* Christian" (emphasis added). Given the religious views of the other philosophes to whom Sainte-Beuve refers, it should be pointed out that there is a great deal of ground between their hostile disbelief and religious enthusiasm.

35. Masson, *La Religion de Jean-Jacques Rousseau*, 50.

36. Elsewhere Rousseau is more demanding of materialists. See, for example, the "Letter to Franquières" of 1769 (CW 8:264) and "Profession of Faith of the Savoyard Vicar" (*Emile*, nn. 273, 279).

37. On this point, see Gouhier, *Les Méditations métaphysiques*, 197.

38. Diderot was persuaded (probably by the police) not to publish this work. The fact that he wrote it during the period of his greatest intimacy with Rousseau makes it highly probable that he showed the work to his friend and discussed it with him.

39. This entire passage of the "Fiction" should be compared with the first part of the "Profession of Faith of the Savoyard Vicar," which follows a similar path and issues in a series of articles on faith.

40. This seems clear even though only four of the statues are described. These four represent pride, prodigality, anger, and avarice.

41. See Pl. 4:1769.

42. For a brief but very useful account of the "son of man" in the Bible, see Gouhier, *Les Méditations métaphysiques*, 202–3.

43. See Pl. 4:1769. Most scholars today do not accept this identification. To the best of my knowledge, Rousseau never mentions Xenophanes in any of his works.

44. See Masson, *La Religion de Jean-Jacques Rousseau*, 2:52–53.

45. See also Starobinski, *Jean-Jacques Rousseau*, 67.

46. D'Alembert, "Preliminary Discourse," 74.

47. Raymond Trousson suggests that these last words reveal a lack of courage on Socrates' part, in *Socrate devant Voltaire, Diderot et Rousseau*, 94. The emphasis in this last scene on the calmness with which Socrates meets death makes this interpretation implausible. Therefore, it is also necessary to reject the view that he endorses that Rousseau presents Socrates as "the first Jesuit there ever was in the universe."

48. On the contradiction to be found on either interpretation of Socrates' behavior, see Gouhier, *Les Méditations métaphysiques*, 199.

49. On the "son of man" as an "exemplar," see Starobinski, *Jean-Jacques Rousseau*, 69. On the difference between Socrates, who reasons and convinces, and Jesus, who engages in "immediate communication," see Trousson, *Socrate devant Voltaire, Diderot, et Rousseau*, 95. See also Miller, *Rousseau*, 5–13; and Shklar, "Rousseau's Images of Authority."

50. On this point, see Gouhier, *Les Méditations métaphysiques*, 203; and Starobinski, *Jean-Jacques Rousseau*, 70.

51. Starobinski thinks that the "Fiction" ends the way it does because Rousseau "does not know what to make of the cross, a symbol of mediation" (*Jean-Jacques Rousseau*, 69). However, elsewhere Rousseau suggests that it is precisely the manner of his death that makes Jesus such a compelling figure. See *Emile* 626. Starobinski is correct in suggesting that Rousseau strips Jesus of most of his significance for Christianity.

52. In *Rousseau's Exemplary Life*, I have argued that the *Confessions* uses Rousseau's own life to combine a moral fable addressed to a popular audience with a concrete example in which is embedded a philosophic teaching.

53. Strauss suggests that in at the case of the *First Discourse*, Rousseau deliberately overstates his skepticism out of his concern to show the danger of philosophy for society ("On the Intention of Rousseau," 272–73).

54. For a more complete account of the illumination, see Kelly, "The *Confessions* as Philosophic Autobiography."

55. For a treatment of the *Letter* in relation to the *Second Discourse*, see Kelly and Masters, "Human Nature, Liberty and Progress." The best treatment of the *Letter* as a whole is Gourevitch, "Rousseau on Providence." In his notes, Gourevitch points to several similarities between the "Fiction" and the *Letter*.

56. Gourevitch points out that in one draft of the *Letter*, Rousseau wrote, "I could not approve of reasoning about such subjects in public in popular language" ("Rousseau on Providence," 292).

Postscript

1. Sorenson, "Natural Inequality," 774.

2. Heinrich Meier, "Why Political Philosophy," unpublished lecture, translated by Marcus Brainard.

3. Starobinski, *Le Remède dans le mal*, 196.

4. Ibid., 165–208.

5. Ibid., 187–200. Starobinski points out that Rousseau mistakenly identified "Henriette" as Suzanne Curchod, who was proposed to by Edward Gibbon and later led an important salon after she married Necker.

6. In the *Confessions* Rousseau says that around this same period he, himself, adopted the slightly more absorbing activity of making laces (*Confessions*, CW 5:503).

7. Starobinski discusses the numerous accounts of the lance of Achilles, which is the only cure for the wounds it inflicts. See *Le Remède dans le mal*, 191–200.

8. For an excellent treatment of the sentiment of existence, see Grace, "The Unbearable Restlessness of 'Being.'"

9. Consider, in particular, his extract from the *Republic* and *Laws*—called "On

Theatrical Imitation"—which was composed while he was working on the *Letter to d'Alembert*.

10. Sorenson, "Natural Inequality," 779. A contemporary like Diderot could claim that reverie was an essential part of scientific investigation, as well as that rigorous rational investigation could stimulate creative activity. See Gourevitch, "Rousseau's Pure State of Nature," 25. For an extended account of Diderot's treatment of the role of a reverie like conjecture in scientific investigation, see Furbank, *Diderot*, 97–121.

11. On this point see Cantor, "The Metaphysics of Botany."

12. See the suggestive remarks made by Strauss in "On the Intention of Rousseau," 289–90.

BIBLIOGRAPHY

Ackerman, Bruce. *Social Justice in the Liberal State.* New Haven: Yale University Press, 1980.

Alembert, Jean Le Rond d'. "Discours préliminaire." In *Encyclopédie (articles choissis).* Vol. 1. Paris: Flammarion, 1986.

———. *Oeuvres complètes.* Geneva: Slatkine Reprints, 1967.

———. *Preliminary Discourse to the Encyclopedia of Diderot.* Trans. Richard N. Schwab. Chicago: University of Chicago Press, 1995.

Anderson, Abraham. *The Treatise of the Three Imposters and the Problem of Enlightenment.* Lanham, Md.: Rowman and Littlefield, 1997.

Baczko, Bronislaw. "Moise Legislateur . . ." In *Reappraisals of Rousseau,* ed. Simon Harvel et al., 111–130. Totowa, N.J.: Barnes and Noble Books, 1980.

Bagley, Paul J. "On the Practice of Esotericism." *Journal of the History of Ideas* 53 (1992): 231–47.

Baker, Felicity. "Eternal Vigilance: Rousseau's Death Penalty." In *Rousseau and Liberty,* ed. Wokler.

Barras, Moses. *The Stage Controversy in France from Corneille to Rousseau.* New York: Phaeton Press, 1933.

Bennington, Geoffrey. *Sententiousness and the Novel: Laying Down the Law in Eighteenth-Century French Fiction.* Cambridge: Cambridge University Press, 1985.

Berman, David. "Deism, Immortality, and the Art of Theological Lying." In *Deism, Masonry, and the Enlightenment,* ed. J. A. L. Lemay, 61–78. Newark: University of Delaware Press, 1987.

Besterman, Theodore. *Voltaire.* New York: Harcourt, Brace, and World, 1969.

Birn, Raymond. "Malesherbes and the Call for a Free Press." In *The Revolution in Print,* ed. Robert Darnton and Daniel Roche, 50–66. Berkeley: University of California Press, 1989.

Bloom, Allan. "Introduction." *Politics and the Arts.* Ithaca: Cornell University Press, 1959.

Boss, Ronald Ian. "Rousseau's Civil Religion and the Meaning of Belief: An Answer to Bayle's Paradox." *Studies in Voltaire and the Eighteenth Century* 84 (1971): 123–83.

Buchanon, Allen E. *Marx and Justice: The Radical Critique of Liberalism*, Totowa, N.J.: Rowman and Littlefield, 1982.

Burgelin, Pierre. *La Philosophie de l'existence de J-J Rousseau*. Paris: Presses Universitaire de France, 1952.

Cameron, David R. "The Hero in Rousseau's Political Thought." *Journal of the History of Ideas* 45 (1984): 397–419.

Cantor, Paul A. *Creature and Creator: Myth-Making and English Romanticism*. Cambridge: Cambridge University Press, 1984.

———. "The Metaphysics of Botany: Rousseau and the New Criticism of Plants." *Southwestern Review* 70 (summer 1985): 362–80.

Chartier, Roger. *The Order of Books: Readers, Authors and Libraries in Europe between the Fourteenth and Eighteenth Centuries*. Trans. Lydia G. Cocherane. Stanford: Stanford University Press, 1994.

Coleman, Patrick. *Rousseau's Political Imagination: Rule and Representation*. Geneva: Droz, 1984.

Condillac, Etienne Bonnot de. *Essai sur l'origin des connaissances humaines*. Paris: Editions Galileé, 1973.

Cranston, Maurice. *Jean-Jacques: The Early Life and Work of Jean-Jacques Rousseau 1712–1754*. Chicago: University of Chicago Press, 1982.

———. *The Noble Savage: Jean-Jacques Rousseau 1754–1762*. Chicago: University of Chicago Press, 1991.

Cranston, Maurice, and Richard S. Peters, eds. *Hobbes and Rousseau*. Garden City, N.Y.: Anchor Books, 1972.

Crocker, Lester G. "Rousseau et la voi du totalitarisme." In *Rousseau et la philosophie politique*. Paris: Presses Universitaire de France, 1965.

———. *Rousseau's "Social Contract": An Interpretive Essay*. Cleveland: The Press of Case Western Reserve University, 1968.

———. "Rousseau's *soi-distant* Liberty." In *Rousseau and Liberty*, ed. Wokler, 244–66.

Cullen, Daniel E. *Freedom in Rousseau's Political Philosophy*. Dekalb: Northern Illinois University Press, 1993.

Darnton, Robert. "Readers Response to Rousseau: The Fabrication of Romantic Sensitivity." *The Great Cat Massacre and Other Episodes in French Cultural History*. New York: Basic Books, 1984.

DeJean, Joan. *Libertine Strategies: Freedom and the Novel in Seventeenth-Century France*. Columbus: Ohio State University Press, 1981.

———. *Literary Fortification: Rousseau, Laclos, Sade*. Princeton: Princeton University Press, 1994.

De Man, Paul. *Allegories of Reading: Figural Language in Rousseau, Nietzsche, Rilke, and Proust*. New Haven: Yale University Press, 1979.

———. *Blindness and Insight: Essays in the Rhetoric of Contemporary Criticism*. New York: Oxford University Press, 1971.

Derrida, Jacques. *Of Grammatology*. Trans. Gayatri Chakravorty Spivak. Baltimore: Johns Hopkins University Press, 1976.

Descartes, René. *Discourse on Method*. In *Discourse on Method and Meditations on First Philosophy*. Trans. Donald A. Cress. Indianapolis: Hackett Publishing, 1980.

Diderot, Denis. *Correspondance*. 16 vols. Ed. Georges Roth. Paris: Editions de Minuit, 1955.

———. *Oeuvres complète*. Ed. J. Assézat and M. Tourneux. Paris: Garnier, 1875–77.

Ellenberg, Stephen. *Rousseau's Political Philosophy: An Interpretation from Within*. Ithaca: Cornell University Press, 1976.

Ellis, Madeleine B. *Rousseau's Socratic Aemilian Myths*. Columbus: Ohio State University Press, 1977.

Emberley, Peter. "Rousseau versus the Savoyard Vicar: The Profession of Faith Considered." *Interpretation* 14 (1986): 299–329.

Encyclopedia: Selections. Ed. Nelly S. Hoyt and Thomas Cassirer. Indianapolis: Bobbs-Merrill Co., 1965.

Fabre, Jean. "Deux frères ennemis: Diderot and Jean-Jacques." In *Diderot Studies*, ed. Otis Fellow and Gita May, 3:155–213. Geneva: Librarie E. Droz, 1961.

Foucault, Michel. "What Is an Author?" In *Language, Counter-Memory, Practice*, ed. Donald F. Bouchard. Ithaca: Cornell University Press, 1977.

France, Peter. *Rhetoric and Truth in France: Descartes to Diderot*. Oxford: Clarendon Press, 1972.

Fréret, Nicolas. *Lettre de Thrasybule à Leucippe*. In *Oeuvres complettes [sic] de M. Fréret*. London: n.p., 1775. Reprint, Westmead, U.K.: Gregg International Publishers, 1972.

Fried, Michael. *Absorption and Theatricality: Painting and Beholder in the Age of Diderot*. Berkeley: University of California Press, 1980.

Furbank, P. N. *Diderot: A Critical Biography*. New York: Alfred A. Knopf, 1992.

Galston, William. "Defending Liberalism." *American Political Science Review* 76 (1982): 621–29.

Gilden, Hilail. *Rousseau's "Social Contract": The Design of the Argument*. Chicago: University of Chicago Press, 1983.

Goldschmidt, Victor. *Anthropologie et politique: Les Principes du système de Rousseau*. Paris: J. Vrin, 1974.

Goodman, Dena. *Criticism in Action: Enlightenment Experiments in Political Writing*. Ithaca: Cornell University Press, 1989.

———. *The Republic of Letters: A Cultural History of the French Enlightenment*. Ithaca: Cornell University Press, 1994.

Gouhier, Henri. *Les Méditations métaphysiques de Jean-Jacques Rousseau*. Paris: J. Vrin, 1970.

———. *Rousseau et Voltaire: Portraits dans deux miroirs*. Paris: J. Vrin, 1983.

Gourevitch, Victor. "The Political Argument of Rousseau's *Essay on the Origin of Languages*." In *Pursuits of Reason: Essays in Honor of Stanley Cavell*, ed. Ted Cohen et al., 21–35. Lubbock: Texas Tech University Press, 1993.

———. "Rousseau on the Arts and Sciences." *Journal of Philosophy* 69 (1972): 737–53.

———. "Rousseau on Lying: A Provisional Reading on the Fourth *Rêverie*." *Berkshire Review* 15 (1980): 93–107.

———. "Rousseau on Providence." In *Literary Imagination, Ancient and Modern: Essays in Honor of David Grene*, ed. Todd Breyfogle, 285–311. Chicago: University of Chicago Press, 1999.

———. "Rousseau's Pure State of Nature." *Interpretation* 16, no. 1 (fall 1988): 23–59.

———, ed. *The Discourses and Other Early Political Writings*. Cambridge: Cambridge University Press, 1997.

Grace, Eve. "The Unbearable Restlessness of 'Being': Rousseau's Protean *Sentiment of Existence*." *History of European Ideas* 27, no. 2 (2001): 133–51.

Grant, Ruth W. *Hypocrisy and Integrity: Machiavelli, Rousseau, and the Ethics of Politics*. Chicago: University of Chicago Press, 1997.

Guy, Basil. *The French Image of China Before and After Voltaire*. In *Studies on Voltaire and the Eighteenth Century*, ed. Theodore Besterman, vol. 21. Geneva: Institut et Musée Voltaire, 1963.

Habermas, Jürgen. *Communication and the Evolution of Society*. Trans. Thomas McCarthy. Boston: Beacon Press, 1979.

———. *The Structural Transformation of the Public Sphere: An Inquiry into a Category of Bourgeois Society*. Trans. Thomas Burger, with Frederick Lawrence. Cambridge: MIT Press, 1989.

Haeringer, Etienne. "L'Esthétique de l'opéra en France au temps de Jean-Phillipe Rameau." *Studies on Voltaire and the Eighteenth Century*. Oxford: Voltaire Foundation, 1990.

Hall, John C. *Rousseau: An Introduction to His Political Philosophy*. London: Macmillan Press, 1973.

Hanley, William. "The Policing of Thought: Censorship in Eighteenth-Century France." *Studies in Voltaire and the Eighteenth Century* 183 (1980): 265–95.

Harvey, Irene. "Exemplarity and the Origins of Legislation." In *Unruly Examples: On the Rhetoric of Exemplarity*, ed. Alexander Gelley, 211–54. Stanford: Stanford University Press, 1995.

Havens, George R. *Voltaire's Marginalia on the Pages of Rousseau: A Comparative Study of Ideas*. Columbus: Ohio State University Press, 1933.

Hobbes, Thomas. *Leviathan*. Ed. Michael Oakeshott. New York: Macmillan, 1962.

Hobson, Marian. *The Object of Art: The Theory of Illusion in Eighteenth-Century France*. Cambridge: Cambridge University Press, 1982.

Hulliung, Mark. *The Autocritique of Enlightenment*. Cambridge: Harvard University Press, 1994.

Isherwood, Robert M. *Music in the Service of King: France in the Seventeenth Century*. Ithaca: Cornell University Press, 1973.

Jackson, Susan K. *Rousseau's Occasional Autobiographies*. Columbus: Ohio State University Press, 1992.

———. "Text and Context of Rousseau's Relation with Diderot." *Eighteenth-Century Studies* 20 (1986): 195–219.

Johns, Adrian. *The Nature of the Book: Print and Knowledge in the Making*. Chicago: University of Chicago Press, 1998.

Kelly, Christopher. "The *Confessions* as Philosophic Autobiography." In *The Cambridge Companion to Rousseau*, ed. Patrick Riley, 302–25. Cambridge: Cambridge University Press, 2001.

———. *Rousseau's Exemplary Life: The "Confessions" as Political Philosophy*. Ithaca: Cornell University Press, 1986.

———. "Rousseau's Philosophic Dream." *Interpretation* 23, no. 3 (spring 1996): 417–44.

Kelly, Christopher, and Roger D. Masters. "Human Nature, Liberty and Progress: Rousseau's Dialogue with the Critics of the *Discours sur l'inegalité*." In *Rousseau and Liberty*, ed. Wokler, 53–69.

———. "Rousseau's *Social Contract*, the Common Good, and the Guilty." *Etudes sur le Contrat Social, Pensée Libre* #2. Ottawa: North American Association for the Study of Jean-Jacques Rousseau, 1989. 107–22.

Keohane, Nannerl. "'The Masterpiece of Policy in Our Century': Rousseau on the Morality of the Enlightenment." *Political Theory* (1977): 457–84.

Kintzler, Catherine. *Jean-Philippe Rameau: Splendeur et naufrage de l'esthétique du plaisir à l'age Classique*. Paris: Le Sycamore, 1983.

Koselleck, Reinhart. *Critique and Crisis: Enlightenment and the Pathogenesis of Modern Society*. Cambridge: MIT Press, 1988.

Lanson, Gustave. "Questions diverses sur l'histoire de l'esprit philosophique en France avant 1750." *Revue d'Histoire Litteraire de la France* 19 (1912): 300–1.

Leibniz, Gottfried Wilhelm. *Writings on China*. Trans. with introduction, notes, and commentary by Daniel J. Cook and Henry Rosemont Jr. Chicago: Open Court, 1994.

Lemos, Ramon. *Rousseau's Political Philosophy: An Exposition and Interpretation*. Athens: University of Georgia Press, 1977.

Loy, J. Robert. *Diderot's Determined Fatalist*. New York: King Crown Press, 1950.

MacIntyre, Alasdair. *After Virtue*. Notre Dame: University of Notre Dame Press, 1981.

Macy, Jeffrey. "'God Helps Those Who Help Themselves': New Light on the Theological Political Teaching in Rousseau's *Profession of Faith of the Savoyard Vicar*." *Polity* 24 (1992): 615–32.

Manent, Pierre. *La Cité de l'homme*. Paris: Fayard, 1994.

Manin, Bernard. "On Legitimacy and Political Deliberation." *Political Theory* 15 (August 1987): 322–47.

Manuel, Frank E. *The Eighteenth Century Confronts the Gods*. Cambridge: Harvard University Press, 1959.

Marks, Jonathan, "Jean-Jacques Rousseau, Michael Sandel and the Politics of Transparency." *Polity* 33, no. 4 (summer 2001): 619–42.

Marshall, Terence. "Art d'écrire et practique politique de Jean-Jacques Rousseau." *Revue de Métaphysique et de Morale* 89, nos. 3 and 4 (1984): 232–61, 322–47.

Masson, Pierre-Maurice. *La Religion de Jean-Jacques Rousseau*. Geneva: Slatkine Reprints, 1970 [reprint of 1916 edition].

Masters, Roger D. *The Political Philosophy of Rousseau*. Princeton: Princeton University Press, 1968.

Matthes, Melissa M. *The Rape of Lucretia and the Founding of Republics: Readings in Livy, Machiavelli, and Rousseau*. University Park: Pennsylvania State University Press, 2000.

McEachern, Jo-Ann E. "*La Nouvelle Héloïse* et la censure." In *Rousseau and the Eighteenth Century: Essays in Memory of R. A. Leigh*, ed. Marion Hobson, J. T. A. Leigh, and Robert Wokler, 83–89. Oxford: Voltaire Foundation, 1992.

Melzer, Arthur M. *The Natural Goodness of Man: On the System of Rousseau's Thought*. Chicago: University of Chicago Press, 1990.

Miller, James. *Rousseau: Dreamer of Democracy*. New Haven: Yale University Press, 1984.

Morgenstern, Mira. "Emile et la révolution dans la vie quotidienne." In *Rousseau "l'Emile" et la Revolution*, ed. Robert Thiéry, 253–69. Paris: Universitas, 1992.

Mungello, D. E. *Curious Land: Jesuit Accommodation and the Origin of Sinology*. Honolulu: University of Hawaii Press, 1989.

Namer, Gérard. *Rousseau Sociologue de la connaissance*. Paris: Editions Klincksieck, 1978.

Negroni, Barbara de, ed. *Correspondance Jean-Jacques Rousseau, Chrétien-Guillaume de Lamoignon de Malesherbes*. Paris: Flammarion, 1991.

Neubauer, John. *The Emancipation of Music from Language: Departure from Mimesis in Eighteenth-Century Aesthetics*. New Haven: Yale University Press, 1986.

Nichols, Mary P. "Rousseau's Novel Education in *Emile*." *Political Theory* 13 (1985): 535–58.

O'Hagan, Timothy. *Rousseau*. London: Routledge, 1999.

Orwin, Clifford. "Democracy and Distrust." *American Scholar* 53 (summer 1984): 313–25.

———. "Rousseau's Socratism." *Journal of Politics* 60, no. 1 (February 1998): 174–87.

Palissot de Montenoy, Charles. *Oeuvres complètes*. Paris: Chez Léopold Collin, 1809.

Pappas, John N. *Voltaire and Diderot*. Bloomington: Indiana University Press, 1962.

Parry, Geraint. "Thinking One's Own Thoughts: Autonomy and the Citizen." In *Rousseau and Liberty*, ed. Wokler, 99–120.

Patterson, Annabel. *Censorship and Interpretation: The Conditions of Reading in Early Modern England*. Madison: University of Wisconsin Press, 1984.

Payne, Harry C. *The Philosophes and the People*. New Haven: Yale University Press, 1976.

Pinot, Virgile. *La Chine et la formation de l'esprit philosophique en France (1640–1740)*. Geneva: Slatkine Reprints, 1971.

Pintard, René. *Le Libertinage érudit dans la première moitié du XVIIe siècle*. Paris: Ancienne Librarie Furne, 1943.

Rawls, John. *A Theory of Justice*. Cambridge: Harvard University Press, 1971.

Ray, William. *Story and History*. Cambridge: Basil Blackwell, 1990.

Robinson, Phillip. "Literature versus Theory: Rousseau's Second Preface to *Julie*." *French Studies* 44 (1990): 403–15.

Roche, Daniel. "Censorship and the Publishing Industry." In *Revolution in Print: The Press in France 1775–1800*, ed. Robert Darnton and Daniel Roche. Berkeley: University of California Press, 1989.

Roosevelt, Grace. *Reading Rousseau in the Nuclear Age*. Philadelphia: Temple University Press, 1990.

Rousseau, Jean-Jacques. *Diskurs über die Ungleichheit/Discours sur l'inégalité*. Ed. Heinrich Meier, dritte, durchgesene Auflage. Paderborn: Verlag Ferdinand Schöningh, 1993.

Saisselin, Remy G. *The Literary Enterprise in Eighteenth-Century France*. Detroit: Wayne State University Press, 1979.

Sandel, Michael J. *Democracy's Discontent: America in Search of a Public Philosophy*. Cambridge: Belknap Press of Harvard University Press, 1996.

Schwartz, Joel. *The Sexual Politics of Jean-Jacques Rousseau*. Chicago: University of Chicago Press, 1984.

Scott, John. "Rousseau and the Melodious Language of Freedom." *Journal of Politics* 59, no. 3 (August 1997): 803–29.

Shackleton, Robert. "Asia as Seen by the French Enlightenment." In *Essays on Montesquieu and on the Enlightenment*, ed. David Gilson and Martin Smith, 231–42. Oxford: Voltaire Foundation, 1988.

———. *Montesquieu: A Critical Biography*. Oxford: Oxford University Press, 1961.

Shaw, E. P. *Problems and Policies of Malesherbes as directeur de la librairie in France, 1750–1763*. Albany: State University of New York Press, 1966.

Shelley, Percy Bysshe. "A Defense of Poetry." In *The Complete Works of Percy Bysshe Shelley*, ed. Roger Ingpen and Walter E. Peck, 7:112. New York: Gordian Press, 1965.

Shklar, Judith. *Men and Citizens: A Study of Rousseau's Social Theory*. London: Cambridge University Press, 1969.

———. "Rousseau's Images of Authority." In *Hobbes and Rousseau*, ed. Maurice Cranston and Richard S. Peters, 333–65. Garden City, N.J.: Anchor Books, 1972.

Smith, D. W. "Helvétius, Rousseau, Franklin and Two New Manuscripts of Fréret's *Lettre de Thrasybule à Leucippe*." In *Enlightenment Essays in Memory of Robert Shackleton*, ed. Giles Barber and C. P. Courtney, 277–82. Oxford: Voltaire Foundation, 1988.

Sorenson, Leonard. "Natural Inequality and Rousseau's Political Philosophy in His *Discourse on Inequality*." *Western Political Quarterly* 43, no. 4 (1990).

Spink, J. S. *French Free-Thought from Gassendi to Voltaire*. London: University of London: Athlone Press, 1960.

Starobinski, Jean. *Blessings in Disguise; or The Morality of Evil*. Trans. Arthur Goldhammer. Cambridge: Harvard University Press, 1993.

———. *Jean-Jacques Rousseau: Transparency and Obstruction*. Trans. Arthur Goldhammer. Chicago: University of Chicago Press, 1998.

———. *Le Remède dans le mal: Critique et légitimation de l'artifice à l'âge de Lumières*. Paris: Gallimard, 1989.

Stendhal. *Racine and Shakespeare*. Trans. Guy Daniels. New York: Crowell-Collier Press, 1962.

Stewart, Philip. *Half-Told Tales: Dilemmas of Meaning in Three French Novels*. Chapel Hill: North Carolina Studies in the Romance Languages and Literatures, 1987.

Strauss, Leo. *Natural Right and History*. Chicago: University of Chicago Press, 1958.

———. "On the Intention of Rousseau." *Social Research* 14 (1947): 455–87.

———. *Persecution and the Art of Writing*. Glencoe, Ill.: Free Press, 1952.

Strong, Tracy. *Jean-Jacques Rousseau: The Politics of the Ordinary*. Thousand Oaks, Calif.: Sage Publications, 1994.

Sullivan, Robert E. *John Toland and the Deist Controversy: A Study in Adaptation*. Cambridge: Harvard University Press, 1982.

Talmon, J. L. *The Origins of Totalitarian Democracy*. New York: Prager, 1960.

Tente, Ludwig, ed. *Die Polemik um den ersten Discours von Rousseau in Frankreich und Deutschland*. 3 vols. Kiel: Christian-Albrechts-Universität zu Kiel, 1974.

Tocqueville, Alexis de. *Democracy in America*. Trans. George Lawrence and ed. J. P. Mayer. New York: Harper & Row, 1969.

Tomlinson, Gary. *Monteverdi and the End of the Renaissance*. Berkeley: University of California Press, 1987.

Topazio, Virgil W. *D'Holbach's Moral Philosophy: Its Background and Development*. Geneva: Institut et Musée Voltaire, 1958.

Trachtenberg, Zev M. *Making Citizens: Rousseau's Political Theory of Culture*. London: Routledge, 1993.

Trousson, Raymond. *Socrate devant Voltaire, Diderot et Rousseau*. Paris: Lettres Modernes Mindard, 1967.

Vanpée, Janie. "Rousseau's *Emile ou de l'education*: A Resistance to Reading." *Yale French Studies* 77 (1990): 156–76.

Vaughan, C. E., ed. *Political Writings of Jean-Jacques Rousseau*. New York: John Wiley and Sons, 1962.

Voltaire. *Lettre au docteur Pansophe*. In *Mélanges de Voltaire*. Paris: Bibliothèque de la Pléiade, 1961.

———. *Les Oeuvres de Voltaire*. Ed. Theodore Besterman. Bandury, Oxfordshire: Voltaire Foundation, 1973.

Walzer, Michael. *Interpretation and Social Criticism*. Cambridge: Harvard University Press, 1987.

Warburton, William. *The Divine Legation of Moses Demonstrated*. New York: Garland, 1978.

Williams, Bernard. *Ethics and the Limits of Philosophy*. Cambridge: Harvard University Press, 1985.

Winthrop, Delba. "Aristotle and Theories of Justice." *American Political Science Review* 72 (1978): 1201–16.

Wokler, Robert, ed. *Rousseau and Liberty*. Manchester: Manchester University Press, 1995.

Zagorin, Perez. *Ways of Lying: Dissimulation, Persecution, and Conformity in Early Modern Europe*. Cambridge: Harvard University Press, 1990.

INDEX

Ackerman, Bruce, 32
Alembert, Jean Le Rond d', 3, 14, 23–24, 29, 30, 34–36, 39, 40, 44, 51, 53–55, 58, 127–30, 132, 135, 166–67, 171, 172
anonymity, 10–21, 25–27, 47, 153
Aristotle, 58, 68, 147, 150, 156–57
atheism, 38–39
Athenaeus, 69
Augustine, Saint, 2, 106

Bacon, Francis, 85
Bagley, Paul, 148
Bayle, Pierre, 143–45
botany, 178–80
Brutus, 70, 105, 110
Buffon, George Louis Leclerc, comte de, 31

Calvin, Jean, 34
Cameron, David R. 84–85, 87
censorship, French system of, 13–16
"Citizen of Geneva," 12, 42, 116, 128, 172
Constant, Benjamin, 117
Crocker, Lester, 118, 125
Cullen, Daniel, 125, 192 n. 12
Cyrano de Bergerac, Savinien de, 143

DeJean, Joan, 143
de Man, Paul, 114
Derrida, Jacques, 5
Deschamps, dom Léger-Marie, 141
Diderot, Denis, 2, 3, 11, 13, 16, 17, 19, 24, 25, 107, 112, 127, 145–48, 151–53, 156– 57, 160–61, 168, 174, 188 n. 16, 195 n. 38, 197 n. 10
Duclos, Charles, 22, 31, 143
Dworkin, Ronald, 32

Encyclopédie, 3, 34, 51, 53, 127, 146–48, 161
esoteric doctrine, 142–54, 193 n. 3, 194 n. 21

Formey, Jean-Henri-Samuel, 147
Foucault, Michel, 14, 19, 27
France, Peter, 145
Frederick the Great, 43–44, 167
Fréret, Nicolas, 143

general will, 118–21, 124, 126, 130, 132–33
Goodman, Dena, 191 n. 21
Gourevitch, Victor, 12, 143, 146, 151
Grimm, Friedrich Melchior von, 151
Grotius, Hugo, 26

Habermas, Jürgen, 6, 32
Helvétius, Claude-Adrien, 11, 13, 15, 124
"Henriette" (pseud.), 175–76, 196 n. 5
Holbach, Paul-Henri-Dietrich, baron d', 15
Hume, David, 11, 153

imitation, 53–55, 58–61, 64, 66–77, 89–95, 100

Jesus, 66, 80–81, 155, 160, 164–65
Juvenal, 1

Keith, George, 167

La Fontaine, Jean de, 61
La Rochefoucauld, François, duc de, 57
legislator, 62–72, 78–82, 84, 90–91, 137, 164–66, 188 n. 19
Livy, 105
Locke, John, 43, 145
Longobardi, Nicholas, 144
Loy, J. Robert, 145
Lycurgus, 76

Machiavelli, Niccolò, 84–85
Malebranche, Nicolas de, 144–45
Malesherbes, Chrétien-Guillaume de Lamoignon de, 13–15
Marshall, Terence, 42
Masson, Pierre-Maurice, 155, 161
Meier, Heinrich, 22, 171
Melzer, Arthur M., 86
Meyer, Eugène, 145
moeurs, 31
Mohammed, 65
Montesquieu, Charles Louis de Secondat, baron de, 3, 11, 12, 26, 145
Moses, 65, 69
music, 3, 52, 53–54, 69–72, 104

Nietzsche, Friedrich, 78
Numa (king), 70

Omar (caliph), 29
Orwin, Clifford, 151
Ovid, 105

Palissot de Montenoy, Charles, 21
Pétau, Denis, 144–45
philosophic pride, 149–50, 154–65, 171, 178
Plato, 140–41, 171
  Apology, 135
  Crito, 160
  Phaedo, 160
  Republic, 2, 71, 84, 177
Plutarch, 61, 89, 93–94, 190 n. 11
Primary Colors (anon.), 12
Pythagoras, 88, 143–44, 149, 155–56, 160

Racine, Jean, 107
Rameau, Jean-Philippe, 3, 71–72

Rawls, John, 32
Raynal, Guillaume-Thomas-François, abbé de, 103
responsibility, 26–28, 49, 140
Rey, Marc-Michel, 12, 19
Ricci, Matteo, 144
Richardson, Samuel, 107
Robinson Crusoe, 93–94, 97
Rousseau, Jean-Jacques
  Confessions, 2, 6–7, 98–99, 108, 141, 144, 151, 167–69, 178
  Considerations on the Government of Poland, 73–76, 89–90
  The Death of Lucretia, 104–12
  Dictionary of Music, 69
  Discourse on the Origin of Inequality (Second Discourse), 11, 22, 23, 42, 66–68, 92, 140–41, 145, 150, 176
  Discourse on the Sciences and the Arts (First Discourse), 2, 3, 16, 17, 20, 30, 51–52, 79, 86, 87, 150, 163, 169
  Discourse on the Virtue Most Necessary for a Hero, 83–88
  Emile, or On Education, 2, 7, 15, 29, 61, 86, 92–98, 113, 169
  Emile and Sophie, or The Solitaries, 96–97
  Essay on the Origin of Languages, 67–70, 78–79
  "Fiction, ou Morceau allégorique sur la révélation," 155–65
  "Idea of the Method in the Composition of a Book," 4
  Julie, or the New Heloise, 2, 22, 24–25, 42, 98, 102–15
  Letter to Beaumont, 15, 19, 23, 47–48
  Letter to d'Alembert on the Theatre, 14, 19, 34–36, 40–41, 57–60, 74–76, 102–3, 106, 127–36, 138, 166–67, 176
  "Letter to Franquières," 38, 80
  Letter on French Music, 78
  Letter from a Symphonist, 17
  "Letter to Voltaire," 37, 169–71, 173–74, 176
  Letters Written from the Mountain, 9–10, 23, 25–27, 65, 120–22, 133–38
  "Lettres morales," 102
  Observations by Jean-Jacques Rousseau of Geneva on the Reply Made to His Discourse, 20–21, 148–50

"On Theatrical Imitation," 64
Le Persiffleur, 16, 21
Project for Perpetual Peace, 22
Reveries of the Solitary Walker, 4, 12, 64, 140–41, 178
Rousseau Judge of Jean-Jacques: Dialogues, 28, 81, 113, 152–53, 181
Social Contract, 12, 15, 29, 32, 37, 42, 62–64, 69–70, 78–80, 103, 117–22, 125–27, 130, 132–33
The Village Soothsayer, 22

Saint-Pierre, Charles-Irénée Castel, abbé de, 22, 99–101, 110
Sainte-Beuve, Charles-Augustin, 155, 195 n. 34
Sandel, Michael J., 117–18
Schiller, Friedrich von, 77
sentiments of sociability, 32–42, 45–46, 51, 63, 117
Shaftesbury, Anthony Ashley Cooper, 3rd earl of, 146
Shelley, Percy Bysshe, 77
Socrates, 24, 84, 135, 155, 156, 161–64, 173, 195 n. 47
Sorenson, Leonard, 171, 175, 178
Spinoza, Baruch, 15
Stanislaus (king of Poland), 20–21, 148, 174
Starobinski, Jean, 5, 174–75
Stendhal, 19
Stewart, Philip, 114
Strauss, Leo, 193 n. 3

strength of soul, 80, 85–92, 96–98, 107, 110–11, 115, 176

Tacitus, 4
Tasso, Torquato, 103
Tocqueville, Alexis de, 39, 97
Toland, John, 146, 153
Trachtenberg, Zev, 192 n. 13
True System or the Key to the Metaphysical and Moral Puzzle (Deschamps), 141–42

Vernes, Jacob, 11
virtue, natural, 86
vitam impendere vero, 1, 174
Voltaire, 8–13, 15–16, 19–20, 23, 24, 34–35, 49, 58, 128, 153, 170–71, 174, 176
 Candide, 171
 Letter from M. de Voltaire to Mr. Hume, 11
 Lettre de M. de Voltaire au docteur Jean-Jacques Pansophe (Letter from Mr. Voltaire to Mr. Jean-Jacques Rousseau), 11, 52
 Oath of the Fifty, 9, 10, 27
 Sentiment of the Citizens, 10

Warburton, William, 143, 147

Xenocrates, 140, 141
Xenophanes, 160

Yvon, Claude (abbé), 146–47

www.ingramcontent.com/pod-product-compliance
Lightning Source LLC
Chambersburg PA
CBHW050905300426
44111CB00010B/1381